IMAGES
of America

KELLEYS ISLAND

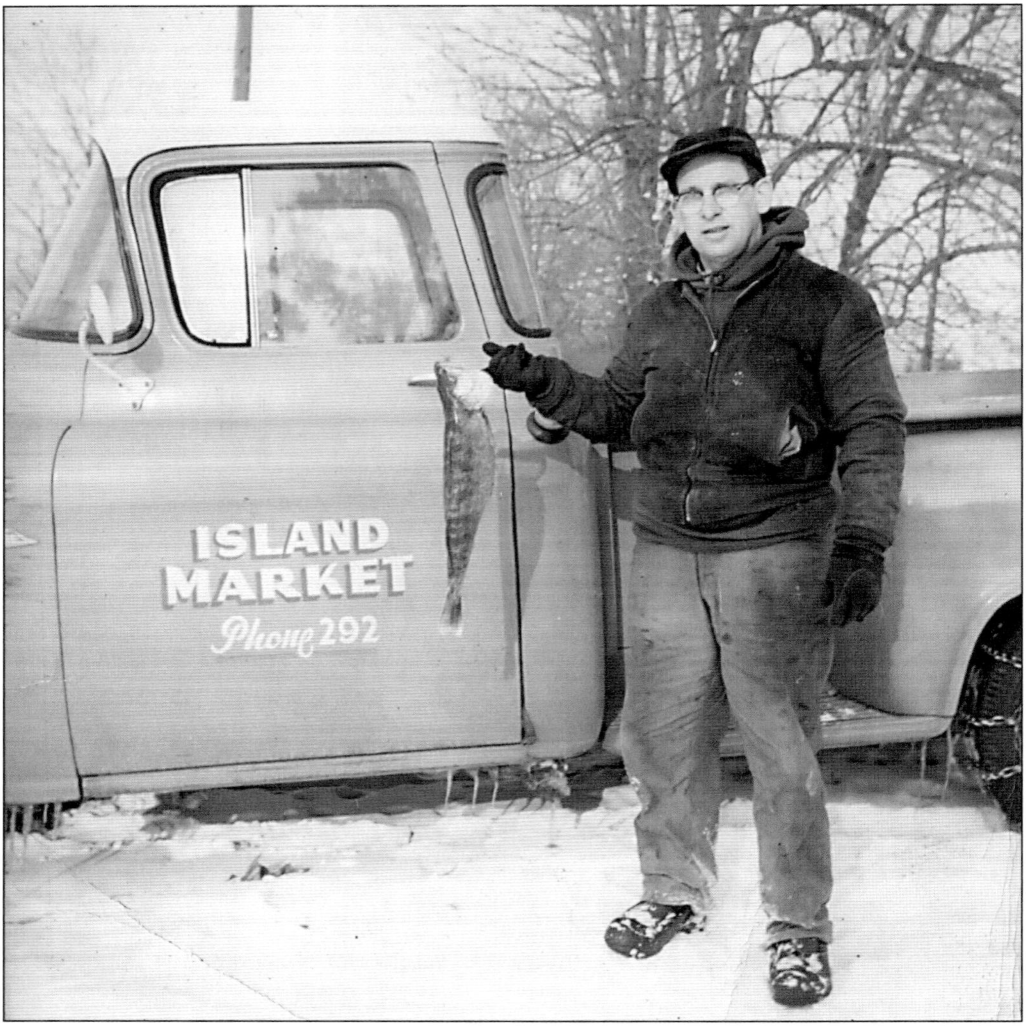

Frank Pohorence summed up most of what can be said about Kelleys Island and the typical islander. A quiet and friendly gentleman, Frank was always willing to lend his skills and talents to a project or to help someone out of a tough situation. As the owner and operator of the Island Market for 37 years, he believed in treating people fairly and making all of his customers feel welcome. Long-time islanders will remember the tabs he kept for regular customers, whom he knew would always pay. This book is especially dedicated to Frank, who spent several hours talking about island history and explaining the stories behind photographs, and who sadly passed away while this book was being prepared. (Courtesy of Laura Jean Pohorence.)

On the Cover: Inscription Rock, on Kelleys Island's south shore just east of the village center, has become a symbol for the island. This 1934 photograph shows the rock long before it was covered to protect it from weather and tourists. The source of the 1914 date is unknown, although the high school class of that year might be suspect. The sunbathers are unidentified. (Courtesy of the Cleveland Public Library Photograph Collection.)

IMAGES
of America

KELLEYS ISLAND

John T. Sabol

ARCADIA
PUBLISHING

ISBN 978-0-7385-9885-7

Published by Arcadia Publishing
Charleston, South Carolina

Printed in the United States of America

Library of Congress Control Number: 2012951820

For all general information, please contact Arcadia Publishing:
Telephone 843-853-2070
Fax 843-853-0044
E-mail sales@arcadiapublishing.com
For customer service and orders:
Toll-Free 1-888-313-2665

Visit us on the Internet at www.arcadiapublishing.com

To my parents, Florence and John Sabol, who passed on to their children and grandchildren their love of Kelleys Island

Contents

Acknowledgments

I am grateful to the following individuals and organizations for their help and advice in preparing this book: the archives of the Adrian Dominican Sisters, Adrian, Michigan; the knowledgeable Ted Blatt; Doug Boldon; Bill and Sis Bradburn; Claudia Brown; Dave Sellers, executive director, and the staff at Camp Patmos; Dagmar Celeste; Margaret Baughman and the staff at the Cleveland Public Library Photograph Collection; William C. Barrow and Lynn Duchez Bycko of the Cleveland Press Archives at Cleveland State University; Judy Du Shane; Dale Lybarger and the Erie County 4-H Camp; Gary and Jackie Finger; Ed and Carol Frindt; Karen Becker Grubaugh; Chuck Herndon; Jack and Linda Hostal; the Kelleys Island Historical Association; Paulette and Richard McMonagle; Jim Miller; Kevin Pape—especially for his advice and historical perspective—and the Pape family collection; Carol Perruchon; Nan Card and the staff at the Frohman Collection, Rutherford B. Hayes Presidential Center; the Sandusky Library Follett House Museum Archives; Bob and Carol Schnittker; Barbara Schock; Larry Sennish; the Slovak Institute and Library; Chris and Frank Yako, and any others I may have inadvertently overlooked.

A special note of tribute goes to the memory of Frank Pohorence, who passed away while this book was in the final stages of preparation and who had spent time with his wife, Laura Jean, identifying and telling stories about many of the photographs they contributed.

And a special thank-you goes to my wife, Jeanne Sabol, who understands more than anybody what a collaborative effort a book like this can be.

Introduction

When I was young—well, younger than I am now—my parents and I and several assorted relatives visited Kelleys Island for two wonderful weeks each summer. This was a time full of anticipation, so much anticipation that I would be out of bed by 6:00 a.m. just to look at the maps showing how to get there, as well as the map of Kelleys Island itself, so I could dream of the places I would visit. For a city kid, this was a magical place, surrounded by water, full of stories, and loaded with things I would never see in my own neighborhood. And it was only 75 or 80 miles away. That was the attraction when I was a kid, and for many, myself still included, that is the attraction today. And I am convinced that was the attraction for those trendsetters in the 1800s who had the foresight to settle on Kelleys Island.

The official history of Kelleys Island begins in 1803 with a French fur trader named Cunningham, who settled on the 3,000-acre island. At that time, the heavily forested land showed remnants of at least two Native American settlements, one of which, possibly Ojibway, apparently left its own history on Kelleys' south shore, carved into a 32-foot-by-21-foot rock, telling a tale of island life before Cunningham.

Archaeological evidence suggests 10,000 years of human occupation on Kelleys Island. With increasing European settlements in the East in the 1600s, life began to destabilize for Native Americans. Attracted to Kelleys Island's abundant resources and its position as a stepping-stone to cross the lake, they took advantage of its position as they migrated farther west. These rapid migrations make it nearly impossible to ascribe tribal identity to the people who occupied these archaeological sites.

An 1817 map shows the island as Cunningham Island, so Cunningham was probably living there before that year. According to an island history published in 1925, Cunningham was injured in an Indian raid in 1812 and escaped to the mainland.

Fast-forward to 1833 and enter the Kelleys, brothers Datus and Irad, who were attracted by the prospect of quarrying limestone on the island. They eventually purchased all 3,000 acres over the next three years, for between $1.50 and $5 per acre, from individual landowners. While both brothers were involved in island life, it appears that Datus spent most of his time on the island, building docks and establishing a variety of industries. The island's limestone became the source for an incipient quarry industry. Its numerous cedar trees became fence posts or fuel. At one time, the island blossomed with a number of wheat fields, and grapes brought to the island by Datus Kelley became the basis for a huge grape industry, which eventually grew into at least 26 wineries. The Kelleys attracted other family members to the island, and other investors sought land there; by 1840, it was renamed for the Kelleys.

Undoubtedly, one of the first things that the Kelleys and their cohorts discovered about their eponymous paradise was that it was a rock—seemingly one huge rock carved out around 10,000 BC. This discovery gave birth to a stone quarry industry that continued into the 21st century. The island's thick forest of cedar trees quickly became another asset, spawning a forestry industry that supplied logs to the mainland and even wooden hulls for ships. The walls of some of the early island dwellings contain native cedar.

Another asset, as ubiquitous as the rock, was Lake Erie, which eventually gave birth to a thriving commercial fishing industry. Island pioneers also discovered that the waters warmed cold breezes, extending the island's growing season to just the right length to support a grape-growing operation, eventually begetting a huge wine-making industry.

These industries attracted population, which exceeded 2,000 by 1900. Luring settlers from nearby mainland communities, the island also became home to a number of European immigrants, who worked mainly in the quarries, at wine-making, and in other trades. At one time, the island had five schools and four churches. Many who came to Kelleys Island seeking employment eventually stayed, and their families either reside or own property on Kelleys to this day.

Through the 1900s, the island gradually lost much of its industrial base. Competitive pressures from grape and wine markets in California and New York signaled the decline of Kelleys' wine industry, which could not compete with the production volume of larger markets. The commercial fishing industry gradually died out along with the commercial fishermen. And the quarries eventually lost out to mainland stone.

But the 1800s also brought another industry that appears to have never left the island—tourism. The wine industry brought visitors, and excursion boats dropped off passengers to visit the island's many wine cellars. Local entrepreneurs encouraged this link between wine and tourism, and many winery owners also owned hotels. In other cases, owners of island guesthouses manufactured their own wine for their summer patrons.

Today, island historical attractions, primarily Inscription Rock and the one-of-a-kind Glacial Grooves, still draw tourists, and the island continues to attract families seeking its atmosphere, with its sandy beach, hiking trails, and healthy sportfishing potential. Two camps also draw young people each summer, as they and other organized camps have done for more than 90 years.

Over the years, Kelleys Island has become known as the "quiet island." And that is the major draw for many families, seeking good times but also looking for a quiet getaway. Vacationers often convert to property owners, and many have built new houses or purchased existing homes on the island. Hotels built more than 100 years ago have become private homes. Also, some large private homes now cater to the tourist trade.

Tourism is the main industry on Kelleys Island today, as boat marinas, commercial boat lines, hotels, condominiums, bed-and-breakfast establishments, and private cottages provide their best for visitors, who have expanded their island time beyond the limitations of the summer months. Add to that bars, restaurants, gift shops, and other attractions, and this is Kelleys Island today: where older residents seek to preserve the island they remember and vacationing families try to just get away and grab a piece of the "quiet island."

For residents and visitors alike, Kelleys Island's history, its natural wonders, and its tranquility are inextricably linked.

One

Cornerstones

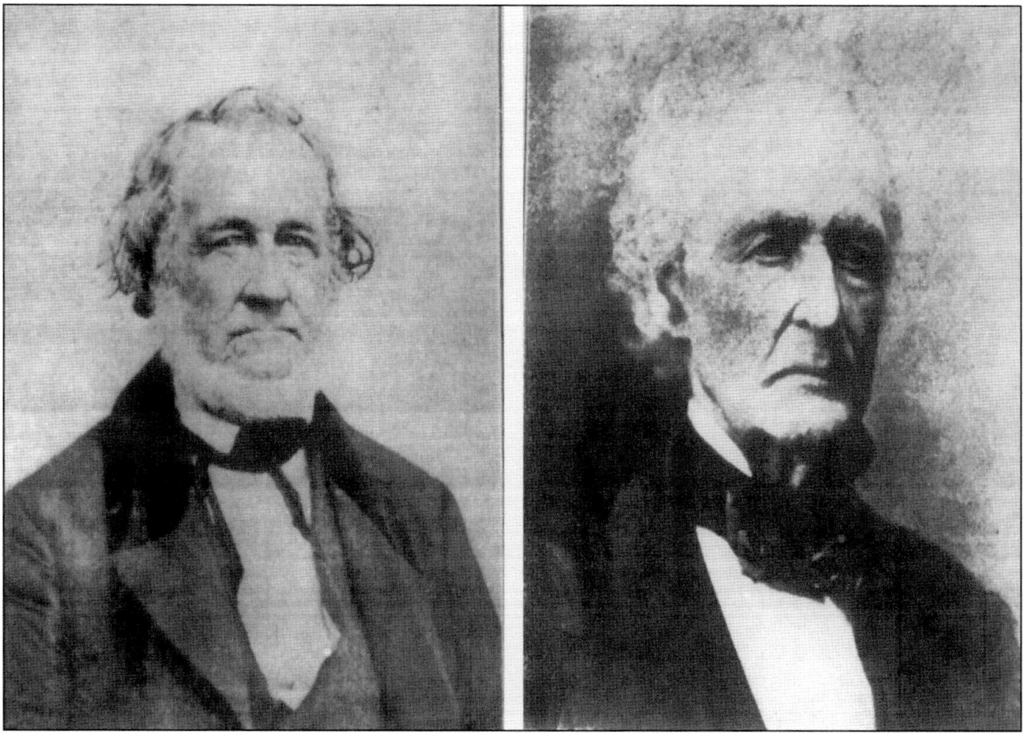

The namesakes of Kelleys Island are brothers Datus (left) and Irad Kelley of Cleveland. The brothers began buying land on Cunningham Island in 1833 and eventually became the principal landowners on the island that would bear their name. Datus died in 1866 and is buried in the island cemetery. Irad remained in Cleveland, where he died in 1875. (Both, courtesy of the Kelleys Island Historical Association.)

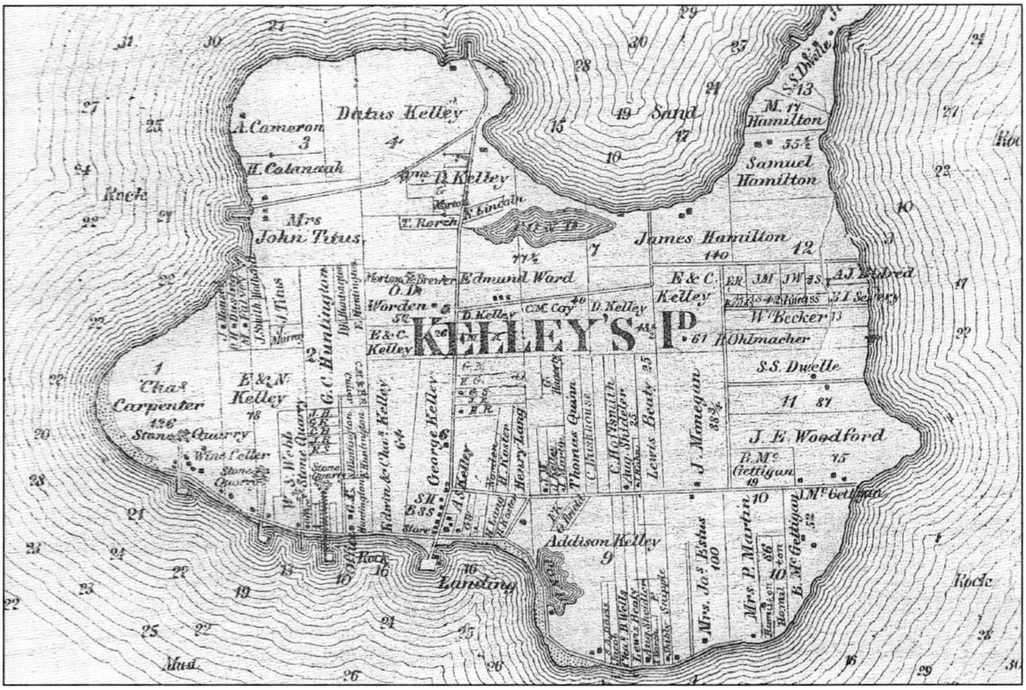

This 1865 map of Kelleys Island shows the extent of the Kelley properties on their namesake island. The holdings became even more extensive, since a portion of the other property was held by relatives of the Kelleys. (Courtesy of the Frohman Collection, Rutherford B. Hayes Presidential Center.)

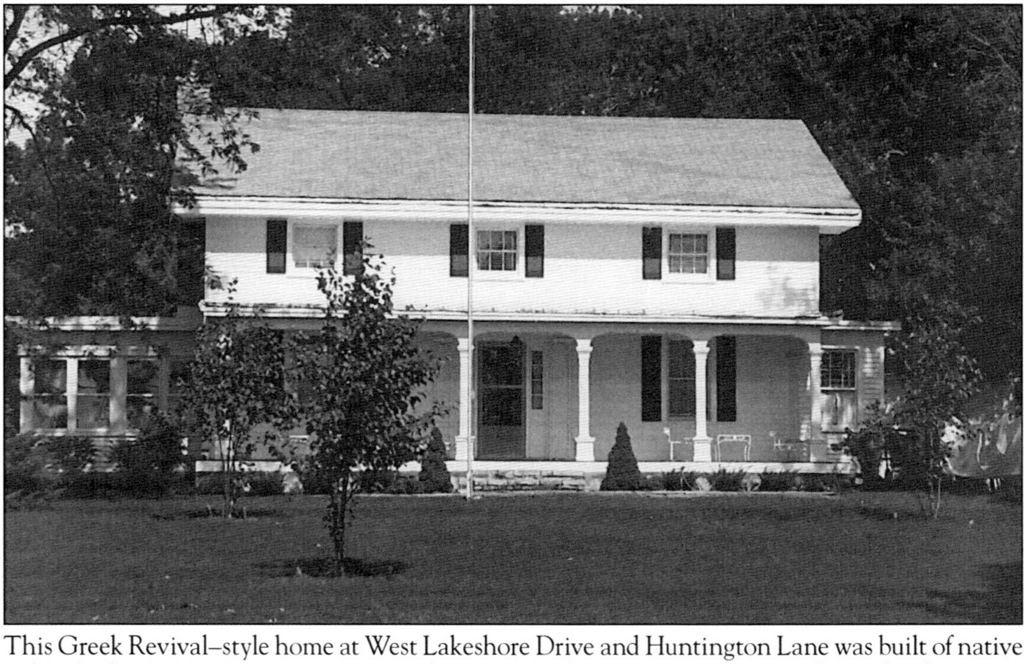

This Greek Revival–style home at West Lakeshore Drive and Huntington Lane was built of native red cedar by George Huntington around 1842, according to Kevin Pape's Kelleys Island Historic District National Register Nomination, 1987. Married to Emeline Kelley, the daughter of Datus and Sara Kelley, Huntington was involved with the island's grape and wine industries and opened one of the island's early quarries. (Courtesy of Jack and Linda Hostal.)

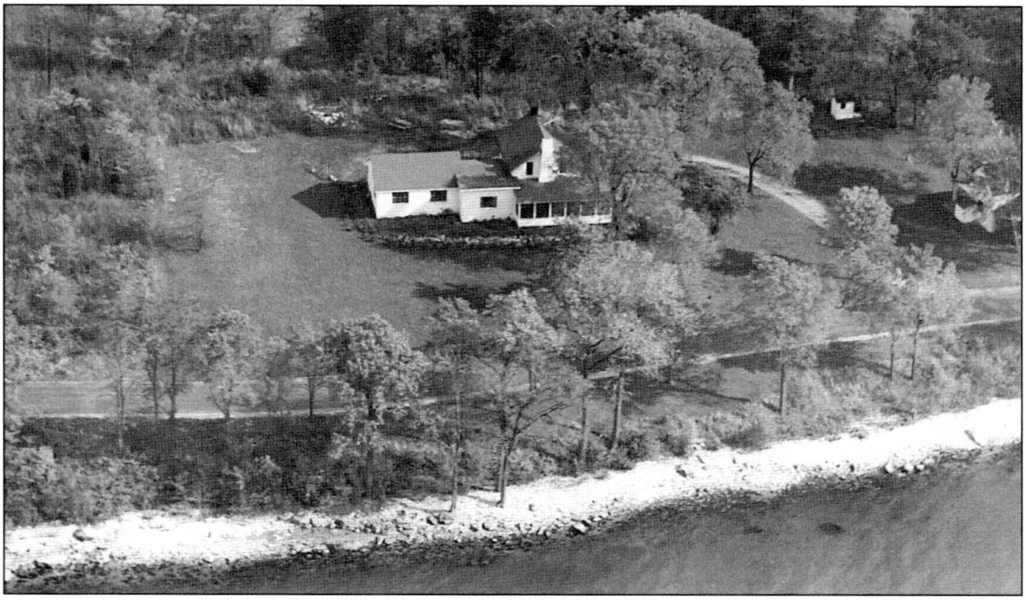

This house, on Carpenter's Point, on West Lakeshore Drive at the extreme western tip of Kelleys Island, was built around 1850 at the western end of Charles Carpenter's 126-acre estate. Built of native limestone, the structure has extremely thick exterior walls. When the house was built, West Lakeshore Drive ended at this point. (Courtesy of Paulette and Richard McMonagle.)

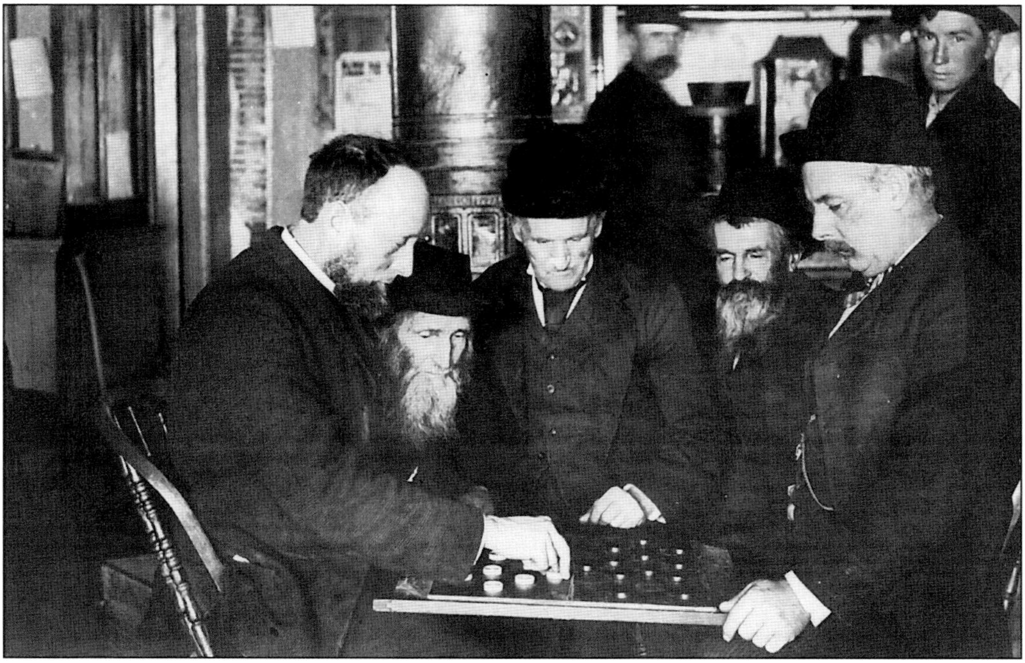

The Store on the Corner, also known as the Lodge, at West Lakeshore Drive and Division Street, was built in the 1850s and became an island gathering place. Seen here from left to right at the checkerboard are Erastus Huntington, Charles Carpenter, J.E. Woodford, Oscar Dean, and Titus Hamilton. Standing in the background are Charles Martin (left) and Charles Erne. The store became Matso's Place and today houses the Captain's Corner Restaurant. (Courtesy of the Kelleys Island Historical Association.)

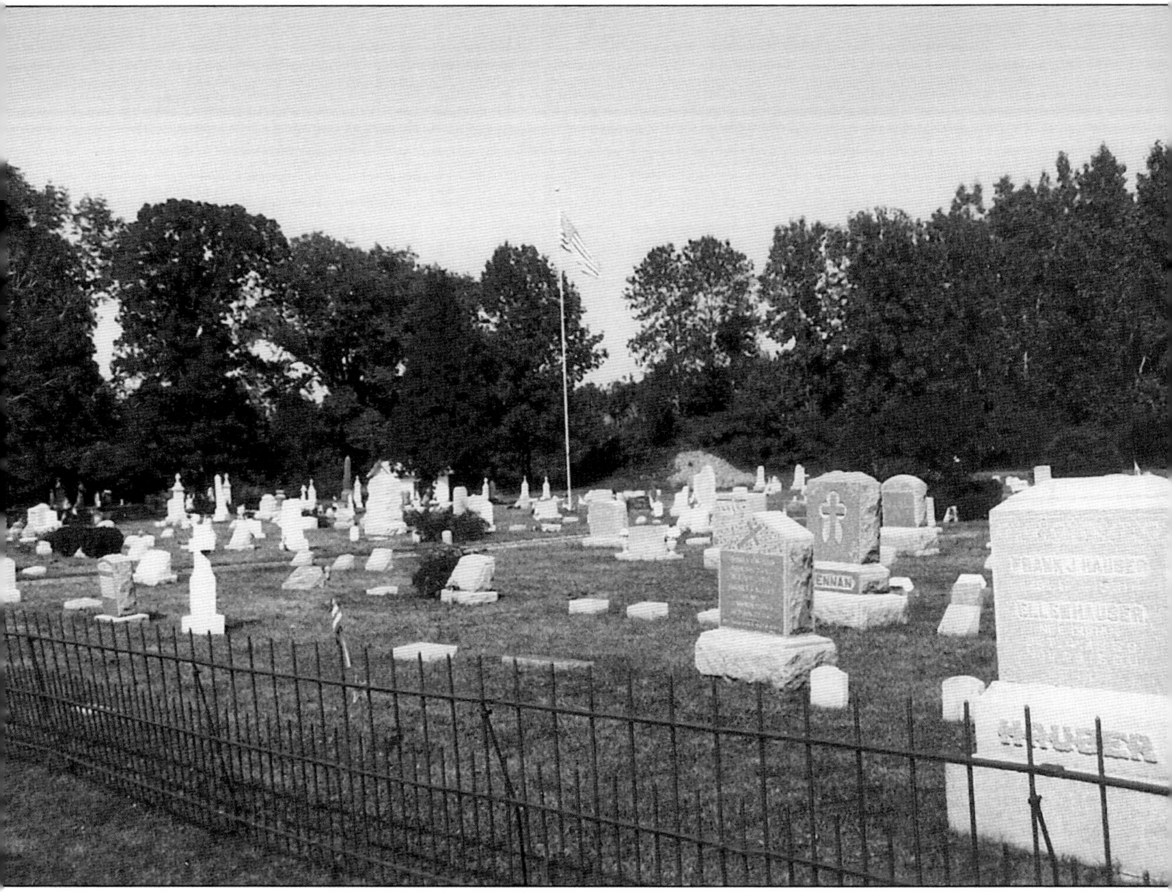

A glimpse of the historical families of Kelleys Island can be found at the cemetery, on the west side of Division Street north of Estes School, in an area of the island known as Sweet Valley. Datus Kelley is buried there along with many other families whose names are attached to historical houses and roads. Land for the cemetery was cleared by John McDonald, who ironically became the first burial after he was killed in a quarry accident in January 1851 at age 26. (Courtesy of Jack and Linda Hostal.)

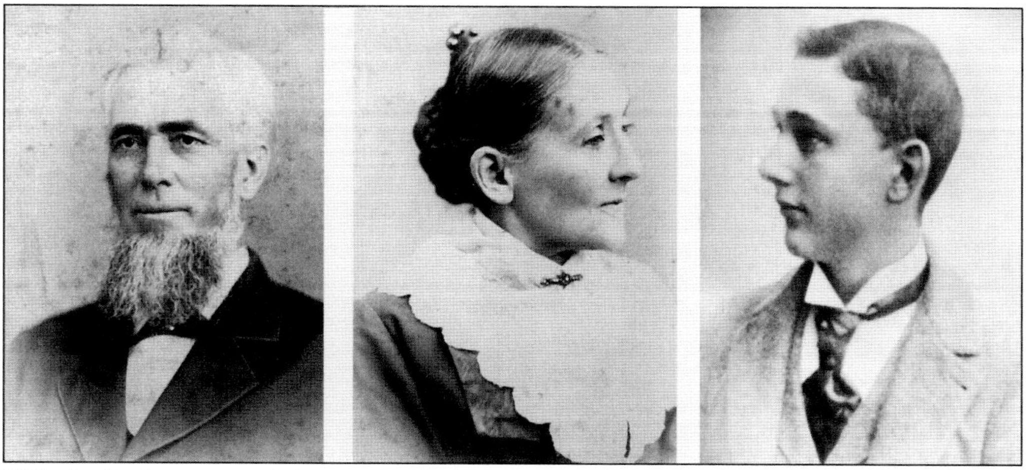

Wilhelm Becker, seen at left sometime before 1888, was born in 1833 in Oberneisen, Germany. He immigrated to America and settled on Kelleys Island in 1852. In 1859, he married Phillipena Katherina Mueller, pictured at center. They raised four sons and six daughters, including Arthur Becker, seen at right at his high school graduation, and established the Becker farm and dairy on Woodford Road in 1905. (All, courtesy of Karen Becker Grubaugh.)

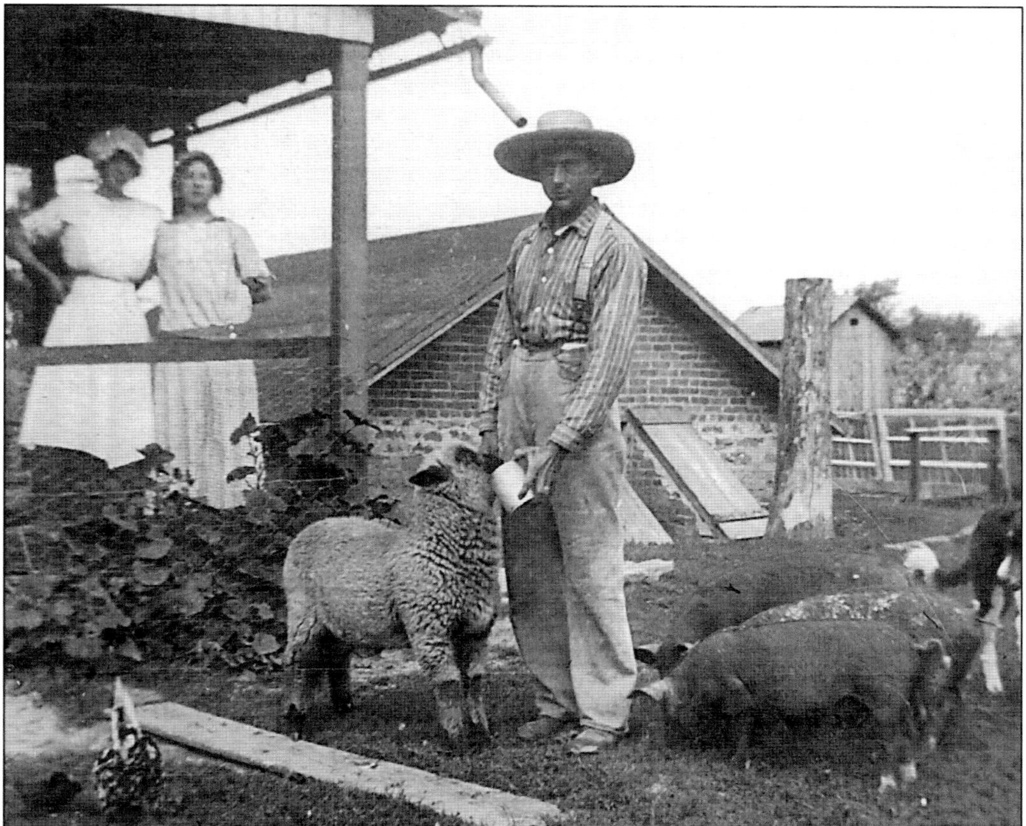

Arthur Becker is hard at work on the Becker farm as Ethel Whitney (left) and Arthur's wife, Laura, look on. The farm was eventually owned and operated by Wilhelm Becker's son George, and then by George's son Reuben, until 1940. (Courtesy of Karen Becker Grubaugh.)

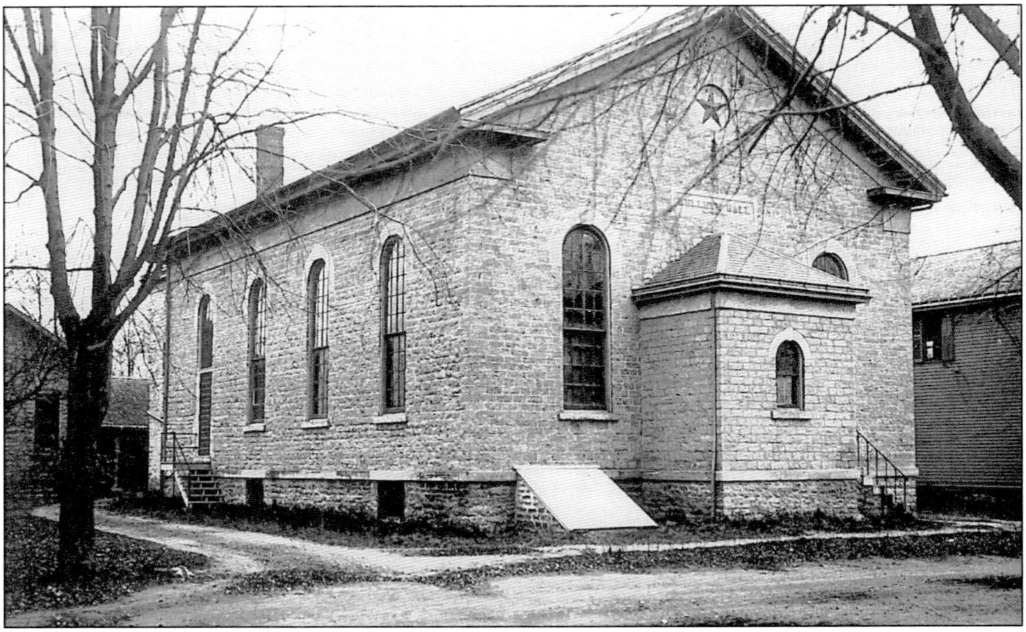

Kelley's Hall, in the center of the village on Division Street, was built and dedicated in 1861. It was a gift to the islanders from Datus Kelley and his wife, Sara, to be used for meetings, theater productions, and other community events. The building is still in use today and has recently been renovated. (Courtesy of the Kelleys Island Historical Association.)

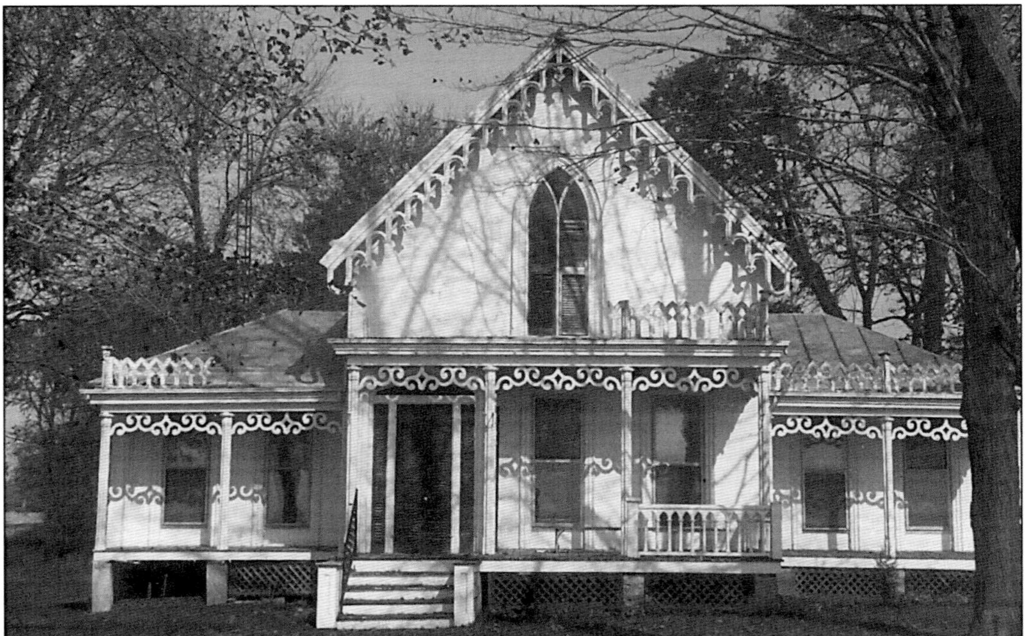

Datus Kelley's youngest son, William, built what came to be known as the William D. Kelley House on West Lakeshore Drive, close to the center of town, in 1861. This unique, eye-catching structure features elaborate scrollwork. William Kelley taught at the island school and served in the Civil War. The house is one of four Kelley family houses in a row along the island's south shore. (Courtesy of Jack and Linda Hostal.)

The Roman Catholic presence on Kelleys Island dates to the 1861 founding of St. Michael Parish. By 1863, this stone church was built at Chappel Street and Addison Road. By 1915, rapid growth resulted in enlarging this structure into the current St. Michael Church building. (Courtesy of the Frohman Collection, Rutherford B. Hayes Presidential Center.)

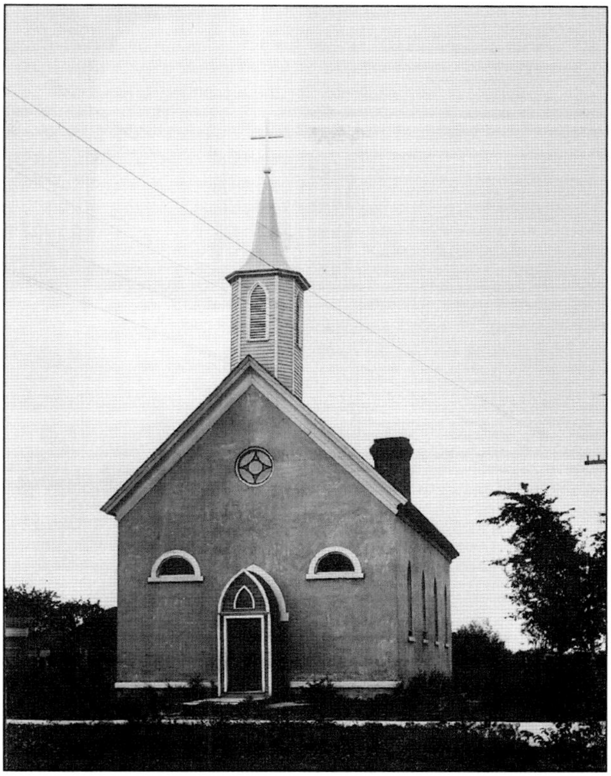

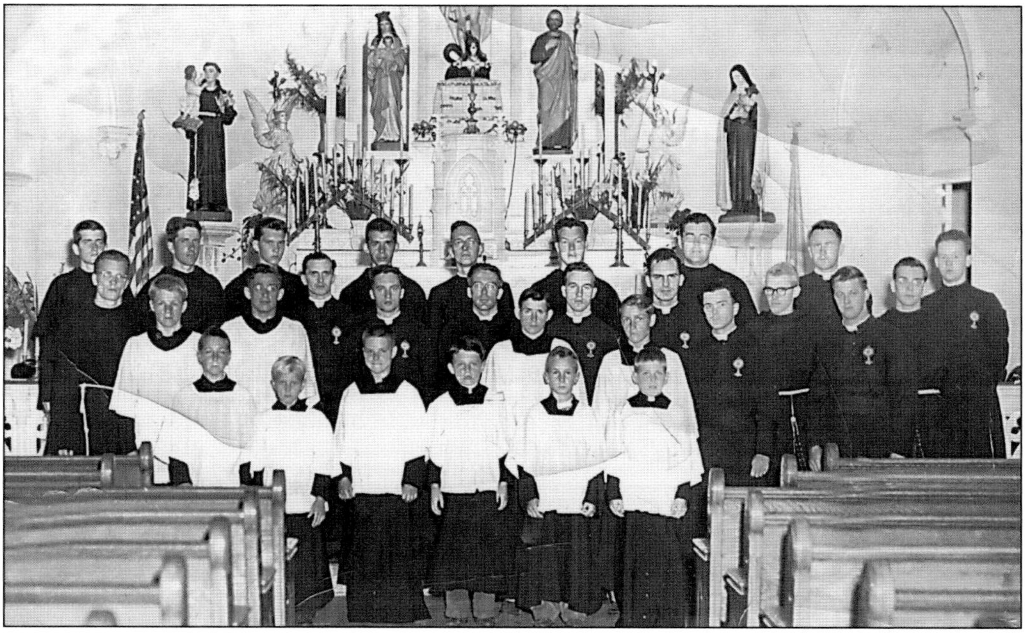

This 1949 view of the interior of St. Michael Church shows off the sanctuary, with its elaborate altar with statues. Servers (in white) are, from left to right, (first row) Jack Schock, David Lenyo, Bill Erne, George Lenyo, unidentified, and Jack Betzenheimer; (second row) Willard Norris, Don Perruchon, Ron Beatty, and Lyle Seeholzer. Also in the photograph are Blessed Sacrament priests, who had a retreat house on Kelleys. (Courtesy of Barbara Schock.)

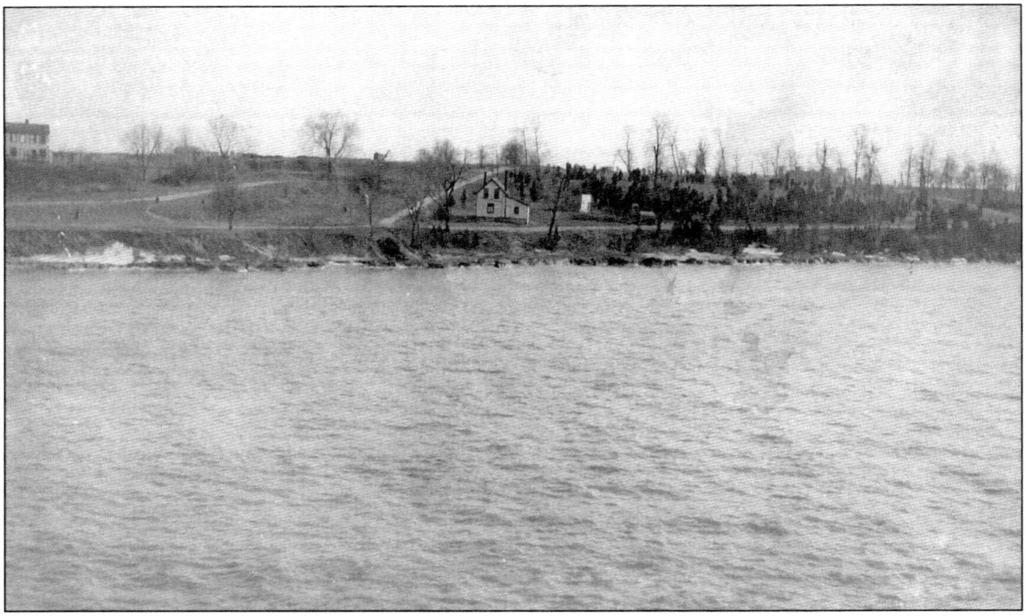

The east shore of Long Point, seen here between 1890 and 1910, had only houses and small roads at the time. At the left edge of the photograph is the house of Joseph and Zepporah Lincoln, who came to the island before 1860. According to the 1880 census, they were neighbors of Robert Hamilton, who owned the land where Camp Patmos is today. (Courtesy of Bob and Carol Schnittker.)

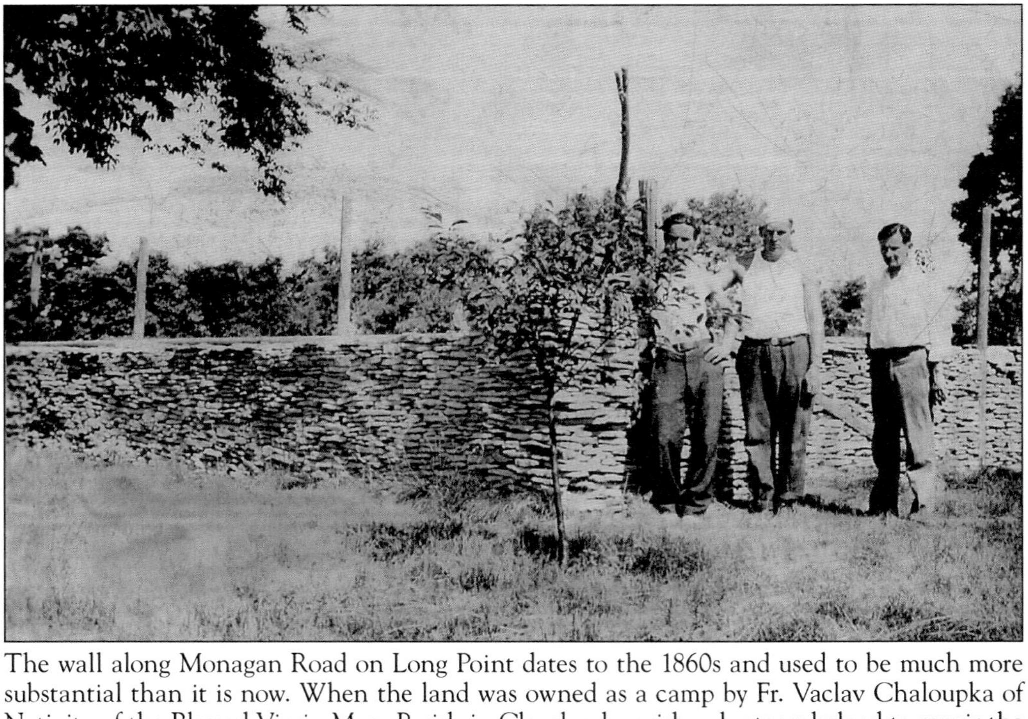

The wall along Monagan Road on Long Point dates to the 1860s and used to be much more substantial than it is now. When the land was owned as a camp by Fr. Vaclav Chaloupka of Nativity of the Blessed Virgin Mary Parish in Cleveland, parish volunteers helped to repair the dry-laid stone wall. Here, John J. Sabol (right) and two other parishioners admire their handiwork in the 1930s. (Courtesy of John T. Sabol.)

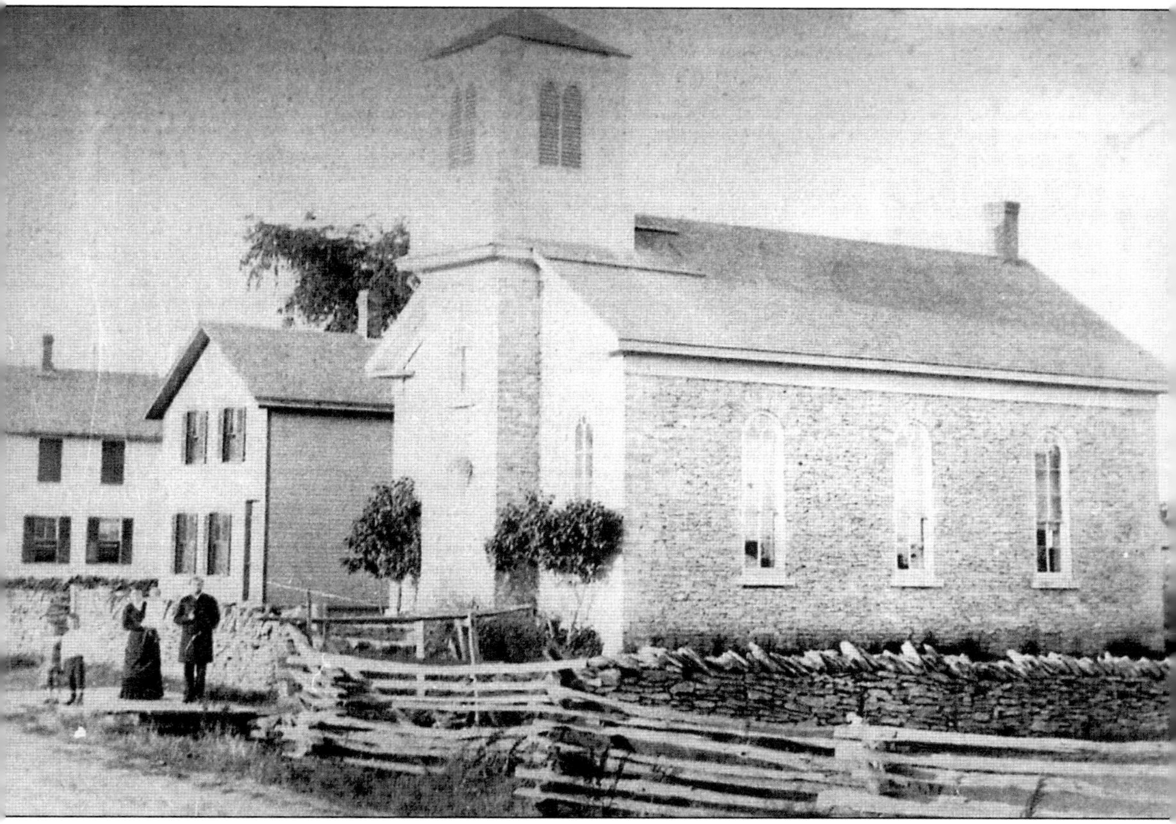

Built in 1865, the German Reformed Church on the east side of Division Street represents the second congregation on Kelleys Island, organized three years after the establishment of St. Michael Catholic Church. It is built of native limestone quarried by hand from the church property. The congregation held regular services until the early 1900s, and the last service was held in 1942. Protestant congregations on the island dwindled with slowdowns and the eventual closing of the quarries in 1943. In 1981, the church was eventually leased to the Kelleys Island Historical Association, which established a museum and shop there. The museum has expanded to a separate building just south of the church, which is still used as a museum. This photograph of the original church shows an early steeple, the predecessor to the more graceful spire that tops the church today. (Courtesy of Bob and Carol Schnittker.)

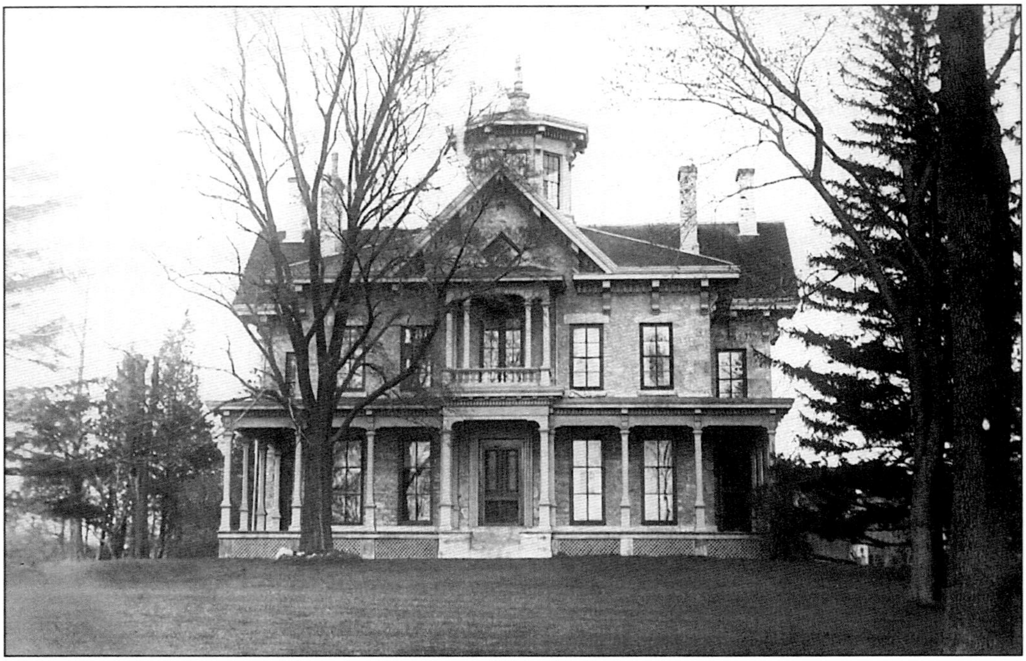

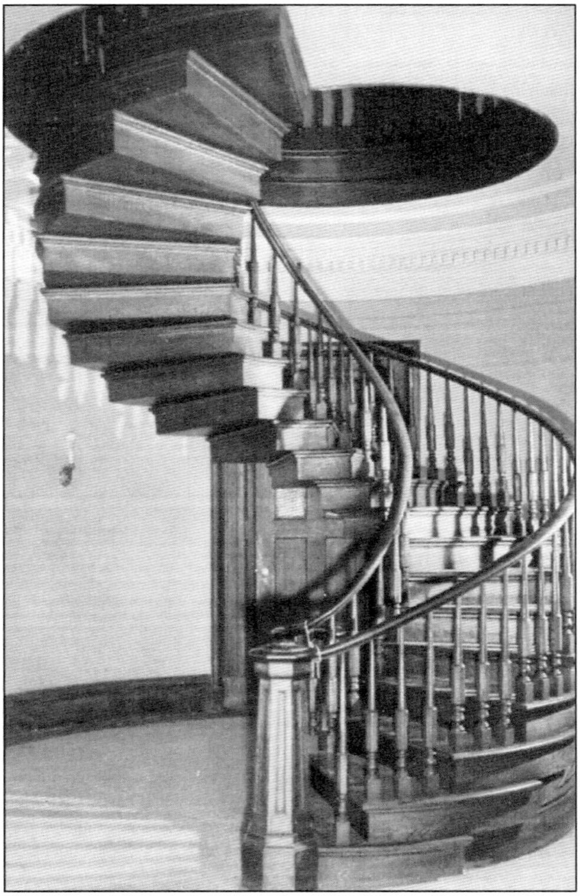

A classic view of the Addison Kelley Mansion at East Lakeshore Drive and Addison Road gives a good idea of how it appeared near the time of its completion in 1867. According to the Kelleys Island Historic District National Register Nomination, 1987, the native limestone mansion was considered "one of the finest pieces of architecture in the state of Ohio." (Courtesy of the Kelleys Island Historical Association.)

The Addison Kelley Mansion features a self-supporting circular staircase, each step balanced on the previous step. The mansion's owner, Addison Kelley, was the son of Datus Kelley, one of the cofounders of Kelleys Island. Construction of the mansion began in 1862 but was delayed because of the Civil War. (Courtesy of John T. Sabol.)

Kelleys Island's First Congregational Church, on the west side of Division Street across from Chappel Street, was built and dedicated in 1877. The congregation, established in 1868, predates this structure, with services originally held in Kelley's Hall. The congregation, like that of the German Reformed Church, dwindled along with the island's population, and the church was torn down in 1934. (Courtesy of Bob and Carol Schnittker.)

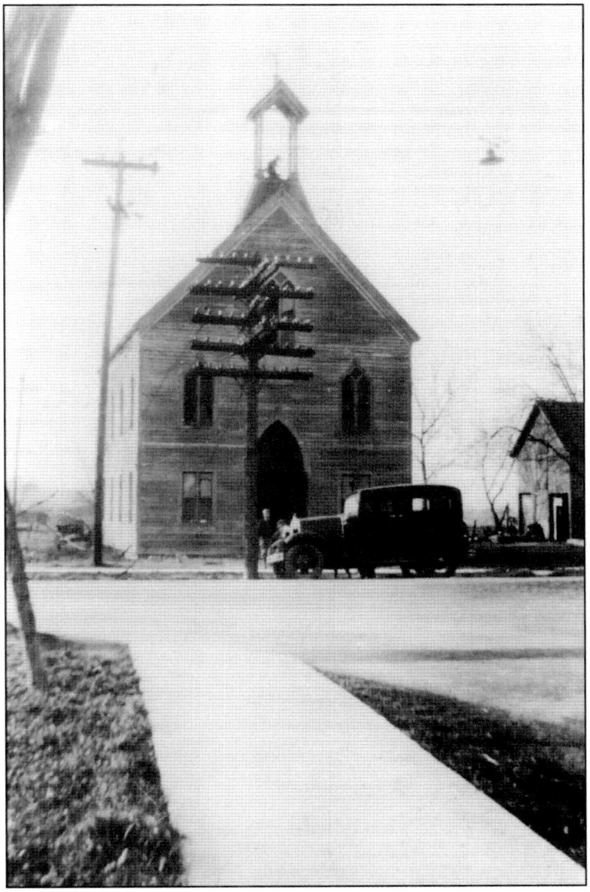

The distinctively structured Casino was opened as a saloon by August Schaedler in 1887. A boathouse and second-floor dance hall on this site date to about 1876 and are the only parts of the original Island House (see page 69) that did not burn, according to the Kelleys Island Historic District National Register Nomination, 1987. Then-owner Charles Himmelein expanded the Casino to its current form in 1901. (Courtesy of the Kelleys Island Historical Association.)

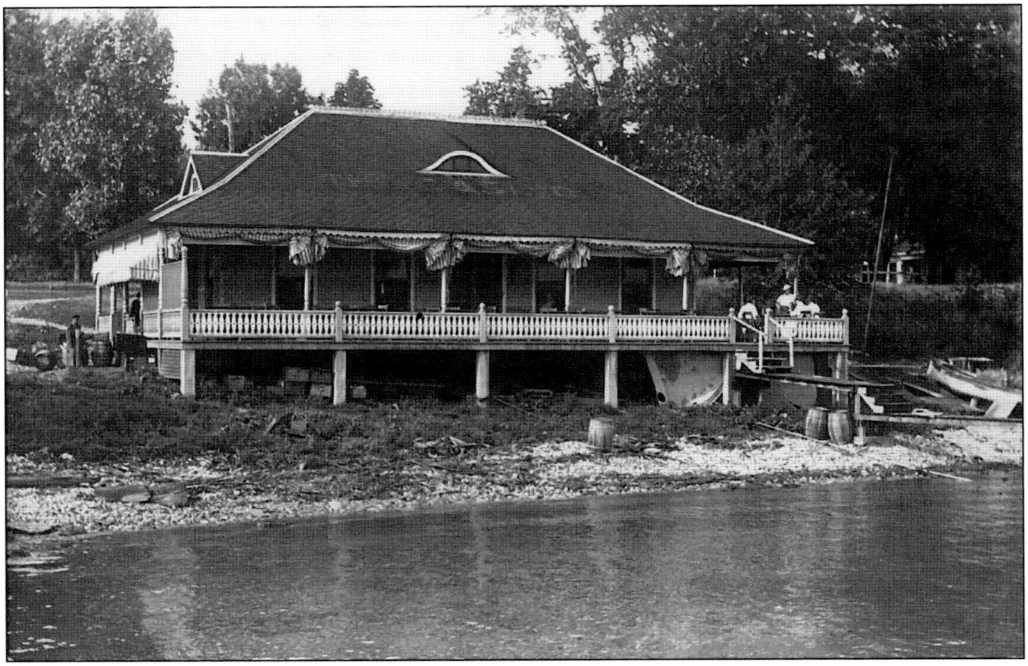

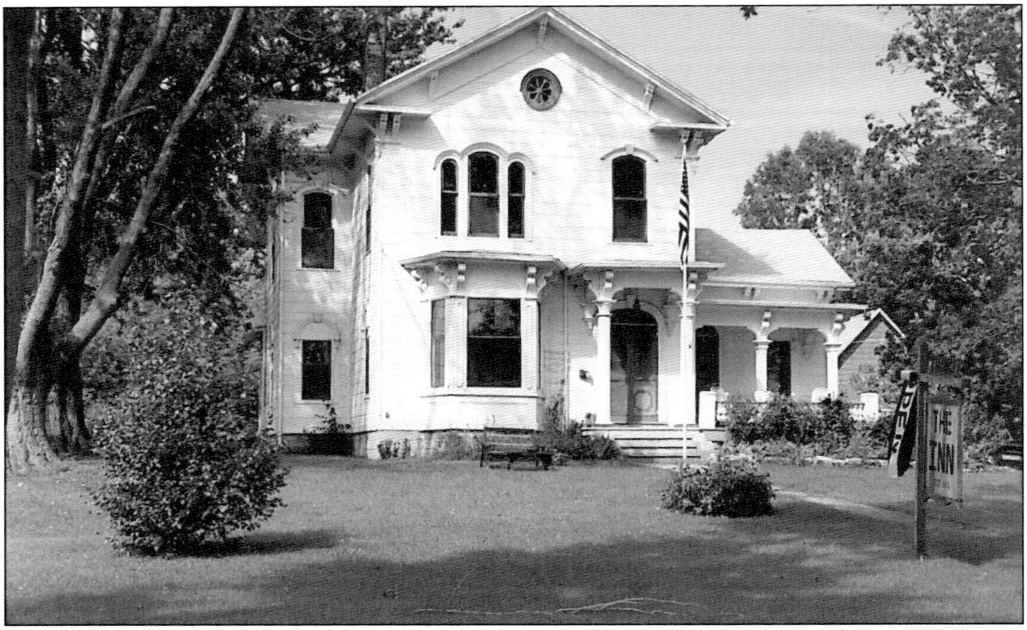

The Inn, on West Lakeshore Drive, has served as a vacation guesthouse for more than 100 years. It was built in 1876 by Erastus Huntington, who operated the island's general store. According to the Kelleys Island Historical Association, Frederina Hamilton opened the residence in 1905 to serve summer visitors. From about 1940 on, Great Lakes ship captain Frank Hamilton and his wife, Katherine, owned it as their personal residence. (Courtesy of Jack and Linda Hostal.)

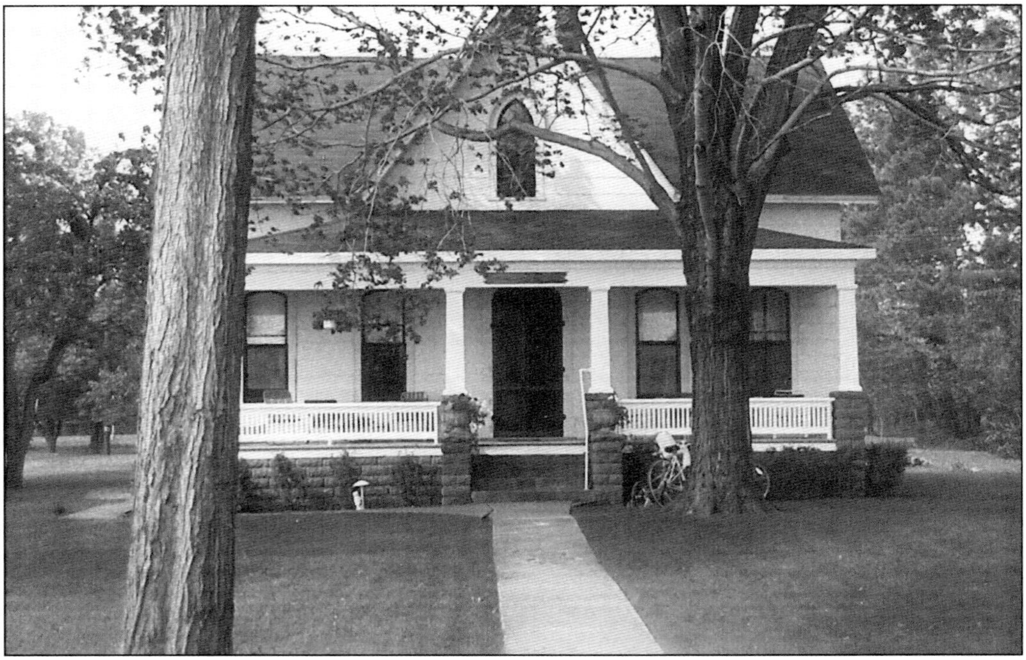

Known as the Old Nest, this house about 1,000 feet from Division Street on West Lakeshore Drive is believed to have been built around 1880 by Charles Farciot, the former superintendent of the Kelleys Island Wine Co. The house was built after he left the company to establish a winery in Sandusky. Today, the house is a vacation rental. (Courtesy of Jack and Linda Hostal.)

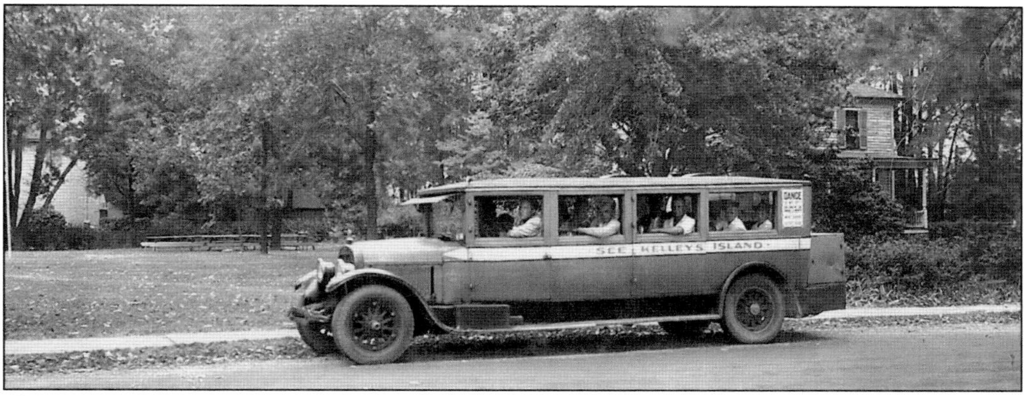

If this photograph from about 1918 is any clue, Kelleys Island is no newcomer to tourism. This tour bus carries passengers and advertised events, as seen by the sign at the back end. According to the Rutherford B. Hayes Presidential Center, tourism probably began on Kelleys Island as early as 1846, when the steamboat *Islander* was making three weekly trips between Sandusky and the island. (Courtesy of the Frohman Collection, Rutherford B. Hayes Presidential Center.)

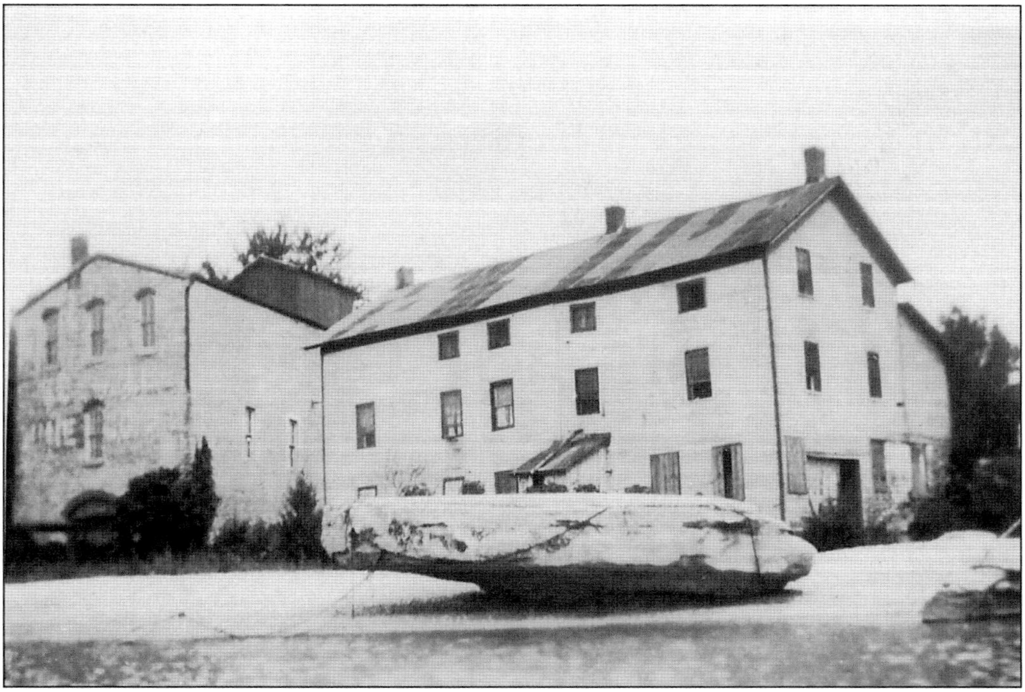

This scene near Inscription Rock would be unrecognizable today were it not for the rock itself. The two buildings on the shore west of the rock have since disappeared. At the left is Koster's Winery, built by Herman Koster in 1883 and razed in 1933. Next door is the Dew Drop Inn, built in 1848 and the home of colorful islander Jake Hays, who also ran a general store there. (Courtesy of Jack and Linda Hostal.)

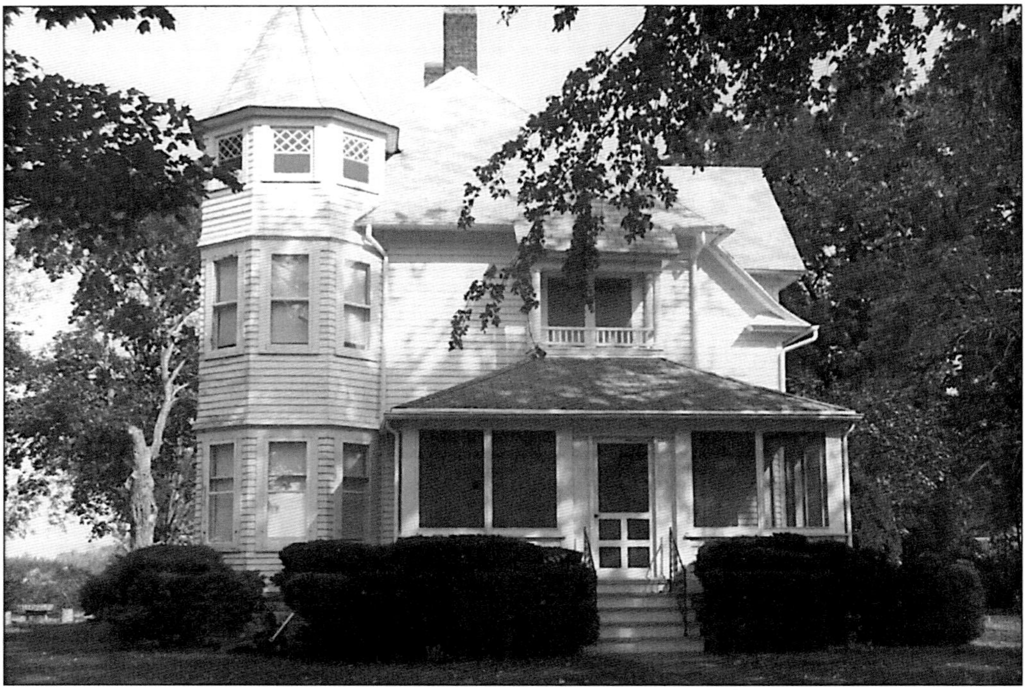

Currently serving as a Lutheran retreat center, Timothy House, on West Lakeshore Drive, was built by Henry Kelley, the grandson of Irad Kelley, in 1883. Henry had worked as a clerk at the Lodge, at the corner of West Lakeshore Drive and Division Street, and later became the assistant superintendent of the Kelley Island Lime & Transport Co. (Courtesy of Jack and Linda Hostal.)

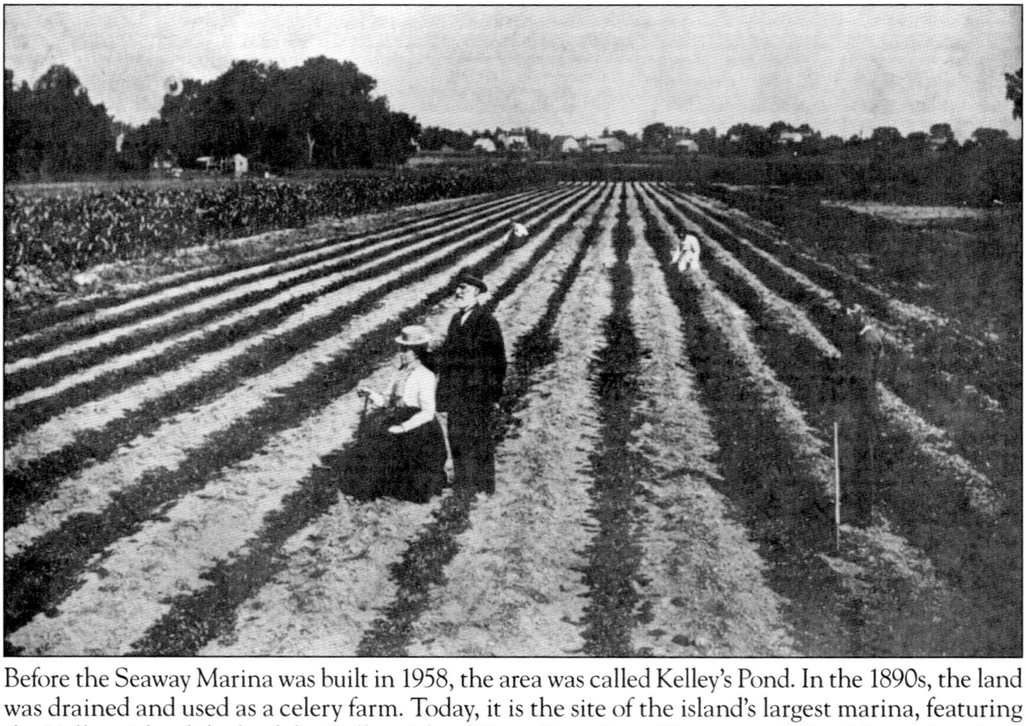

Before the Seaway Marina was built in 1958, the area was called Kelley's Pond. In the 1890s, the land was drained and used as a celery farm. Today, it is the site of the island's largest marina, featuring the Kelleys Island dock of the Kelleys Island Ferry Boat line. (Courtesy of Carol Perruchon.)

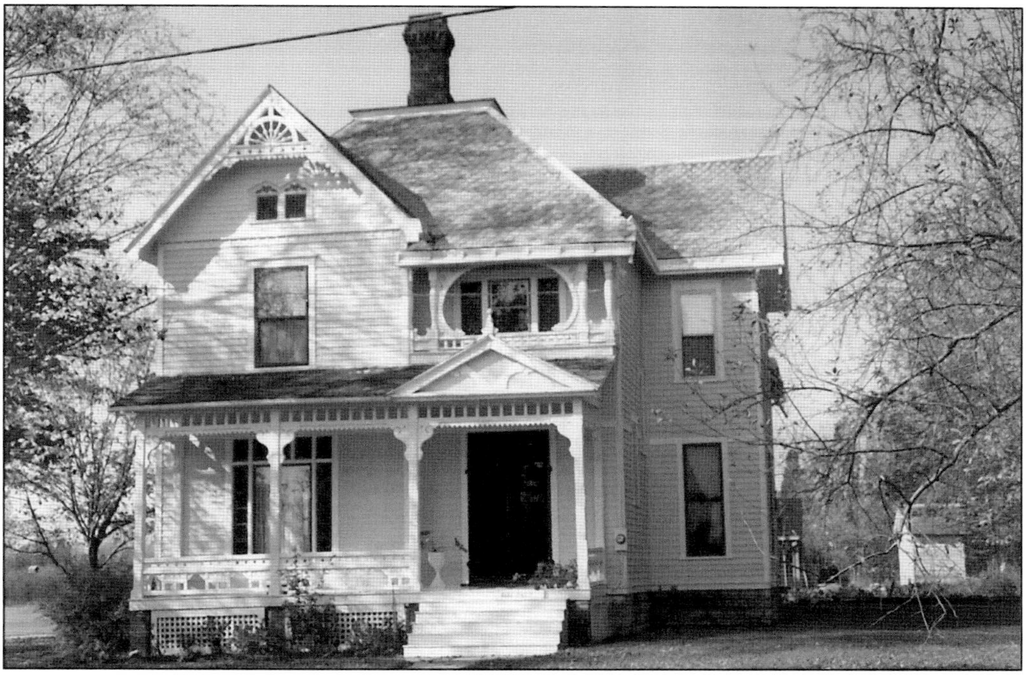

Kevin Pape's Kelleys Island Historic District National Register Nomination, 1987, calls this house, on the west side of Division Street north of the island cemetery, an excellent example of Queen Anne architecture and one of the island's best-preserved residences. The house, in the island's Sweet Valley, was built in 1892 by Otto Brown, who formed the Sweet Valley Wine Co., whose winery ruins stand immediately to the south. (Courtesy of Jack and Linda Hostal.)

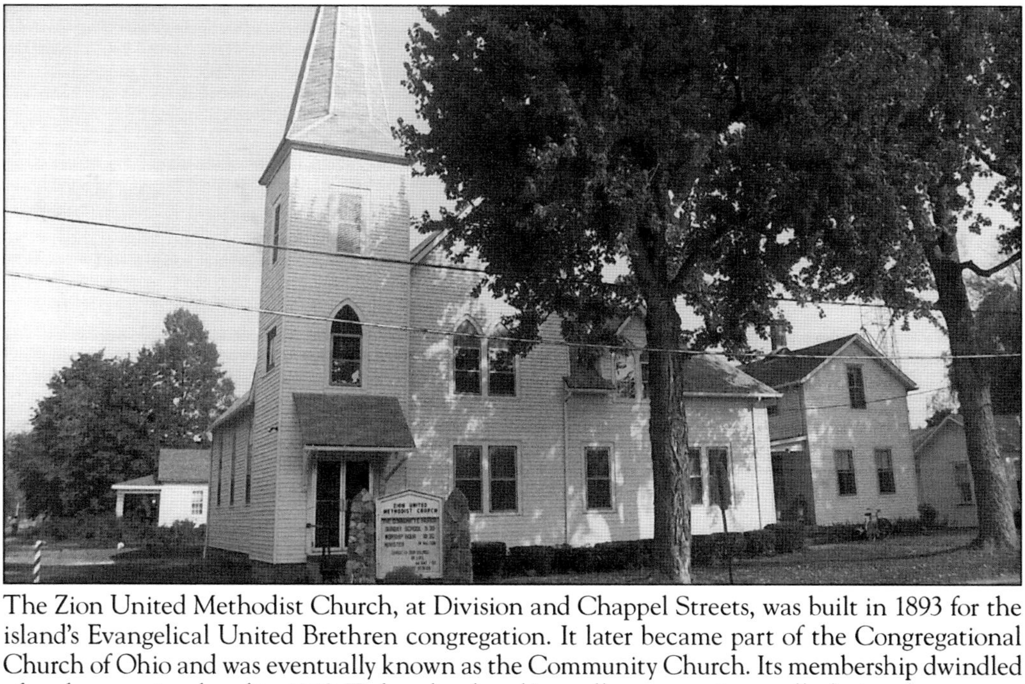

The Zion United Methodist Church, at Division and Chappel Streets, was built in 1893 for the island's Evangelical United Brethren congregation. It later became part of the Congregational Church of Ohio and was eventually known as the Community Church. Its membership dwindled after the quarries closed in 1943. Today, the church's small congregation swells during the summer months. (Courtesy of Jack and Linda Hostal.)

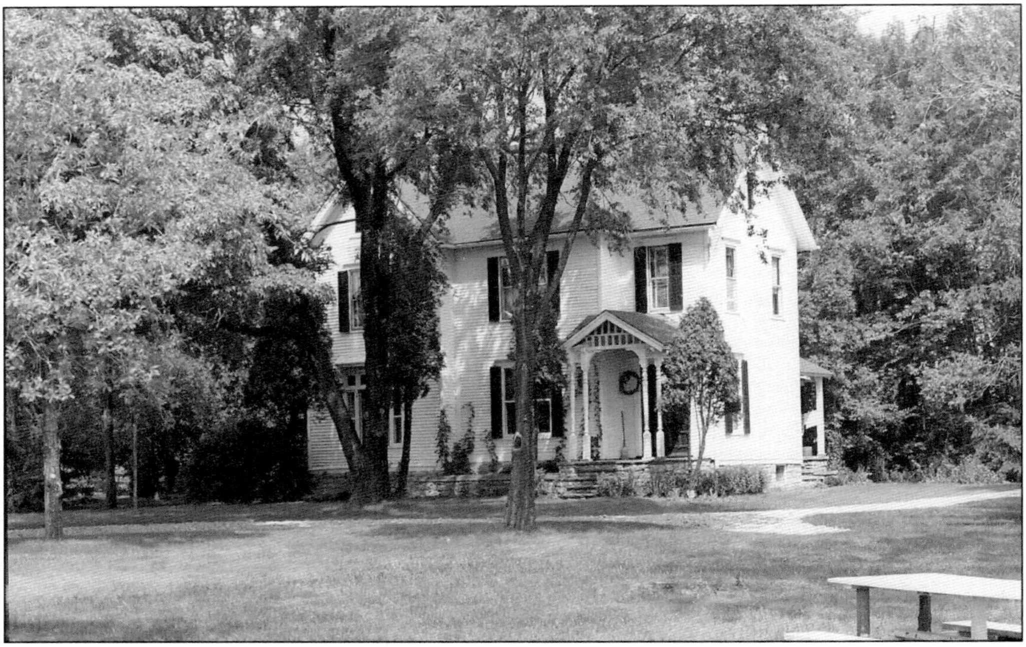

Secluded at the eastern end of Kelleys Island just northeast of the airport, this house was built by Wilhelm Becker in 1893. At the time, Becker's winery and vineyards were producing well and he had become one of the leaders of the German Reformed Church. The house has also been owned by two of the island's mayors and by Richard Celeste when he was governor of Ohio. (Courtesy of Dagmar Celeste.)

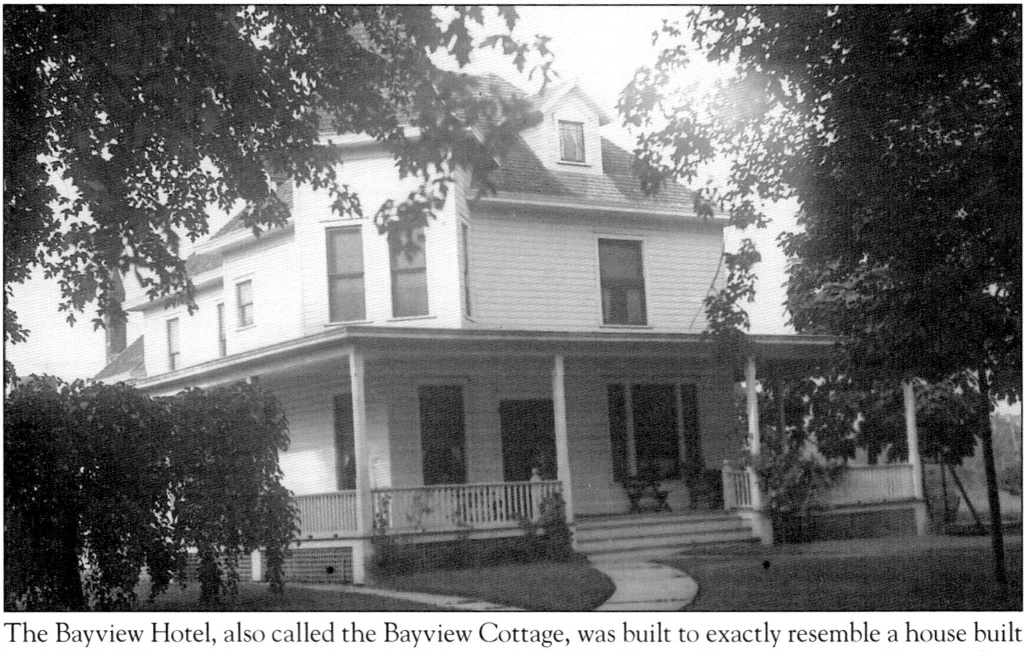

The Bayview Hotel, also called the Bayview Cottage, was built to exactly resemble a house built by Alfred Kelley on the same site, which burned in 1896. The residence was owned by members of the Moysey family until 1950, when it was purchased by William Overcasher, who served as mayor of Kelleys Island from 1957 to 1965. The house is now a private residence. (Courtesy of John T. Sabol.)

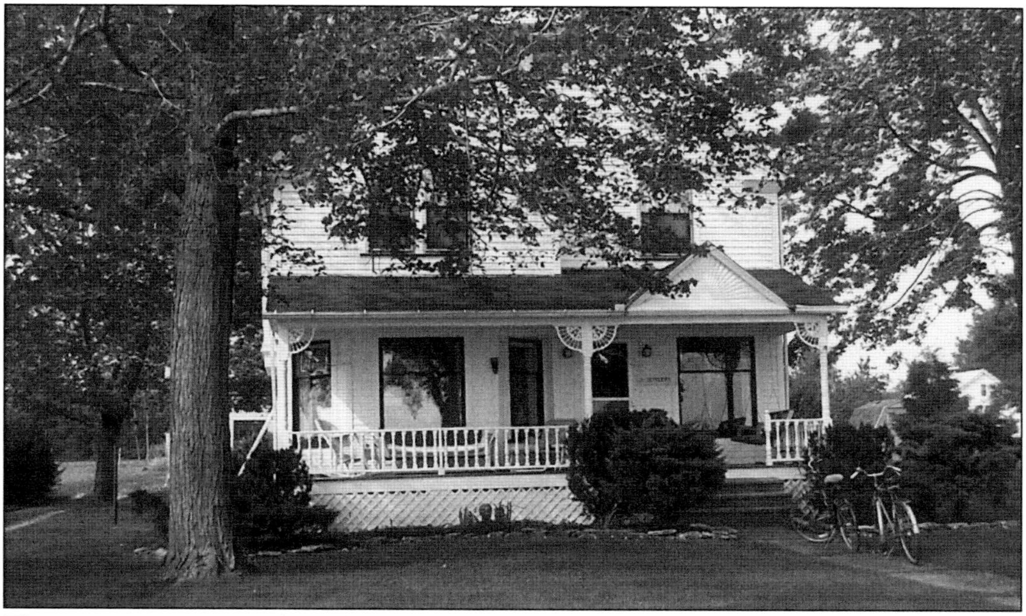

This imposing structure along the island's south shore, about 1,200 feet west of Division Street, once did double duty as a residence and a mortuary, with occasional wakes held in the front parlor. The house was built in 1897 for William Burger, who managed the general store on Division Street. Burger had learned the undertaker's trade at one time and established an undertaker's office at the general store. (Courtesy of Jack and Linda Hostal.)

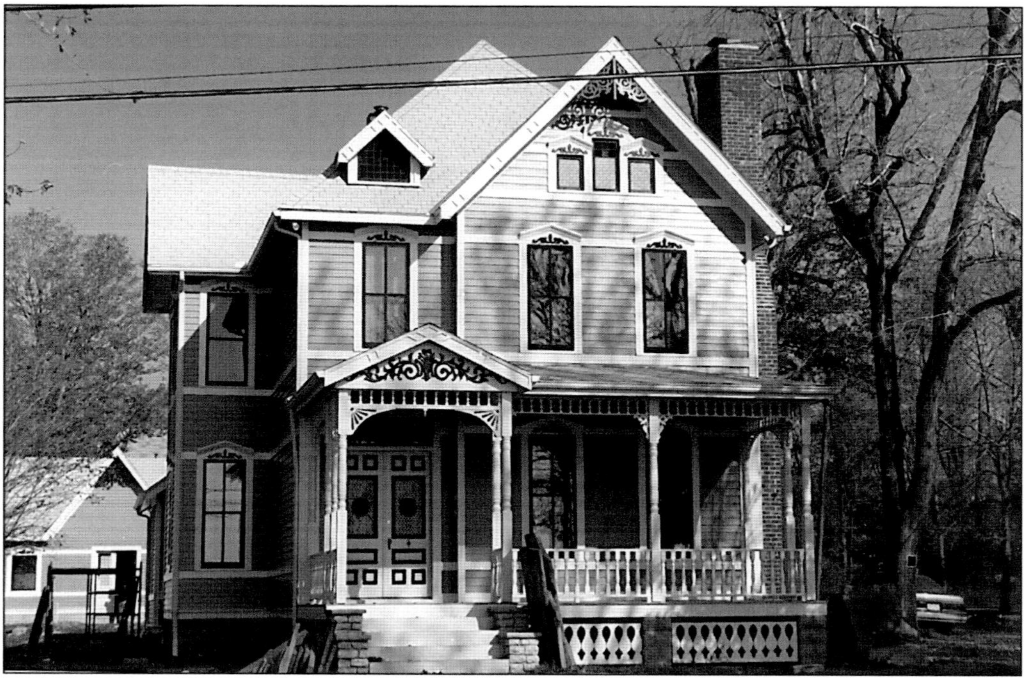

This colorful home at Huntington Lane and West Lakeshore Drive was built in 1898 by Frank Hauser, the superintendent of Kelleys Island Wine Co. Its current owner purchased and restored the house in 1986. A gazebo and an iron fence were added, along with an antique ice cream parlor in the summer kitchen and a vintage barbershop in the garage. (Courtesy of Jack and Linda Hostal.)

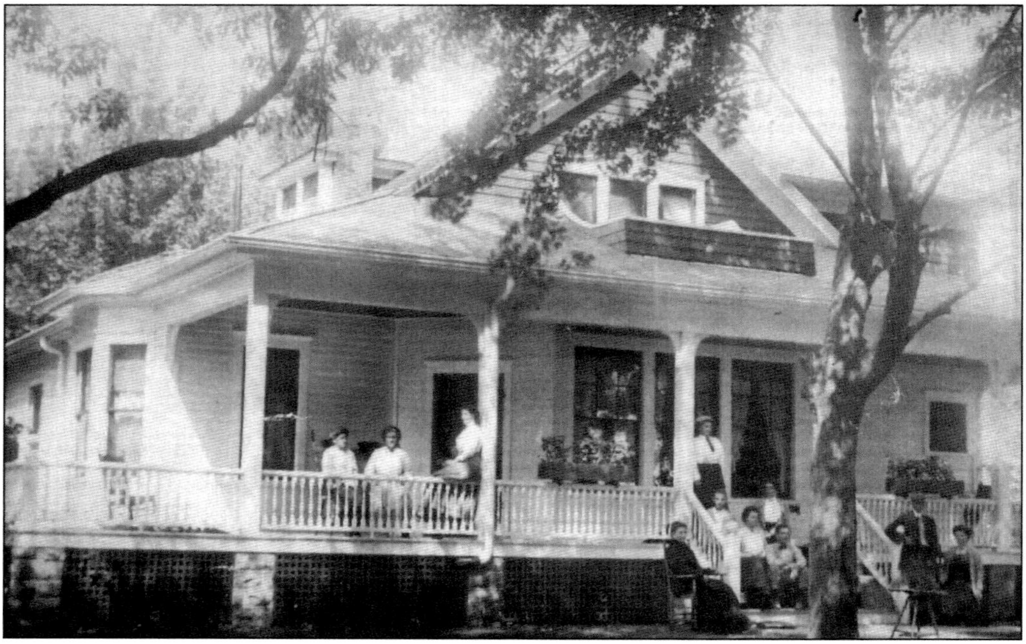

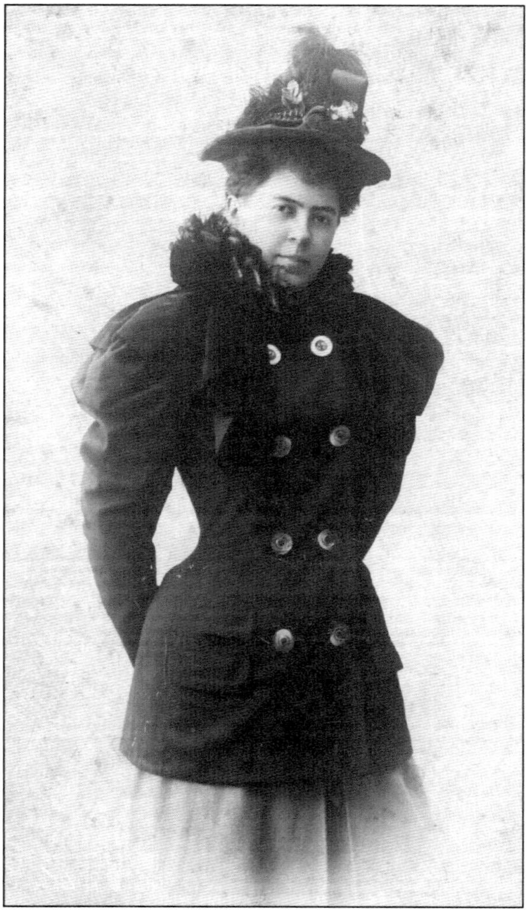

Cricket Lodge, John and Bertha Himmelein's summer retreat, was a getaway for members of the theatrical stock companies that John managed. John's father, Johann, owned the neighboring Himmelein Hotel, which John had managed. Following their theatrical careers, the couple retired in Sandusky and maintained Cricket Lodge, which they built in 1905, as their summer home until Bertha and John died in 1955 and 1956, respectively. The home, which served as a bed-and-breakfast for more than 20 years, is now a private residence. (Courtesy of Chris and Frank Yako.)

John Himmelein and his wife, Bertha Wiles, owned Cricket Lodge, on East Lakeshore Drive just east of Division Street. The Himmeleins were a theatrical family: John owned several theaters in northwest and north-central Ohio as well as several stock companies, and Bertha sang and performed as a dramatic actress, comedian, and vaudevillian under the stage name Beatrice Earle. (Courtesy of Chris and Frank Yako.)

Vaudevillians from John Himmelein's stock company, the Ideals, spent their summers at the Himmelein Hotel perfecting their craft. Here, an unidentified actor or magician from the company performs one of his tricks on the hotel's front lawn. (Courtesy of Fritz Pape's photo album, Pape family collection.)

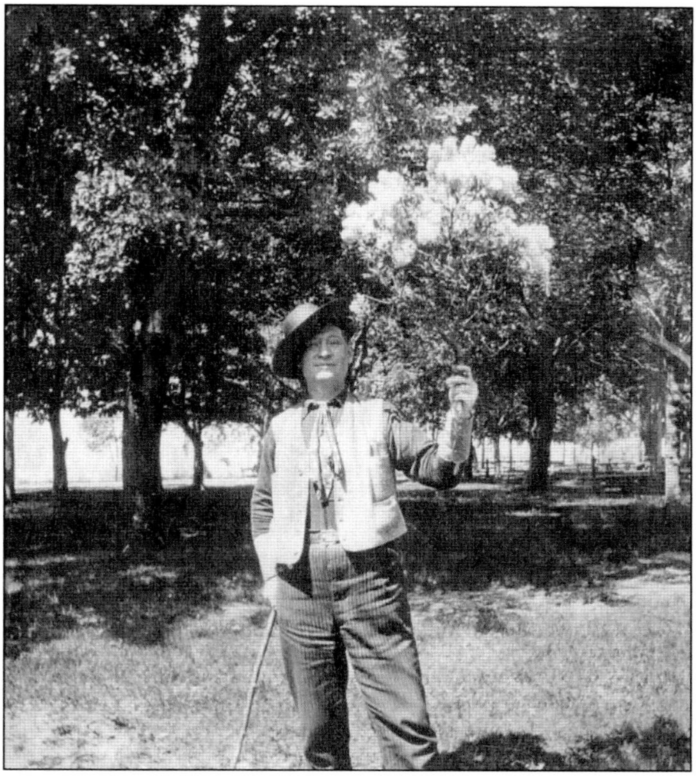

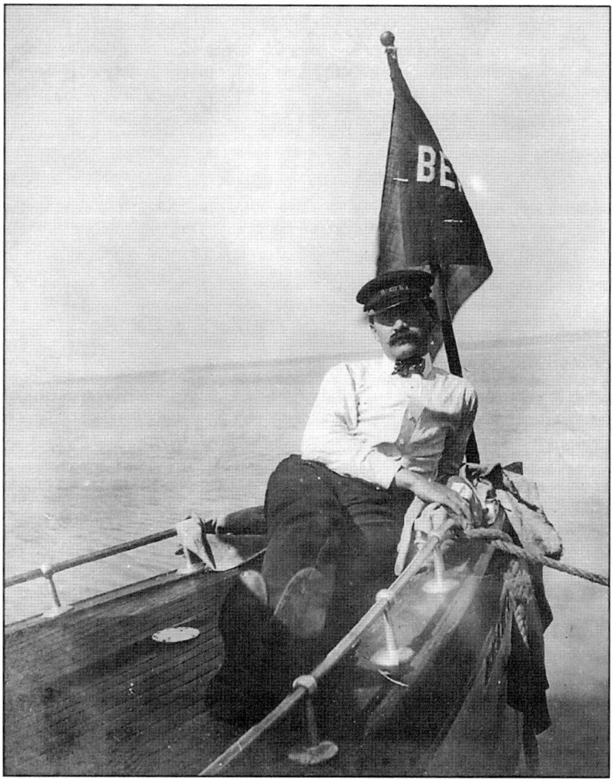

John Himmelein, seen here on his boat off of Kelleys Island, was the son of Johann and Johanna Himmelein, the proprietors of the Himmelein Hotel. In 1890, John left the family hotel business and began working with Howard Wall's Model Comedy Company as the company's agent, later partnering with Wall to create the Ideals. John Himmelein married his leading lady, Bertha Wiles, who used the stage name Beatrice Earle. (Courtesy of Chris and Frank Yako.)

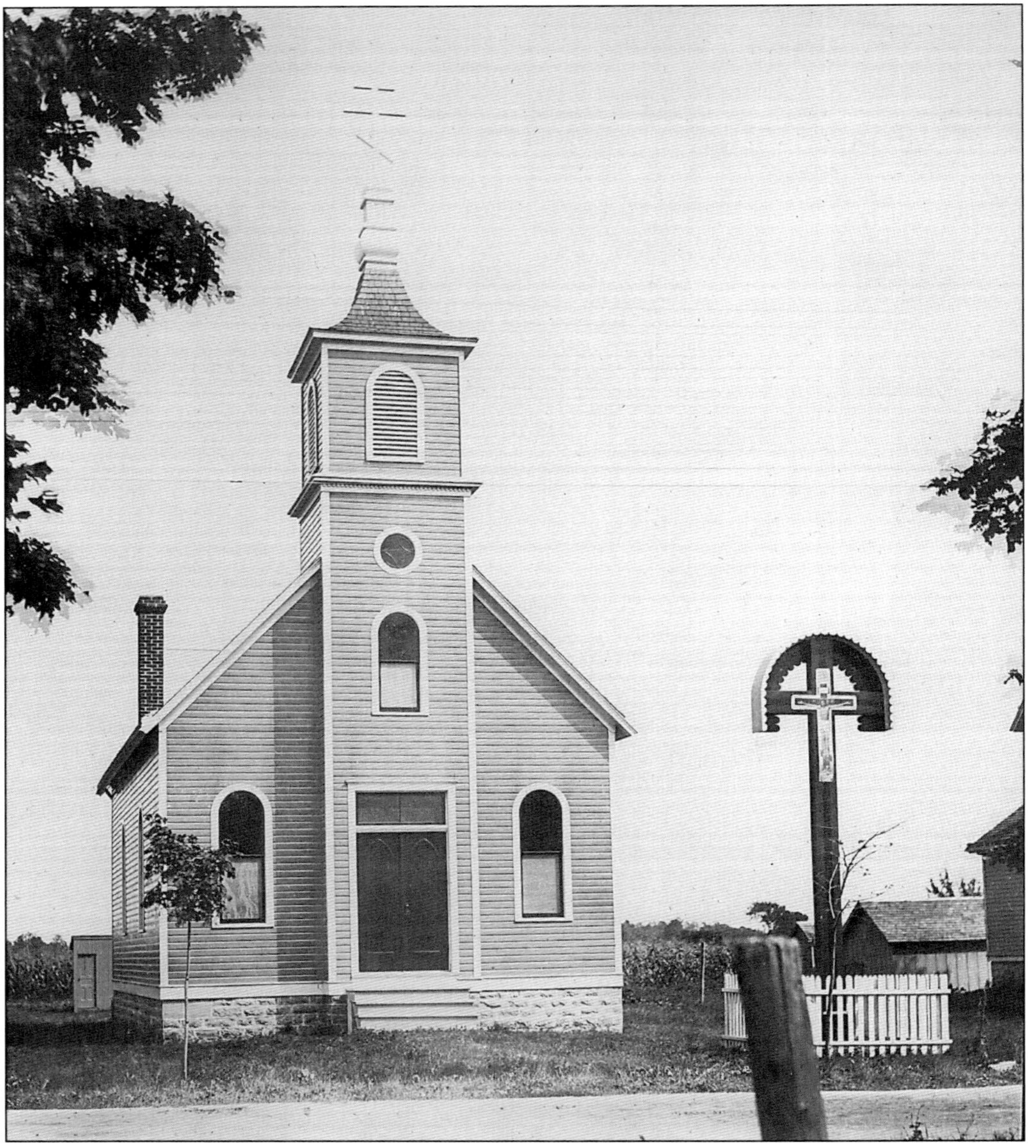

Carpatho-Rusyn quarry workers on Kelleys Island organized a Greek Catholic church around 1900. This building on the east side of Division Street served the congregation, which appears to have shifted from the Greek Catholic to the Russian Orthodox faith, possibly depending on the availability of clergy. The congregation dwindled, particularly after the quarries began to shut down in 1940, and the church was razed in 1941. Curiously, this church predates a Greek Catholic church established in Marblehead, on the mainland, by several years. A Greek cross remains as a memorial on the property where the church once stood. The marker is a tribute to these hardy immigrants, many of whose descendants still reside on the island. (Courtesy of the Frohman Collection, Rutherford B. Hayes Presidential Center.)

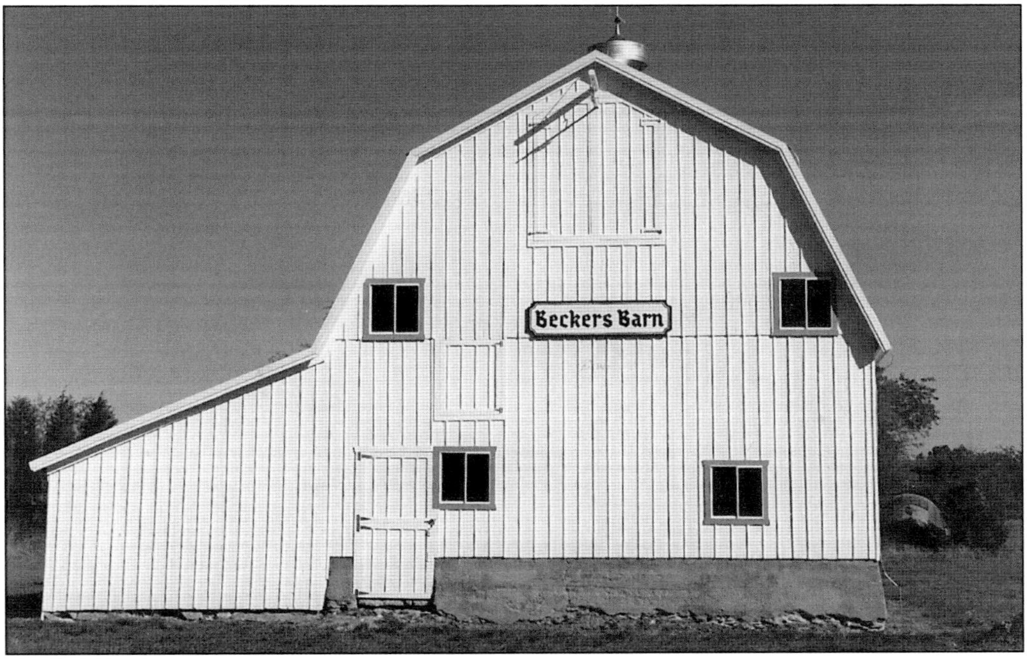

A remnant of Kelleys Island's agricultural economy is Becker's Barn, on the north side of Woodford Road. Operated by George Becker from about 1905 to 1940, the dairy farm specialized in Jersey cattle. The Kelleys Island Historical Association points out that the farms on the island supported the pheasant population, which attracted hunters each year. Once the farms died out, the pheasants' food supply and the pheasant population dwindled. (Courtesy of Jack and Linda Hostal.)

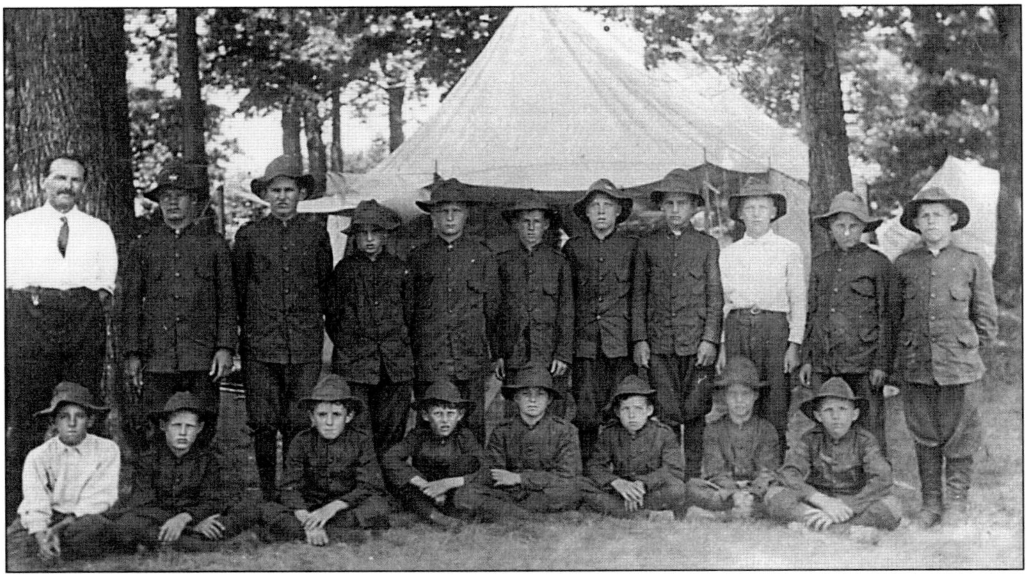

Posing around the time of World War I, this group from the German Reformed Church includes, from left to right, (first row) Ted Suhr, Ted Neumeister, George Suhr, Clayton Huges, Kari Klaaske, Zenus Mapes, Leroy Neumeister, and Bill Burger; (second row) Rev. Matthew Neumeister, Christ Kurtz, Ruben Becker, Fritz Schlumbohm, Webb Gibeaut, Henny Beatty, Bill Schnittker, Wess Trieschman, John Reinheimer, Butch Schaedler, and Boiler Kurtz. (Courtesy of the Kelleys Island Historical Association.)

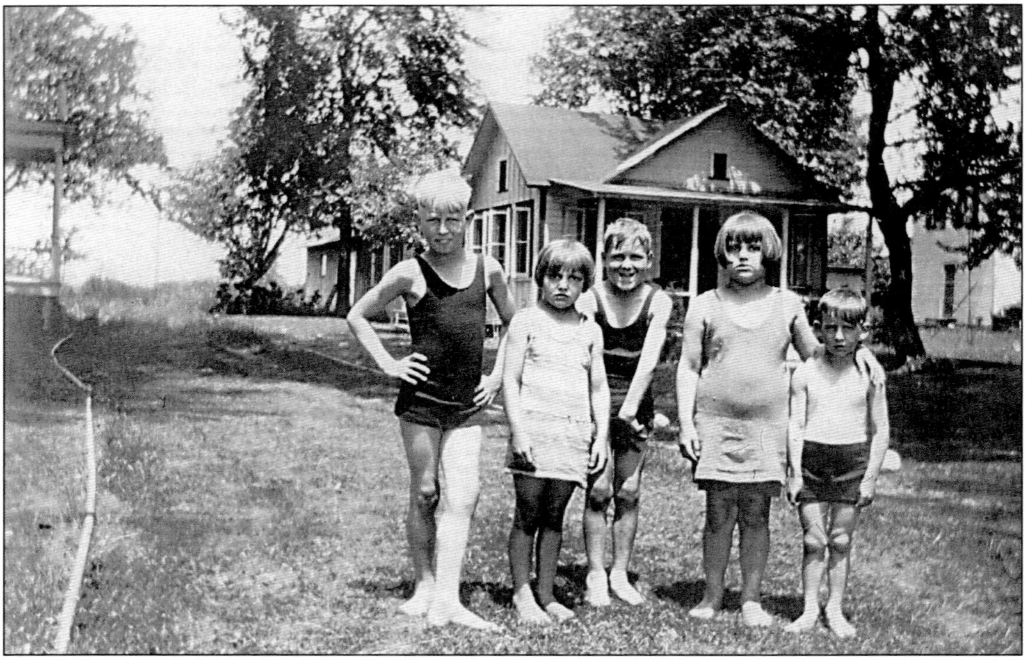

The Pape cottage, on East Lakeshore Drive about 500 feet west of Addison Road, was originally a two-lane bowling alley serving patrons of the Himmelein Hotel next door. Posing for a photograph taken by Bill Pape around 1930 are, from left to right, Teddy Himmelein, Florence Pohorence, Jimmy Himmelein, Josephine Pohorence, and Frank Pohorence, who became the owner of the Island Market from 1946 to 1983. (Courtesy of Bill Pape's photo album, Pape family collection.)

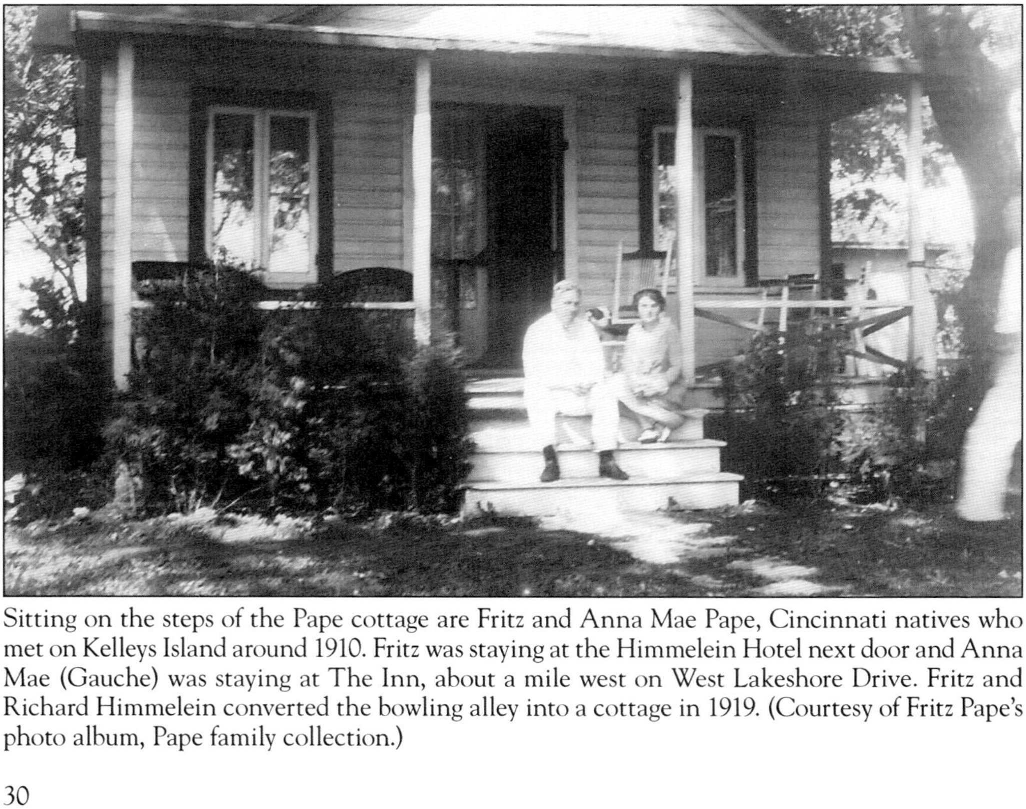

Sitting on the steps of the Pape cottage are Fritz and Anna Mae Pape, Cincinnati natives who met on Kelleys Island around 1910. Fritz was staying at the Himmelein Hotel next door and Anna Mae (Gauche) was staying at The Inn, about a mile west on West Lakeshore Drive. Fritz and Richard Himmelein converted the bowling alley into a cottage in 1919. (Courtesy of Fritz Pape's photo album, Pape family collection.)

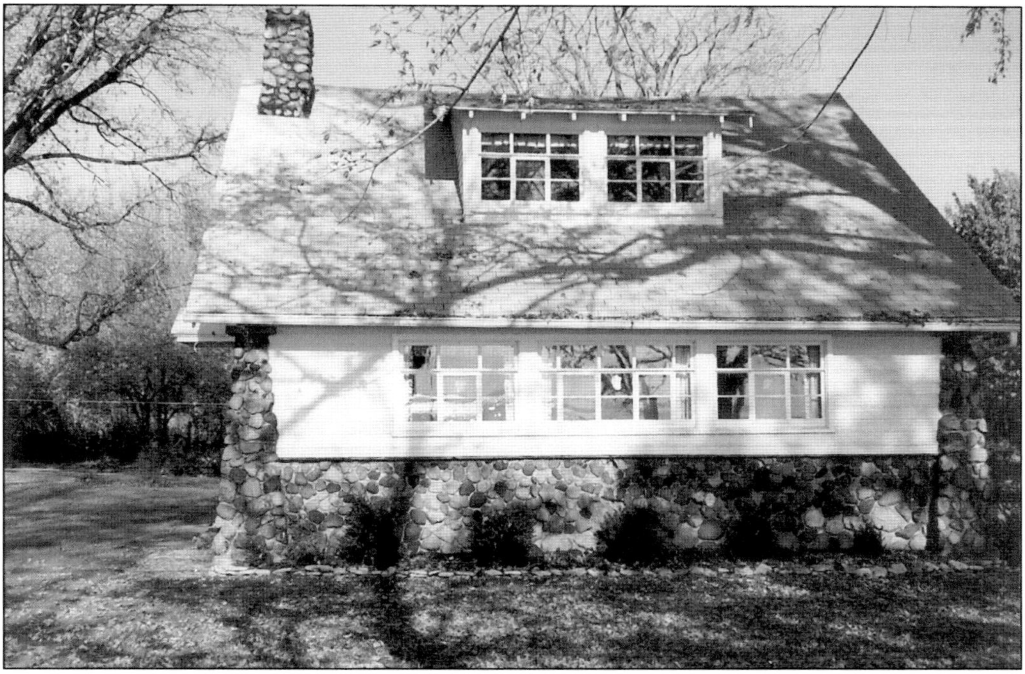

This house, on East Lakeshore Drive just west of the Seaway Marina, was one of the first on the island to be constructed as a vacation home. Dr. Robert Hummell of Western Reserve (now Case Western Reserve) University built the house in 1925. Dr. Hummell was part of a group that purchased the nearby Kelley Mansion and operated it from 1927 to 1932 as the Kelleys Island Sportsmen's Club. (Courtesy of Jack and Linda Hostal.)

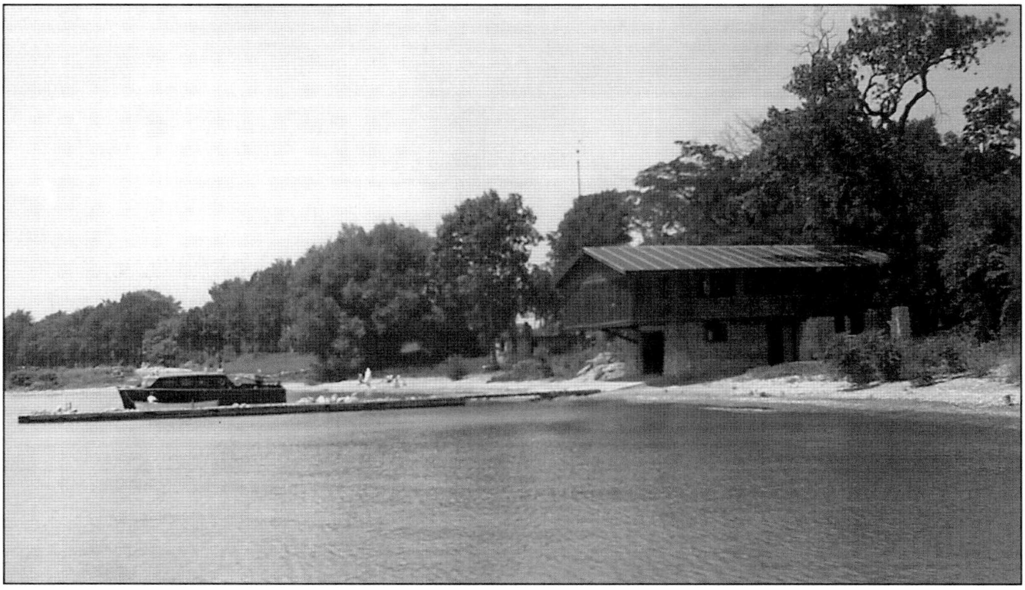

The Huber cottage, on East Lakeshore Drive east of the Addison Kelley Mansion, is one of the few dwellings built directly on the island's south shore. The cottage was constructed by Alic Huber in 1932. It is said that Native American inscriptions have been found on a large rock in the foundation. The boat in this 1935 photograph is the *Dun Dee*, owned by the Kelley family. (Courtesy of Jack and Linda Hostal.)

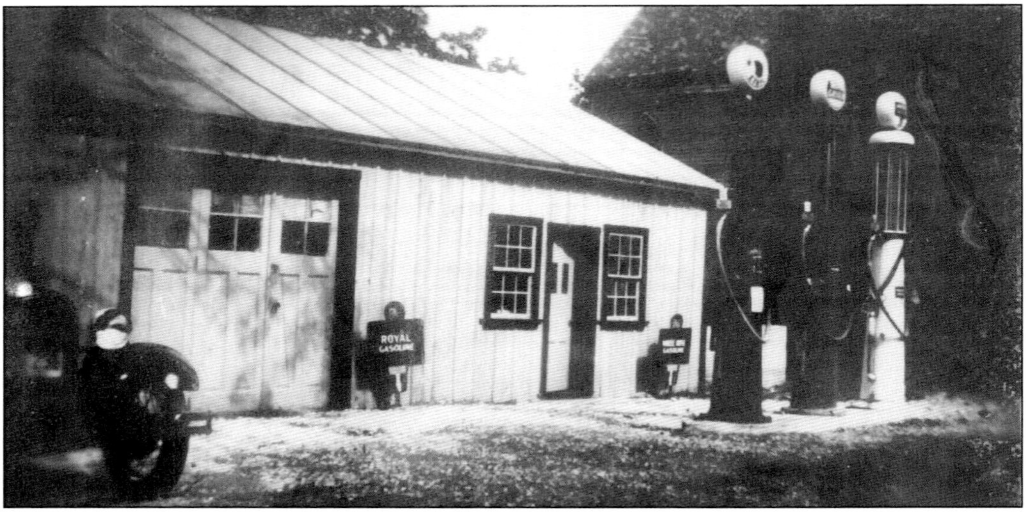

This service station and garage on the west side of Division Street, Myers Garage, stood almost across from the intersection with Chappel Street. It was owned by Sam Myers, and after this building burned, he moved a quarry worker's house from Bookerman Road onto the foundation. That dwelling still stands on this site and is a private residence. (Courtesy of Gary and Jackie Finger.)

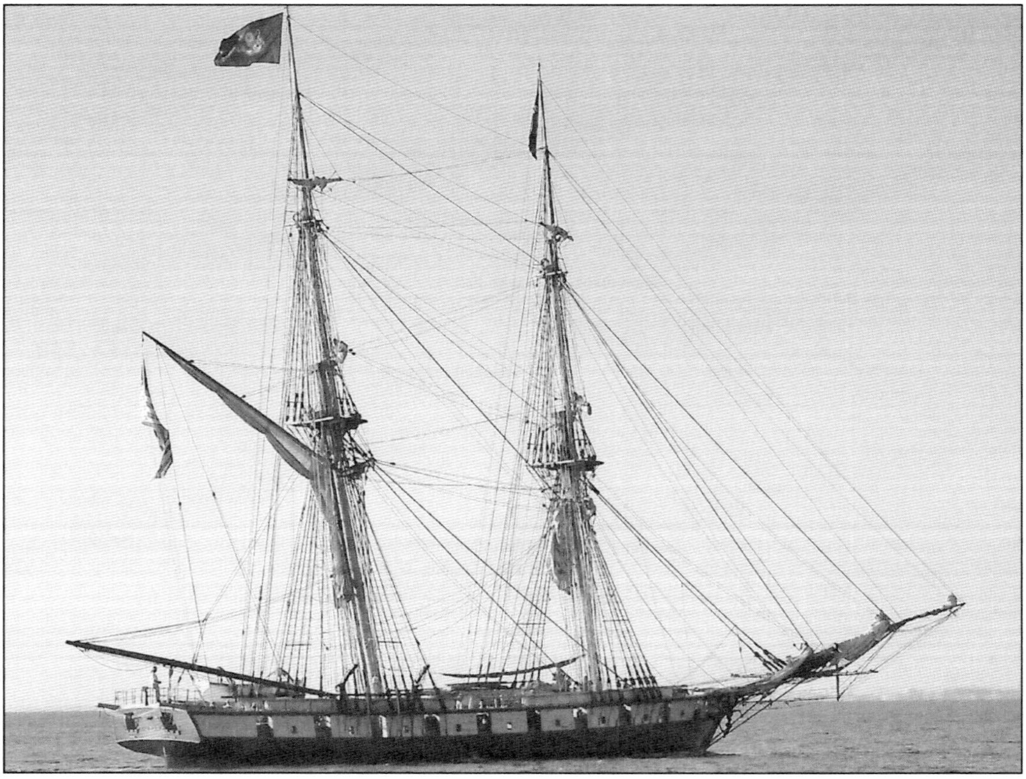

The year 2013 marked the 200th anniversary of the Battle of Lake Erie, a pivotal encounter between the United States and Great Britain during the War of 1812. In advance of this anniversary, a replica of the *Niagara*, the flagship of Commodore Oliver Hazard Perry during the battle, visited Kelleys Island. The island played an important role before the battle, as observers there reported back to the US fleet about British movements. (Courtesy of Doug Boldon.)

Two

ON THE ROCKS PART I

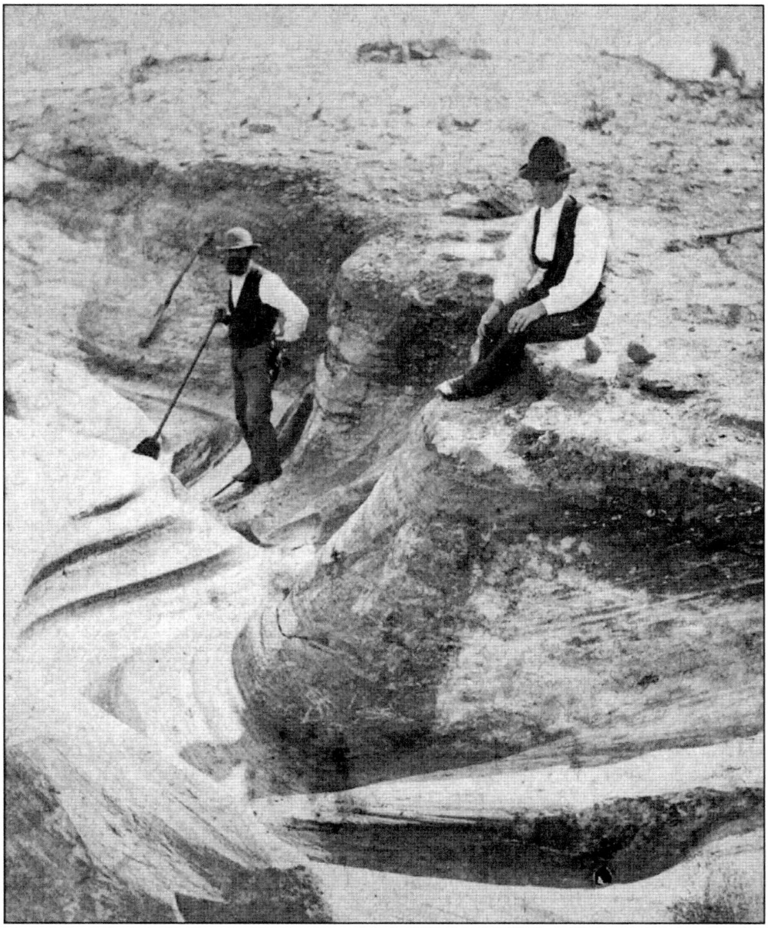

Carved into limestone by mile-high glaciers 10,000 years ago, Kelleys Island's Glacial Grooves, near the north end of Division Street, are an example of the remarkable power of glaciers. Sadly, a considerable portion of the Great Grooves, seen here in the 1890s, was destroyed by quarrying before the operations were halted. (Courtesy of the Sandusky Library Follett House Museum Archives.)

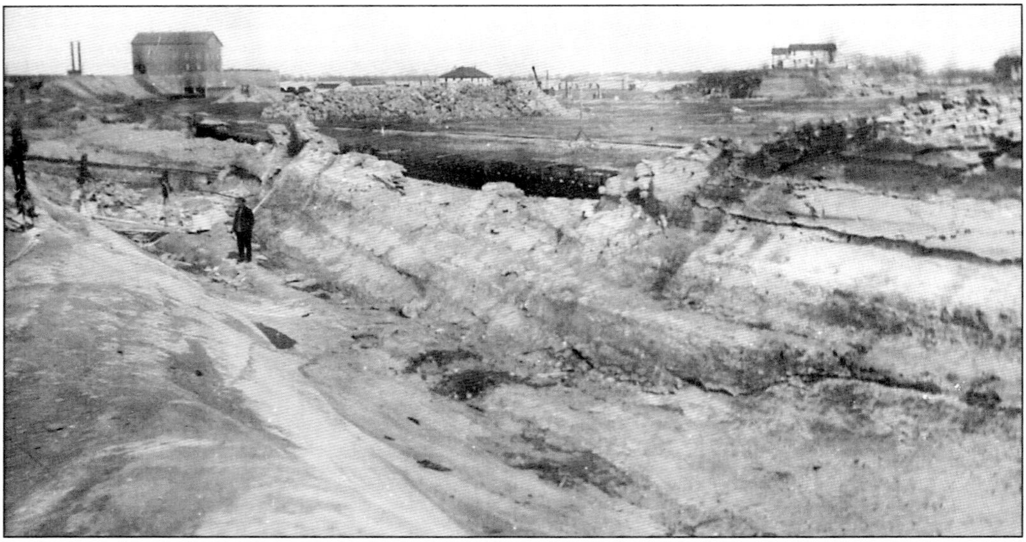

No one will ever visit this portion of the Glacial Grooves. Seen here in 1913, this section—measuring 2,000 feet long, 30 feet wide, and 15 feet deep—was completely quarried out. Seen from left to right in the background are the North Quarry stone crusher, the Kelley Island Lime & Transport Co. general store, and the quarry workers' boardinghouse, which was razed in 1926. (Courtesy of Gary and Jackie Finger.)

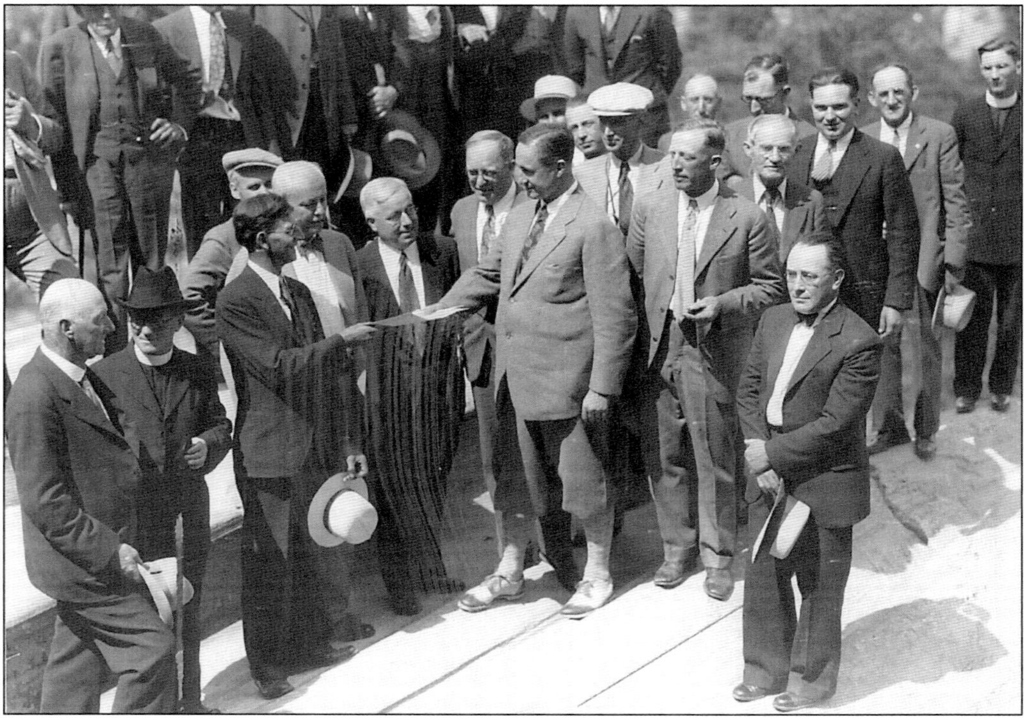

In 1922, Harold T. Clark, the secretary of the Cleveland Museum of Natural History, obtained title to the Glacial Grooves in an effort to preserve them. In June 1932, Clark (center), standing on the grooves, passes the title to H.C. Shetrone, the director of the Ohio State Archaeological and Historical Society. (Courtesy of the Cleveland Press Archives, Cleveland State University Library Special Collections.)

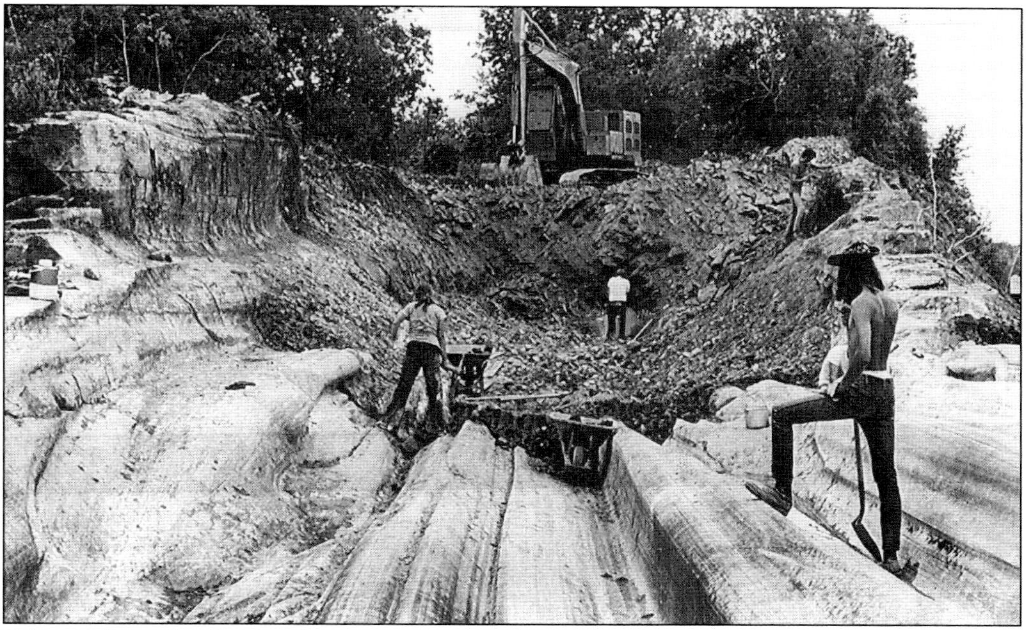

When Kelleys Island's Glacial Grooves were established as a park, only a small section was exposed. In 1972, the Ohio Historical Society uncovered the section that is exposed today, measuring 430 feet long, 35 feet wide, and 15 feet deep. Here, in July 1972, Carl Bennett, a geology major at Ohio State University, stands on the lower right, where the digging began. (Courtesy of the Cleveland Press Archives, Cleveland State University Library Special Collections.)

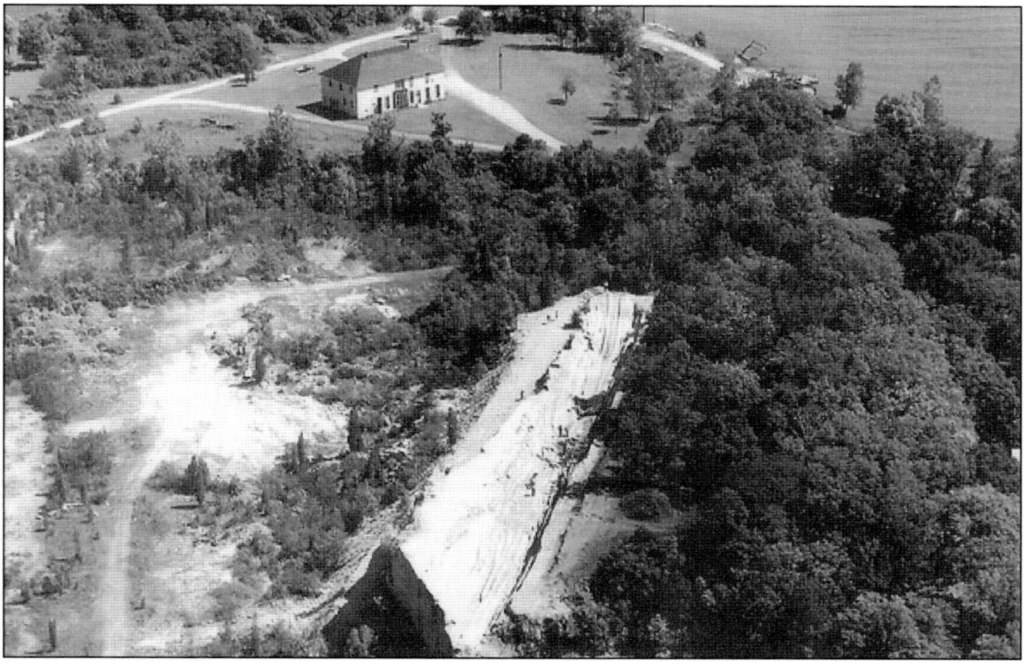

Kelleys Island's Glacial Grooves are seen here fully uncovered in 1972. This view makes it painfully obvious how much of the grooves had already been destroyed before it was realized how important a geological find the grooves were. The structure to the upper left is a former quarry building. (Courtesy of the Kelleys Island Historical Association.)

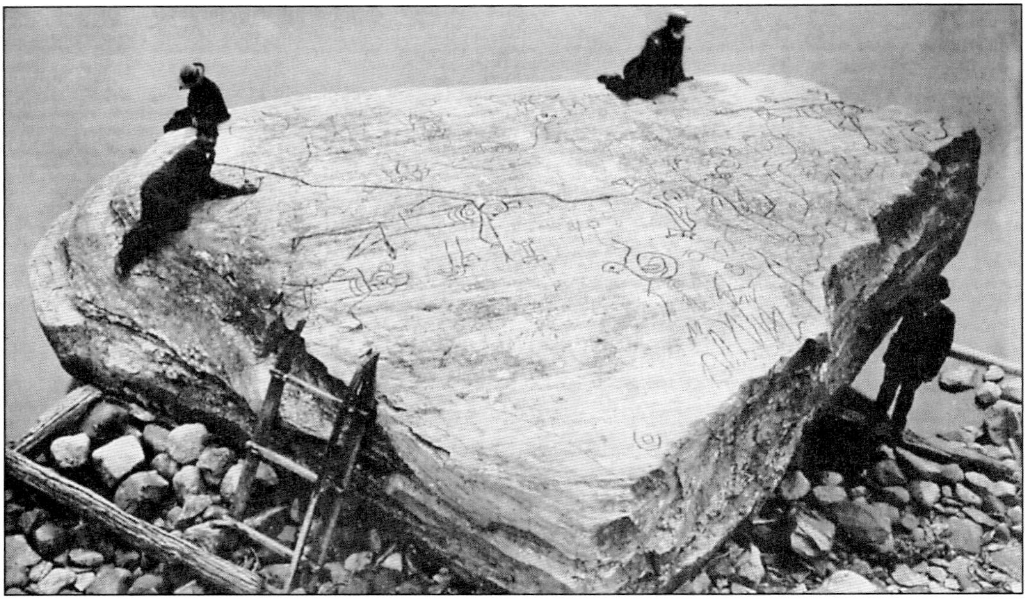

With its 122 pictographs depicting Native American life on the island between 1200 and 1600 AD, the 32-foot-by-21-foot Inscription Rock is a look at the island's prehistory. This view of Inscription Rock from the late 1800s gives a clear view of the pictographs that were once more visible than they are today. (Courtesy of John T. Sabol.)

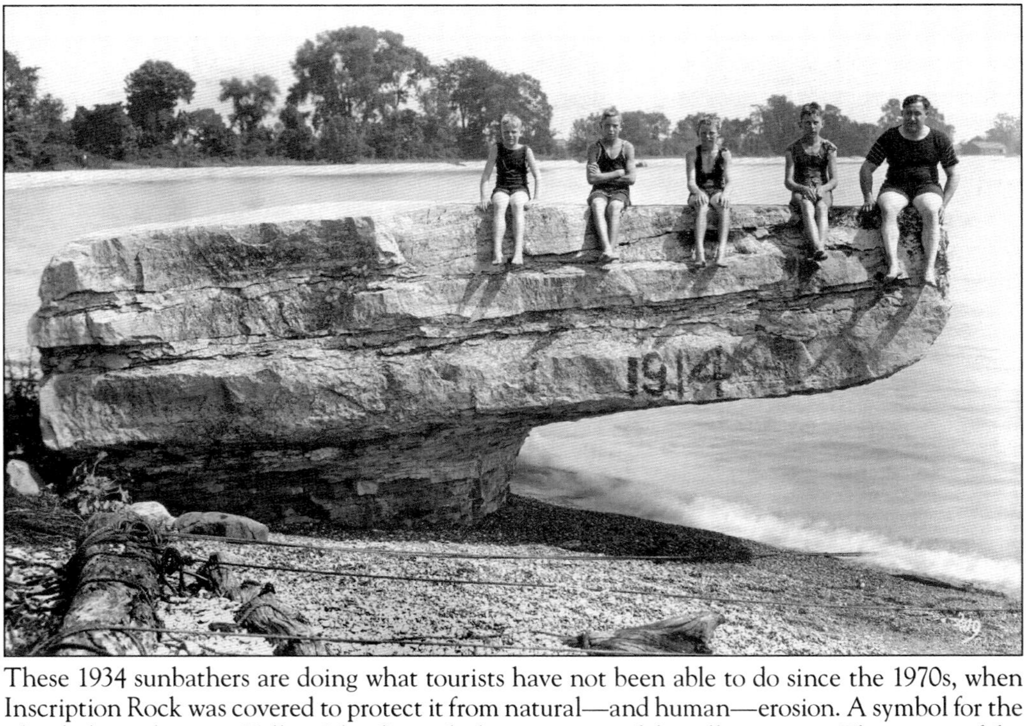

These 1934 sunbathers are doing what tourists have not been able to do since the 1970s, when Inscription Rock was covered to protect it from natural—and human—erosion. A symbol for the island, the rock sits on Kelleys Island's south shore just east of the village center. The source of the 1914 date is unknown—although the high school class of that year might be suspect. The sunbathers are unidentified. (Courtesy of the Cleveland Public Library Photograph Collection.)

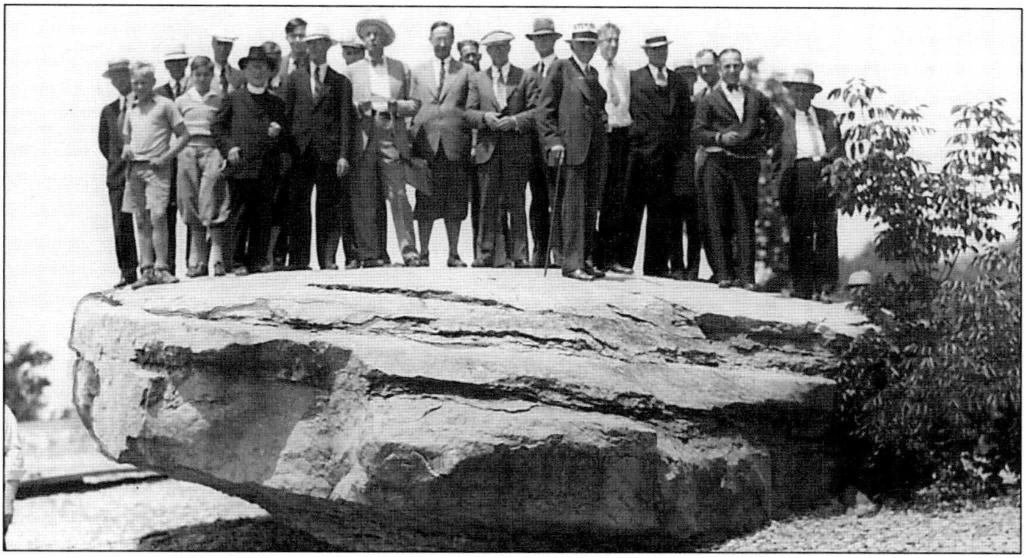

In June 1932, these visitors may have been trying to set a record for the number of people who can stand on Inscription Rock. They are representing the Cleveland Museum of Natural History and the Ohio State Archaeological and Historical Society, and are on the island for the transfer of ownership of Inscription Rock and the Glacial Grooves to the latter group. (Courtesy of the Cleveland Press Archives, Cleveland State University Library Special Collections.)

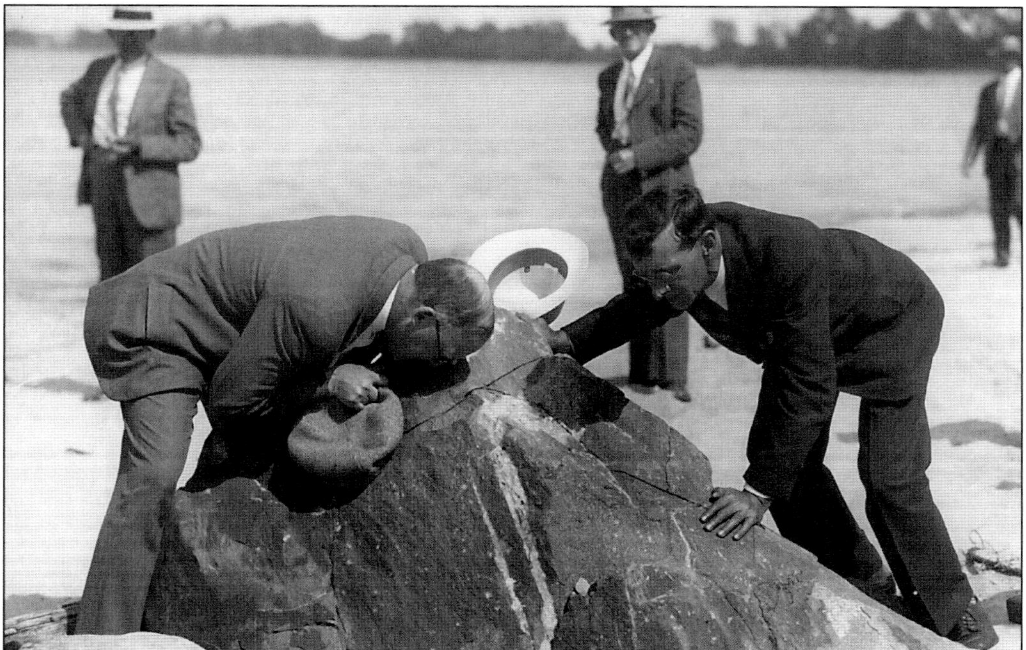

Inscription Rock was complemented by a smaller version at Sandy Beach. The rock disappeared over time, but as late as 1932, in an effort to preserve island landmarks, Harold Madison (left) of the Cleveland Museum of Natural History and H.C. Shetrone (right), the director of the Ohio State Archaeological and Historical Society, visited the island and examined the North Bay Inscription Rock. (Courtesy of the Cleveland Press Archives, Cleveland State University Library Special Collections.)

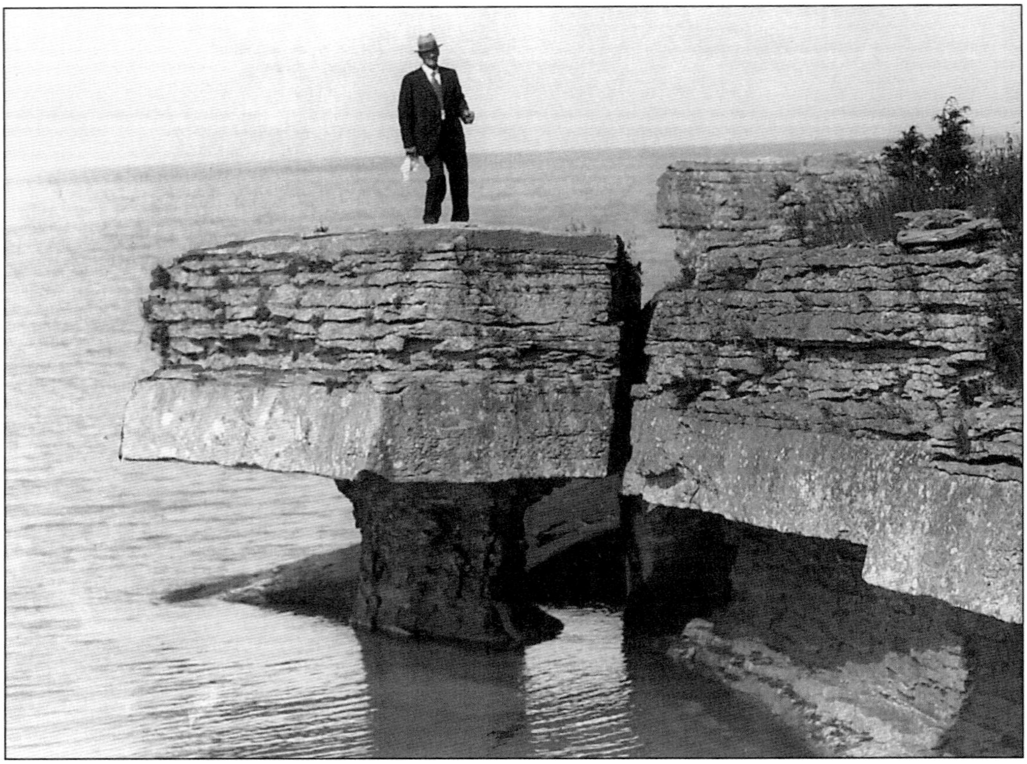

In 1932, according to the *Cleveland Plain Dealer*, people were beginning "to appreciate the beauty of the lake and its richness in scientific and historical lore." Part of this appreciation focused on the island's Table Rock, which formerly graced Kelleys' northwest tip on Long Point. Lake Erie's waves have since tumbled this island landmark. (Courtesy of the Cleveland Press Archives, Cleveland State University Library Special Collections.)

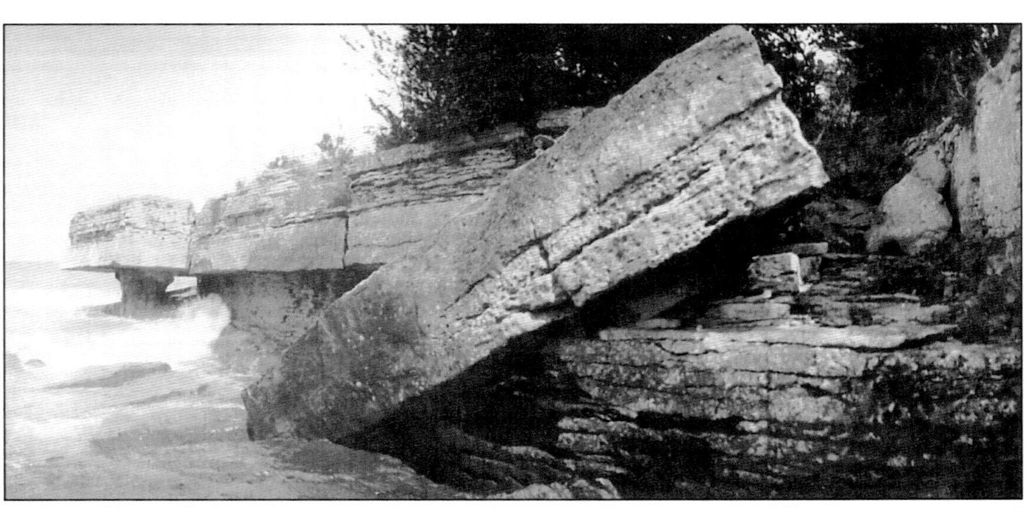

Sadly, Table Rock, long a tourist sight on Kelleys Island's Long Point, fell victim to continued pounding by Lake Erie and began its inevitable tumble into the water in the 1970s. The lake's action on Long Point has made its west shore more treacherous. (Courtesy of Bob and Carol Schnittker.)

Three

Casks and Nets

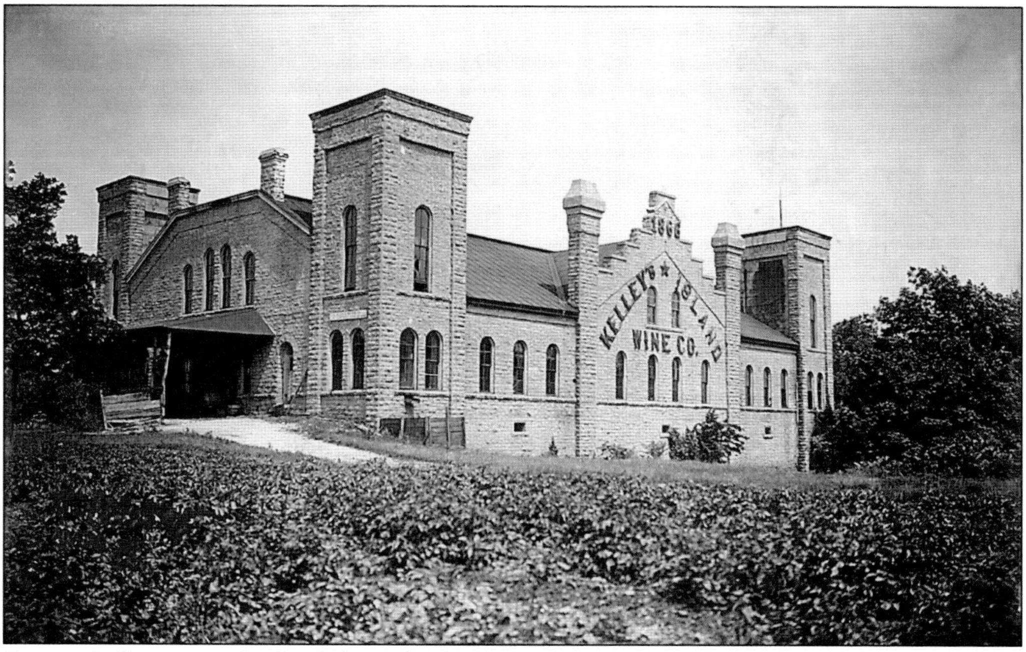

Surrounded by vineyards, the Kelleys Island Wine Co. winery is seen here during its peak production days. The winery was established in 1865 as a cooperative, bringing together the work of several smaller vineyards. By 1872, it was producing 163,500 gallons of wine. This building replaced a smaller facility damaged in an 1876 fire and was able to store 350,000 gallons. (Courtesy of the Cleveland Press Archives, Cleveland State University Library Special Collections.)

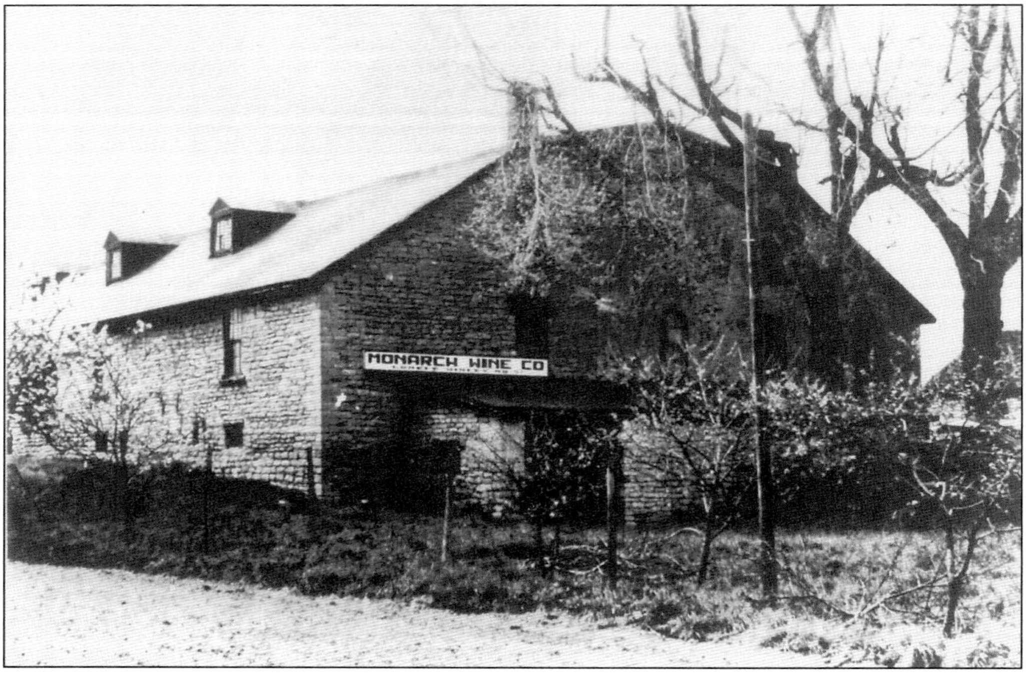

The Monarch Winery, on the west side of Division Street north of Ward Road, had a cellar that held 40,000 gallons of wine plus 2,000 gallons of grape brandy, according to the book *Kelleys Island: A Tour Guide*. The winery, built in 1872 and expanded in 1880, was the only island winery to resume production in 1933 with the end of Prohibition. It closed in 1950, and its ruins are still visible from Division Street. (Courtesy of the Kelleys Island Historical Association.)

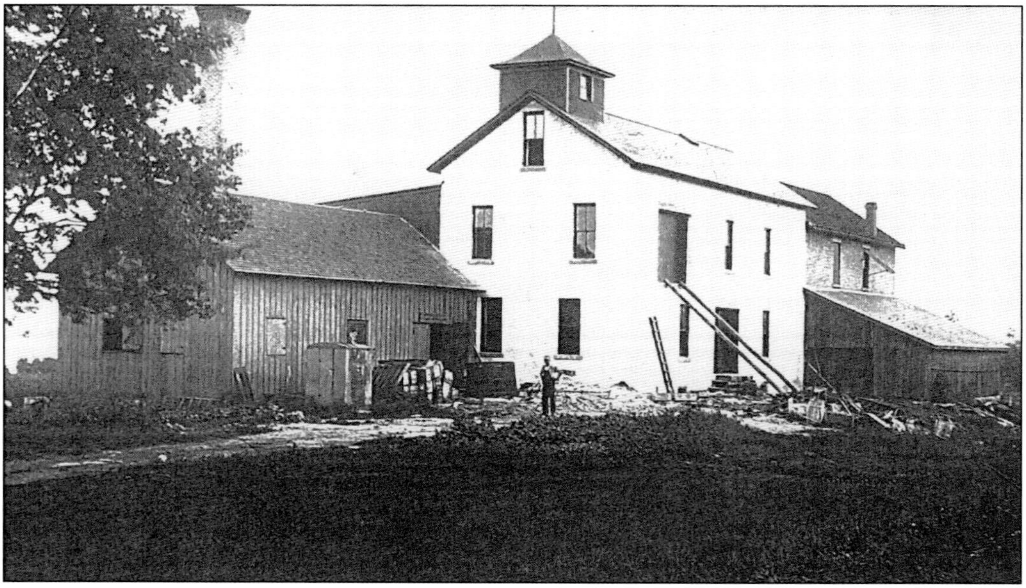

In addition to being involved in farming, Wilhelm Becker also established the W.F. Becker & Co. winery on Ward Road, in a building he purchased from Titus Hamilton in 1882. The winery burned in 1924, and the remains were razed in 1936. Bricks from this building were used to construct the south wing of the Villa, a Catholic camp on Monagan Road (now Camp Patmos). (Courtesy of Karen Becker Grubaugh.)

Koster's dock, just west of Inscription Rock, was originally the shipping point for wine from the Koster Winery and became the home of the Unique Marker Yacht Club. The winery is seen here in 1931. In 1883, Herman Koster built the winery on what is now East Lakeshore Drive and rented it to the Sweet Valley Wine Co. The winery was damaged by fire in 1932 and torn down in 1933. (Courtesy of the Cleveland Public Library Photograph Collection.)

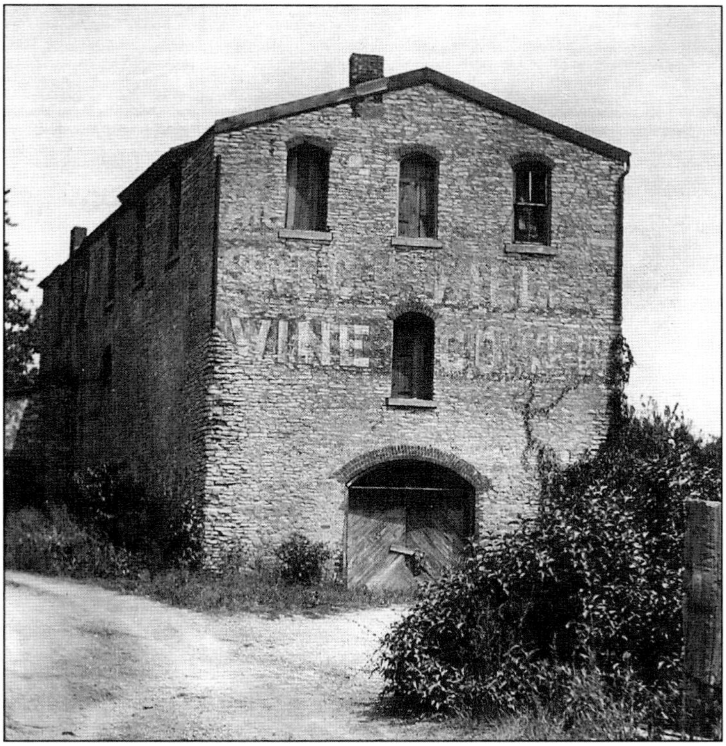

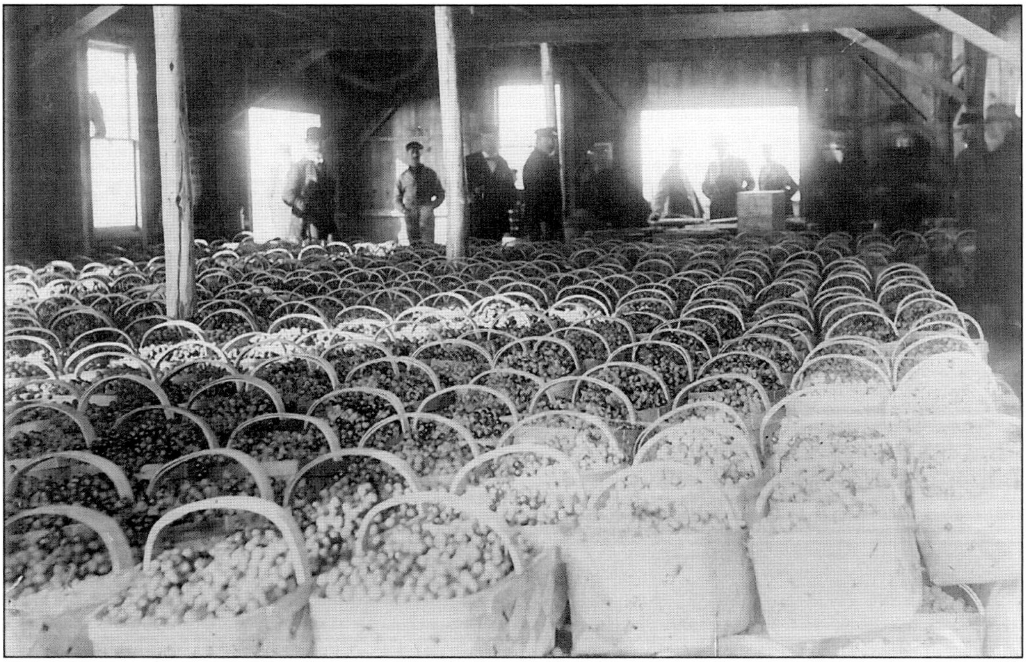

Baskets of grapes await shipment to the mainland. Grapes quickly became an important island industry, beginning with the Kelleys themselves in 1841. They were followed by Datus Kelley's son-in-law Charles Carpenter, who purchased 123 acres from Horace Kelley on the southwest corner of the island in 1846. A host of individual families opened commercial vineyards on the island. (Courtesy of the Kelleys Island Historical Association.)

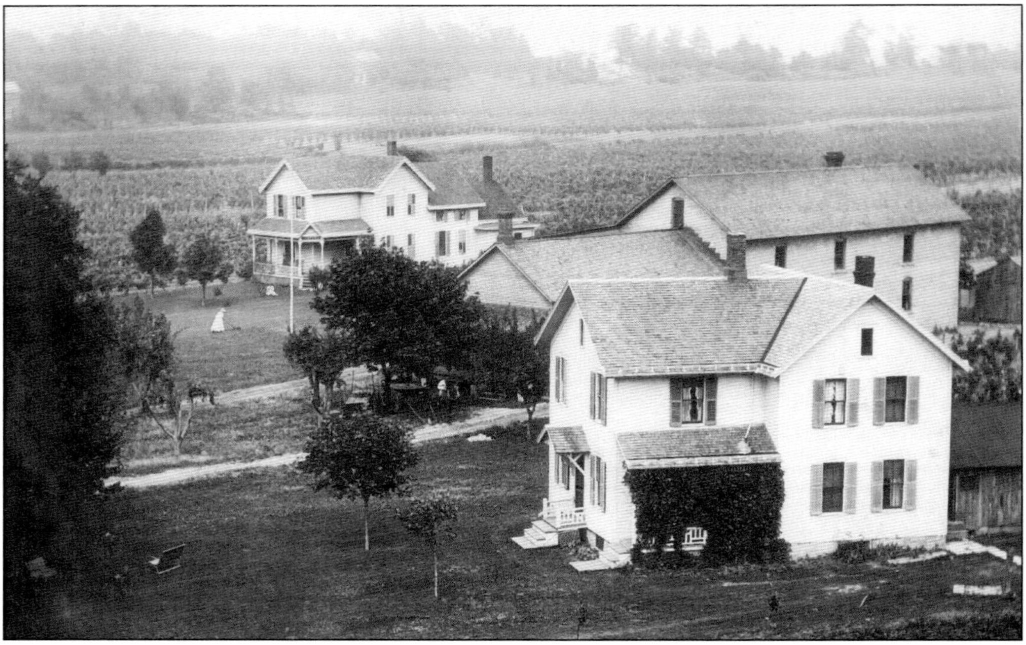

The site of the West Bay Inn is seen here around 1900. The center building in this group of three is the current West Bay Inn—the wing in the front appears to have been removed. At this time, it was the Schaedler and Rhein Winery. The house on the left, John Schaedler's home, was built about 1890. In the foreground is Louis Rhein's house, built in 1886. (Courtesy of the Kelleys Island Historical Association.)

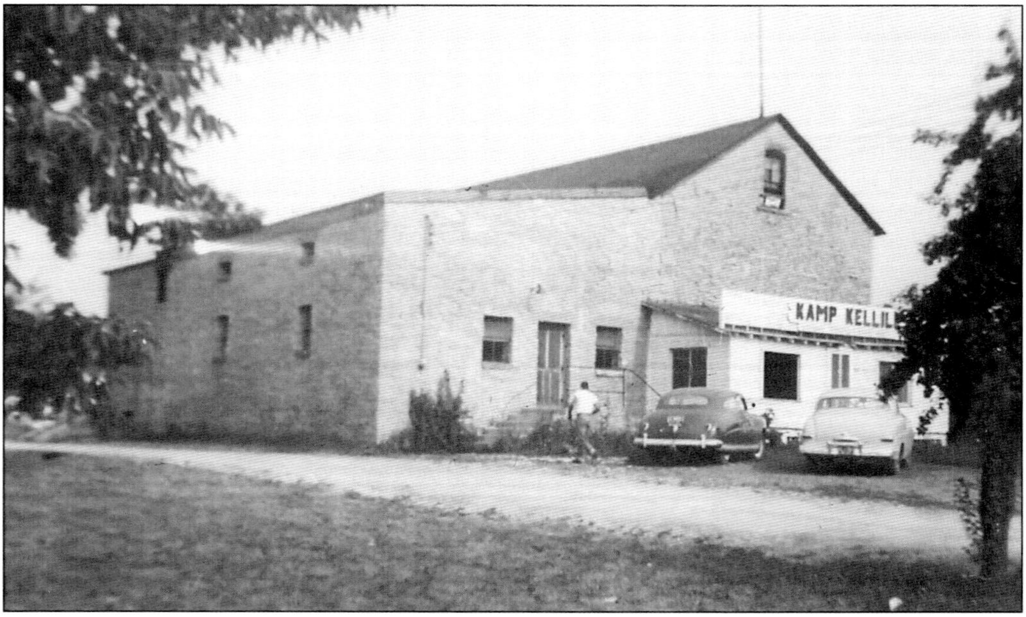

What is now the West Bay Inn was known for many years as Kamp Kellile. Before that, it was the Schaedler and Rhein Winery. The original building, constructed in 1887, is on the right. With a capacity of 80,000 gallons, it was one of the largest wineries on the island. However, it lay vacant from about 1920 until it was purchased in 1935 and reestablished as Kamp Kellile. (Courtesy of Ed and Carol Frindt.)

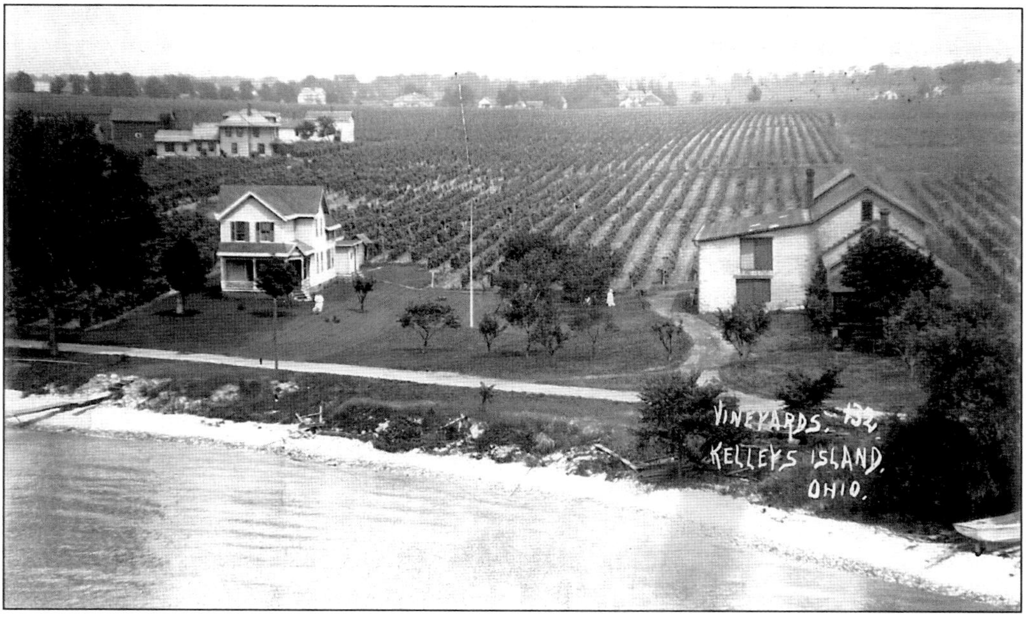

This scene along the West Bay shows the extent of the vineyards in this area, most of which were the property of Frederick Kastning, one of the principal owners of what would become the Sweet Valley Wine Co. The Kastning home is on the left, behind a house owned by Otto Dodge. North Bay is in the distant background. (Courtesy of the Cleveland Press Archives, Cleveland State University Library Special Collections.)

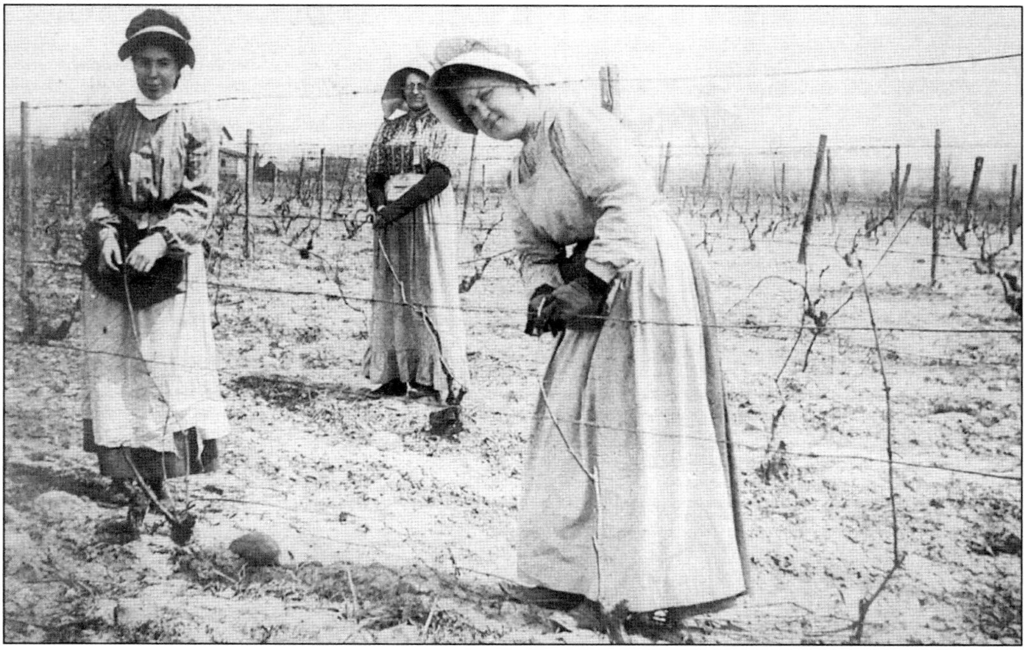

The women in this undated photograph tie up grapes, arguably Kelleys Island's single largest product in the 1800s and early 1900s. A *Cleveland Plain Dealer* report from 1861 details that more than 300 tons of grapes had been shipped off the island—200 tons alone to Cincinnati, St. Louis, Chicago, Boston, New York City, and Washington, DC. (Courtesy of the Kelleys Island Historical Association.)

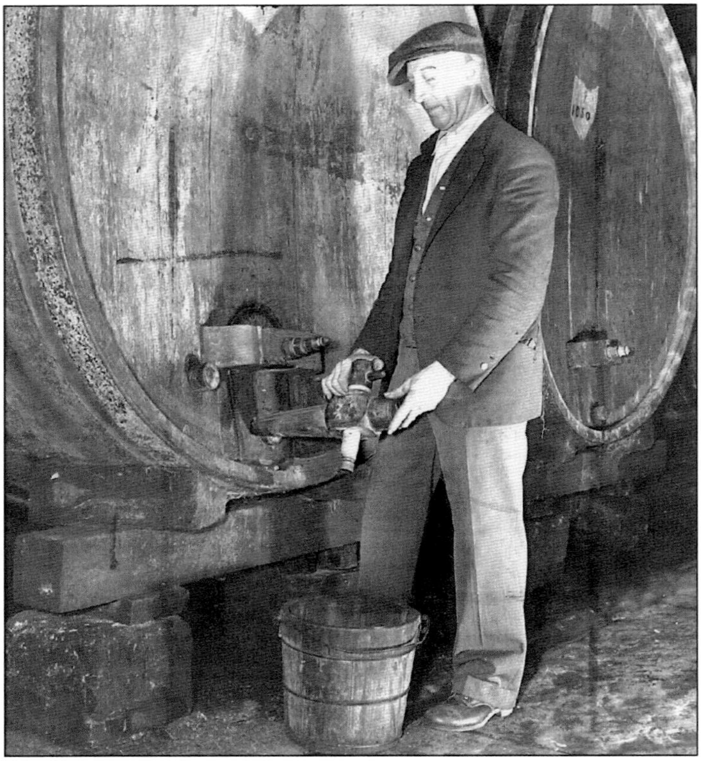

In 1941, farmer and vintner Roland Brown also served as the mayor of Kelleys Island. He is seen here drawing wine from a cask in his wine cellar at the Monarch Winery, on the west side of Division Street. (Courtesy of the Cleveland Press Archives, Cleveland State University Library Special Collections.)

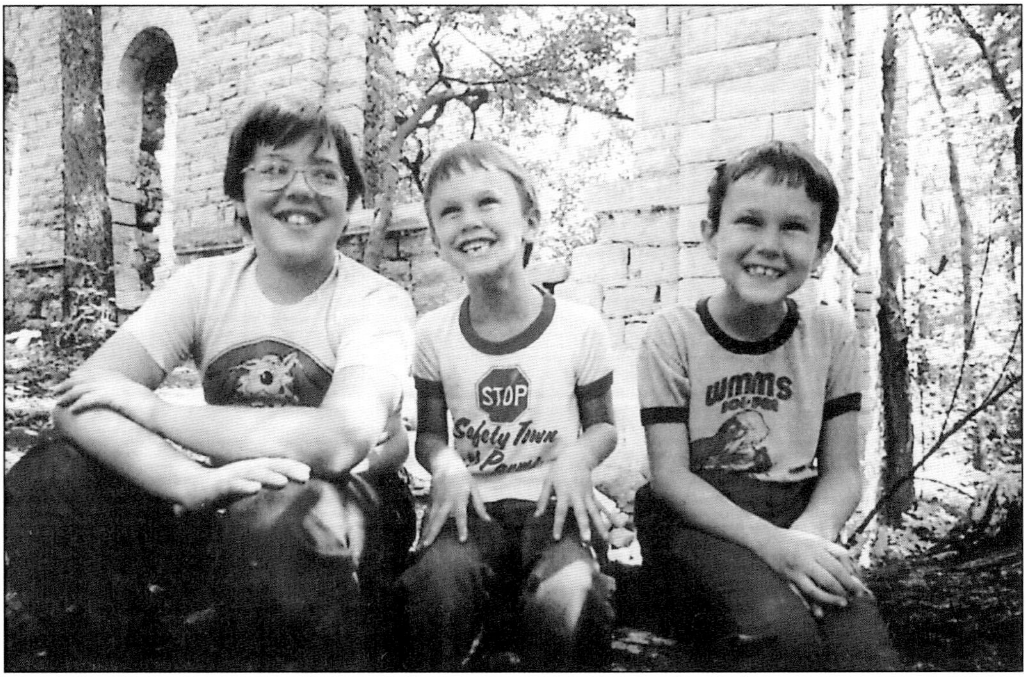

The ruins of the Kelleys Island Wine Co. winery always present a tempting lure for young explorers, as youngsters Stephen (left), David (center), and Tom Sabol learned. Today, the winery ruins, on private property, are unstable and no longer a welcome spot for visitors. (Courtesy of John T. Sabol.)

Finishing their day's work on the island's south shore, these commercial fishermen posing with their nets are, from left to right, (first row) Walter Bickley and Herb Bickley; (second row) Len Bickley and Art Siebert. (Courtesy of Ted Blatt.)

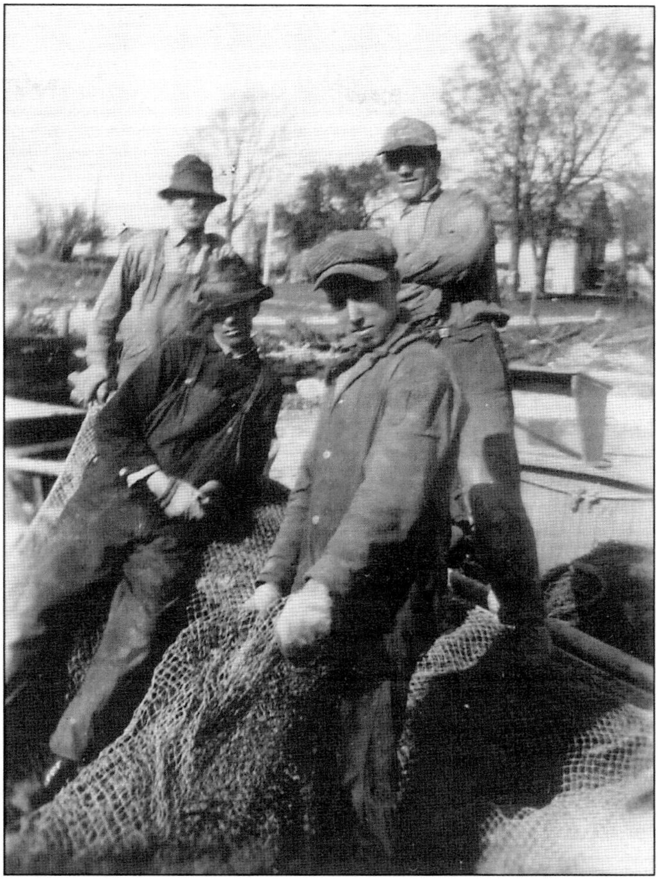

From the looks of the Lay Bros. fishing crew on Kelleys Island, one would not want to cross them, even on a good day. They are, from left to right, David McKillips, Allen McKillips, George McKillips, Allan "Boss" McKillips, Joe Moross, and Steve Lachney. Lay Bros., headquartered in Sandusky, was a large commercial fishing operation on Kelley Island. (Courtesy of the Sandusky Library Follett House Museum Archives.)

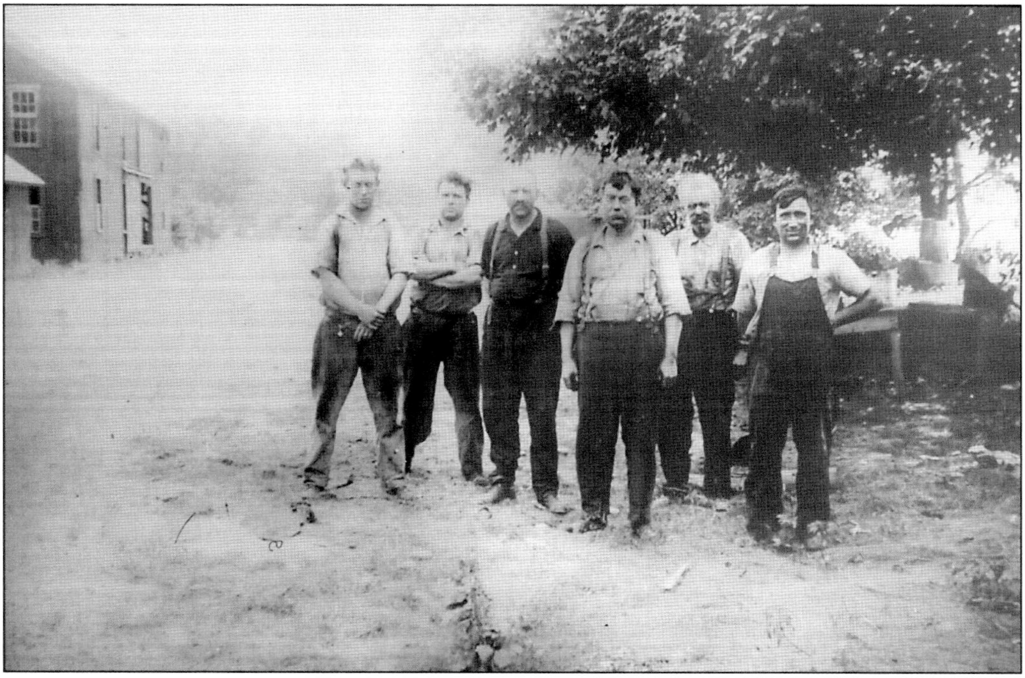

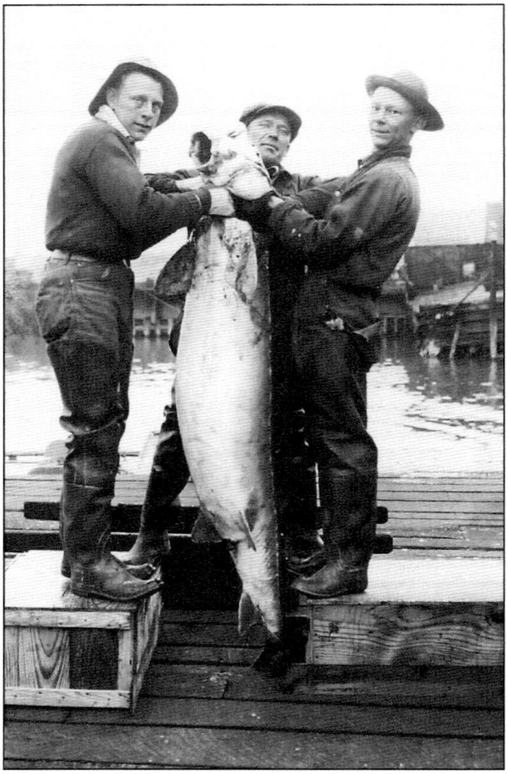

Although the sturgeon is supposed to be a sign of a healthy lake, the fish could turn fishing nets into dental floss. This 180-pound sturgeon, one of the largest ever caught in Lake Erie, was hooked in 1935 by Alfred McKillips (left), Albert Kugler (center), and Sylvester Dwelle. Today, about 30 to 40 sturgeon are spotted in a year, according to the Ohio Department of Natural Resources. (Courtesy of Ted Blatt.)

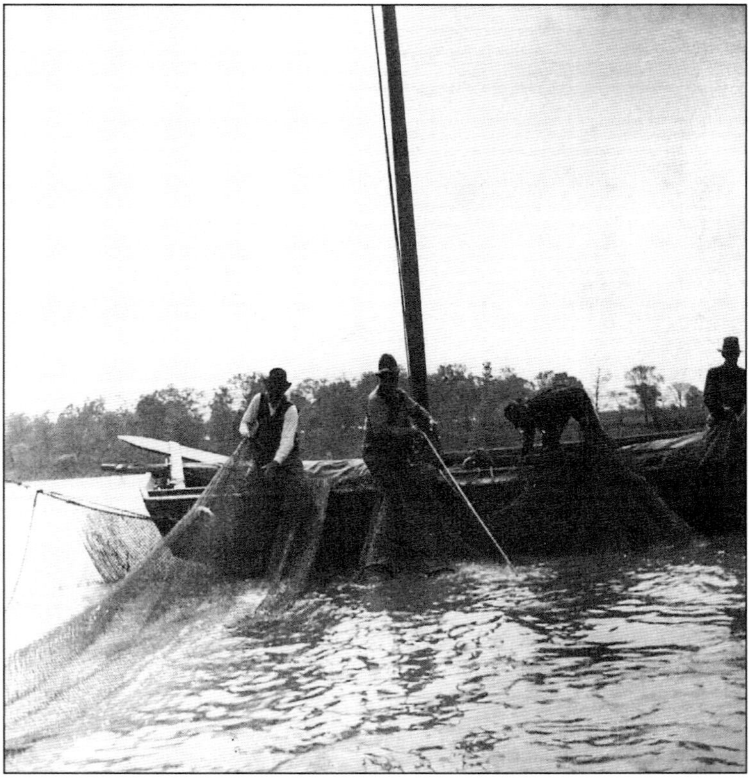

Around 1900, commercial fisherman used pound nets to bring in their daily catches. Pound nets had an impounding area about 20 feet long, and fish were guided into the pound by a series of wings and channels. The nets were attached to stakes 30 feet to 40 feet long. These unidentified fishermen bring in their pound net off of Kelleys Island. (Courtesy of Chris and Frank Yako.)

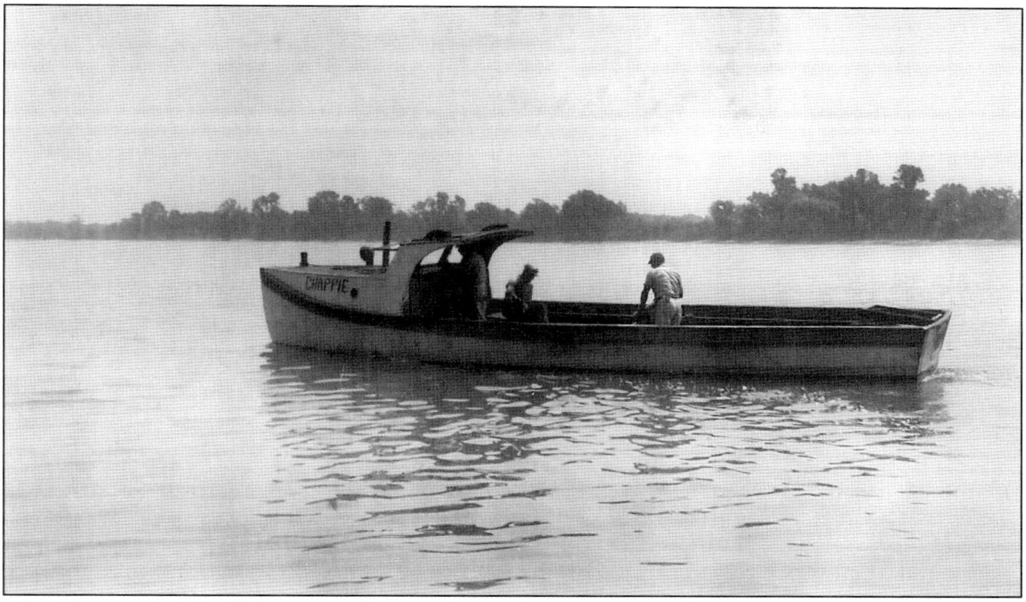

The *Chappie* was a well-known fishing boat on Kelleys Island. The boat was purchased by Henry Beatty and his brother-in-law Sonny Elfers from Henry's brother Art, who built it. The 36.5-foot boat cost $2,250. (Courtesy of the Kelleys Island Historical Association.)

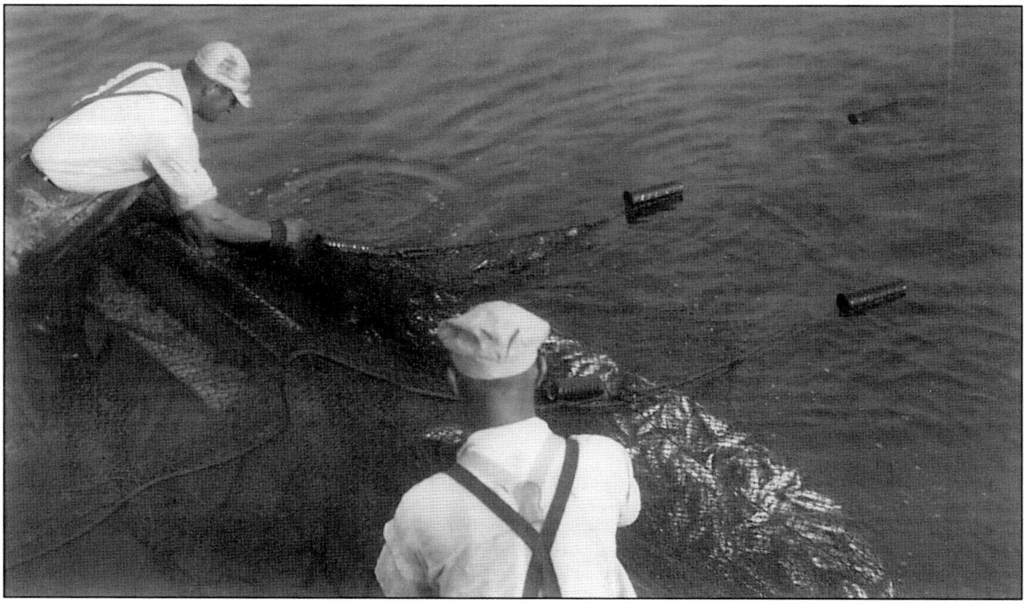
In the 1950s, commercial fishing thrived on Kelleys Island, as illustrated by this full net being hauled in by Jack Betzenheimer (left) and Roy Erne. The two peak years for commercial fishing in Lake Erie were 1935 and 1956. (Courtesy of the Kelleys Island Historical Association.)

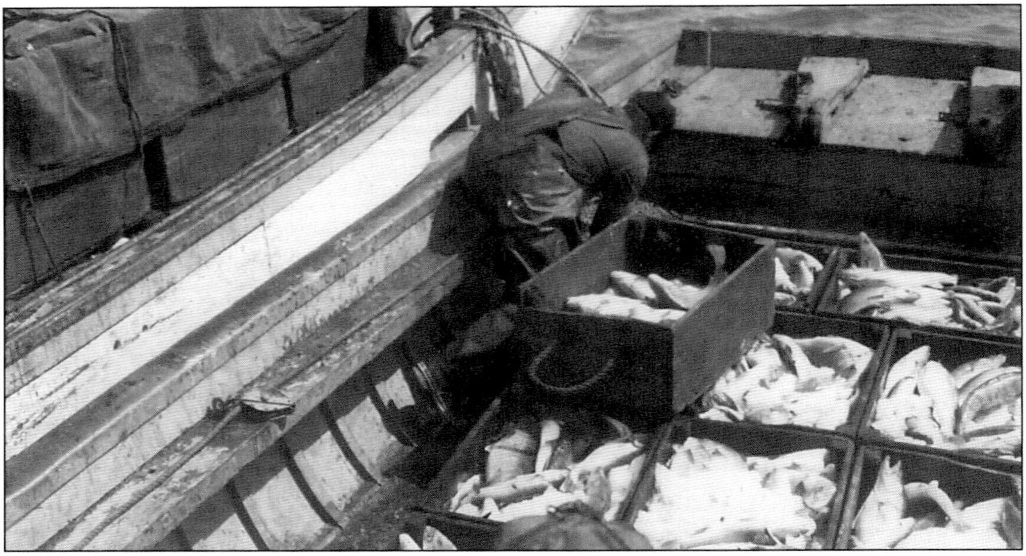

On good days, another boat would come out to transfer fish that had already been caught. Here, fish from the *Chappie* are moved to the *Chief*. The *Chief* was a Lay Bros. fishing boat whose task it was to gather up the nets each day. (Courtesy of the Kelleys Island Historical Association.)

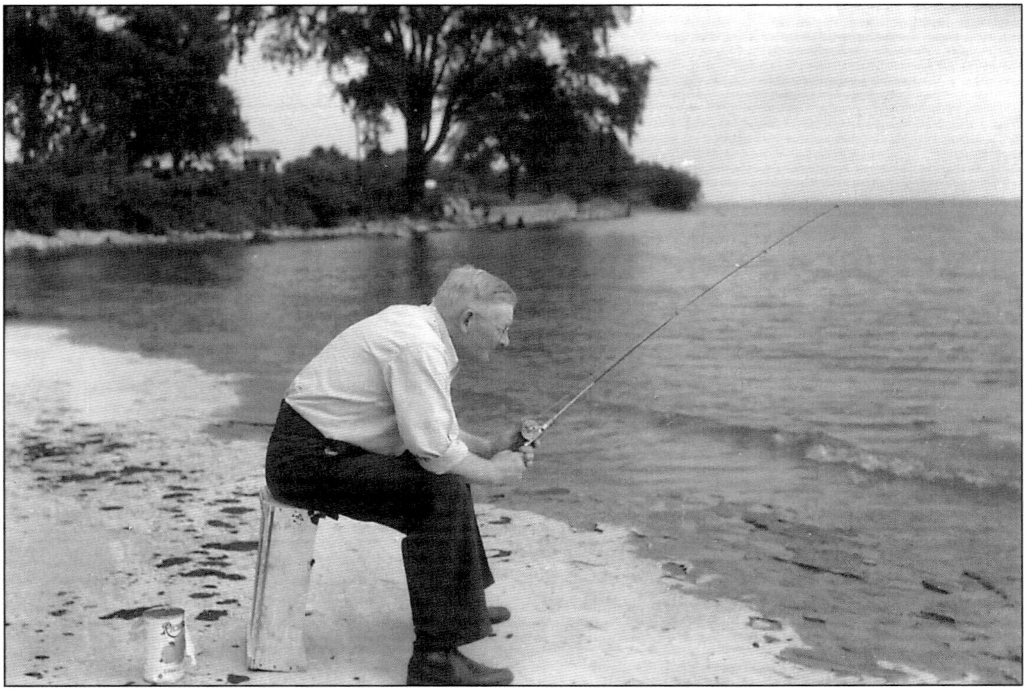

What greater comfort is there than a comfortable seat and a fishing rod? Well, comfort is where a person can find it, and William Charles Smith appears to be enjoying himself as he fishes on Roland Brown's beach on East Lakeshore Drive. When he was not occupied with the angling arts, Smith worked as an engineer on the lake steamer *Arrow*. (Courtesy of Judy Du Shane.)

Four

Island Transportation

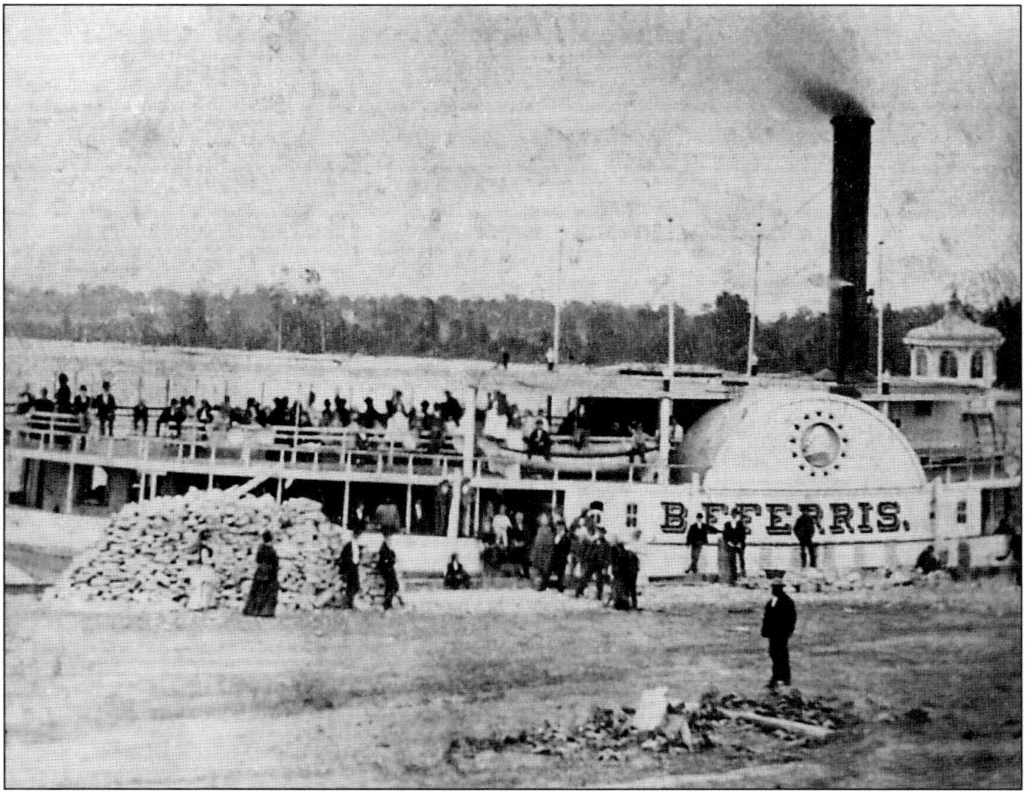

The *B.F. Ferris*, seen here in 1876, carried freight and passengers from the mainland. The boat brought cattle for Henry Trieschman, the owner of what is now the Island Market, every few weeks. Trieschman had a slaughterhouse on Woodford Road. The *B.F. Ferris* suffered several mishaps while in service between Sandusky, Marblehead, and Kelleys, and it was destroyed by fire in June 1891 in Saginaw, Michigan. (Courtesy of the Sandusky Library Follett House Museum Archives.)

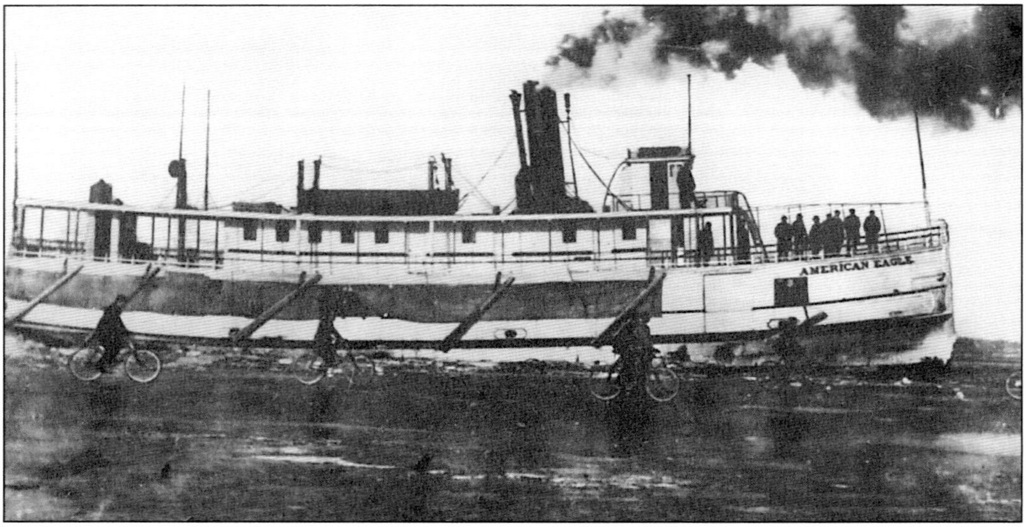

The steamer *American Eagle*, seen here in the winter of 1898–1899, appears to be racing bicyclists on the Kelleys Island shore—a pursuit now taken over by golf carts. The boat was built in 1880 and could cut through 8 inches of ice without stopping, and 24 inches of ice by backing up and bucking the ice. (Courtesy of Gary and Jackie Finger.)

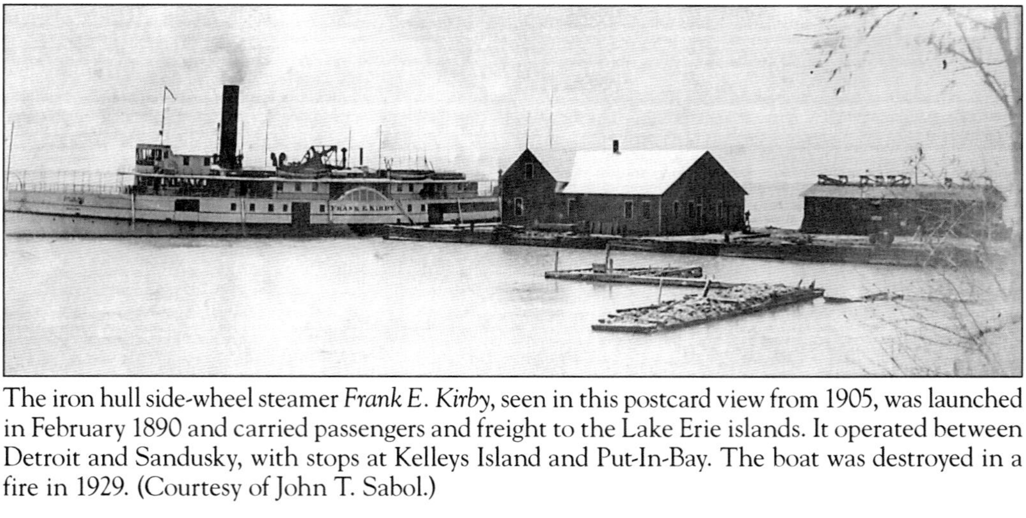

The iron hull side-wheel steamer *Frank E. Kirby*, seen in this postcard view from 1905, was launched in February 1890 and carried passengers and freight to the Lake Erie islands. It operated between Detroit and Sandusky, with stops at Kelleys Island and Put-In-Bay. The boat was destroyed in a fire in 1929. (Courtesy of John T. Sabol.)

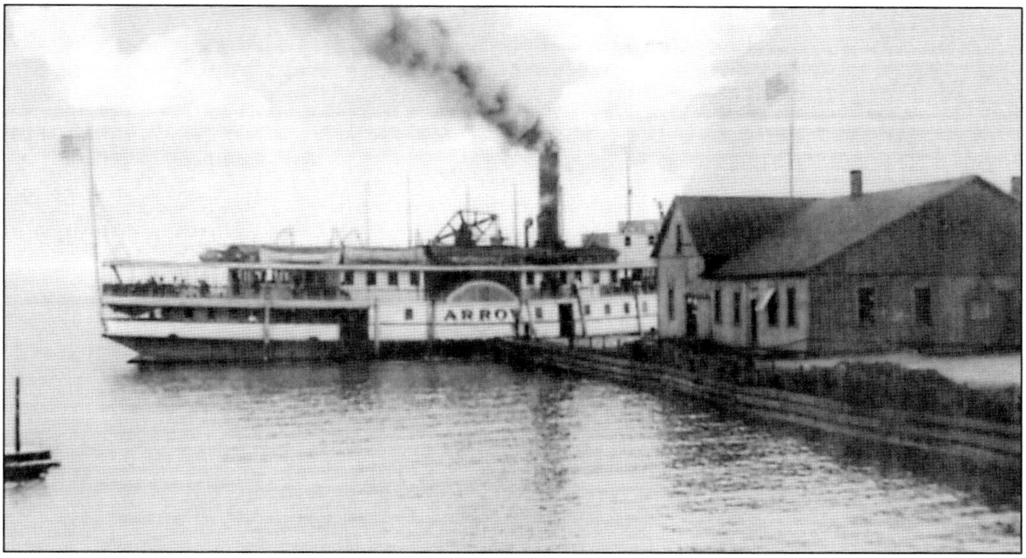

In 1912, round-trip tickets for the steamer *Arrow*, seen here in a 1909 postcard view, cost 50¢. From 1895 to 1922, the *Arrow* took passengers from Sandusky to Kelleys Island, Middle Bass, North Bass, and Put-In-Bay. Its cabin was furnished in light mahogany, and there was a grand piano in the salon. (Courtesy of John T. Sabol.)

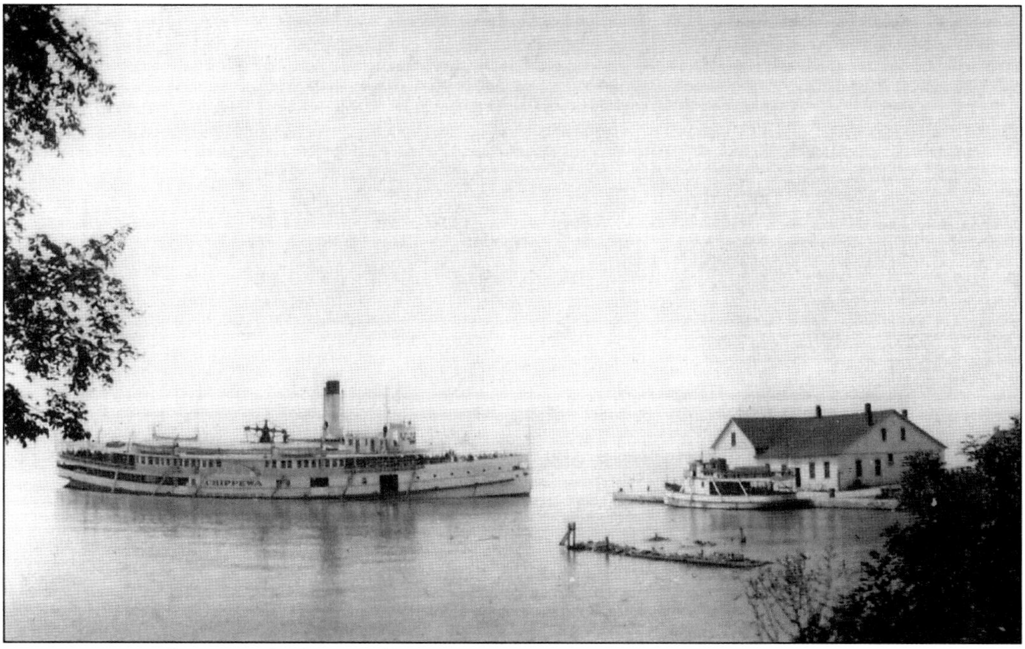

Steaming into the Store dock on Kelleys Island is the *Chippewa*, which began service to the Lake Erie Islands in 1923 and continued until 1938. According to the Rutherford B. Hayes Presidential Center, the boat was originally christened the *William P. Fessenden*, a US revenue cutter, in 1883. Already docked in this photograph is the Neuman Boat Line's *Mascot*, which served the island from 1925 until the early 1950s. (Courtesy of Bob and Carol Schnittker.)

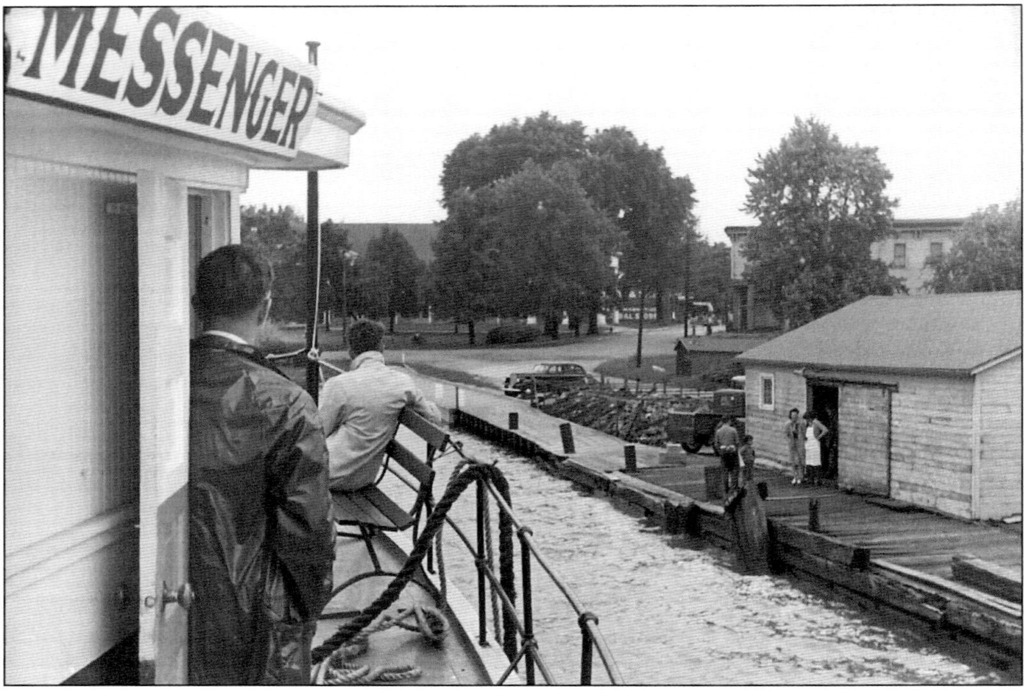

The Neuman Boat Line ferry *Messenger* approaches the ferry dock in Sandusky following a trip from Kelleys Island in the late 1940s. For almost 50 years, Neuman served Kelleys Island from this dock in Sandusky. In the early-to-mid 1950s, Neuman also made use of flattop car-carrying ferries from another dock in Marblehead. (Courtesy of the Cleveland Public Library Photograph Collection.)

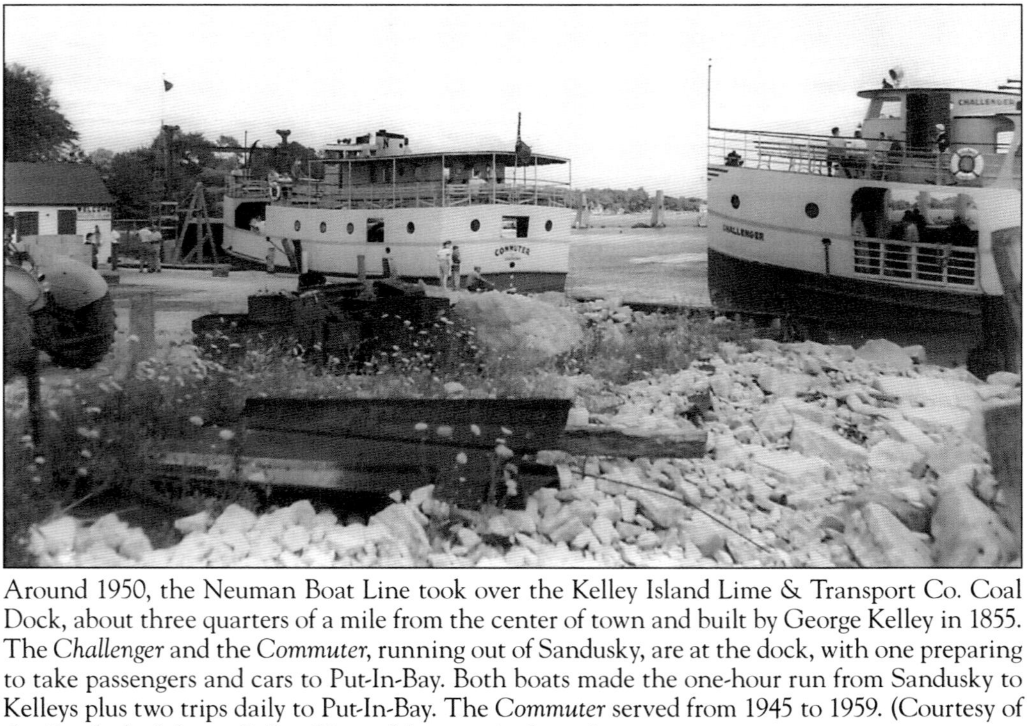

Around 1950, the Neuman Boat Line took over the Kelley Island Lime & Transport Co. Coal Dock, about three quarters of a mile from the center of town and built by George Kelley in 1855. The *Challenger* and the *Commuter*, running out of Sandusky, are at the dock, with one preparing to take passengers and cars to Put-In-Bay. Both boats made the one-hour run from Sandusky to Kelleys plus two trips daily to Put-In-Bay. The *Commuter* served from 1945 to 1959. (Courtesy of the Sandusky Library Follett House Museum Archives.)

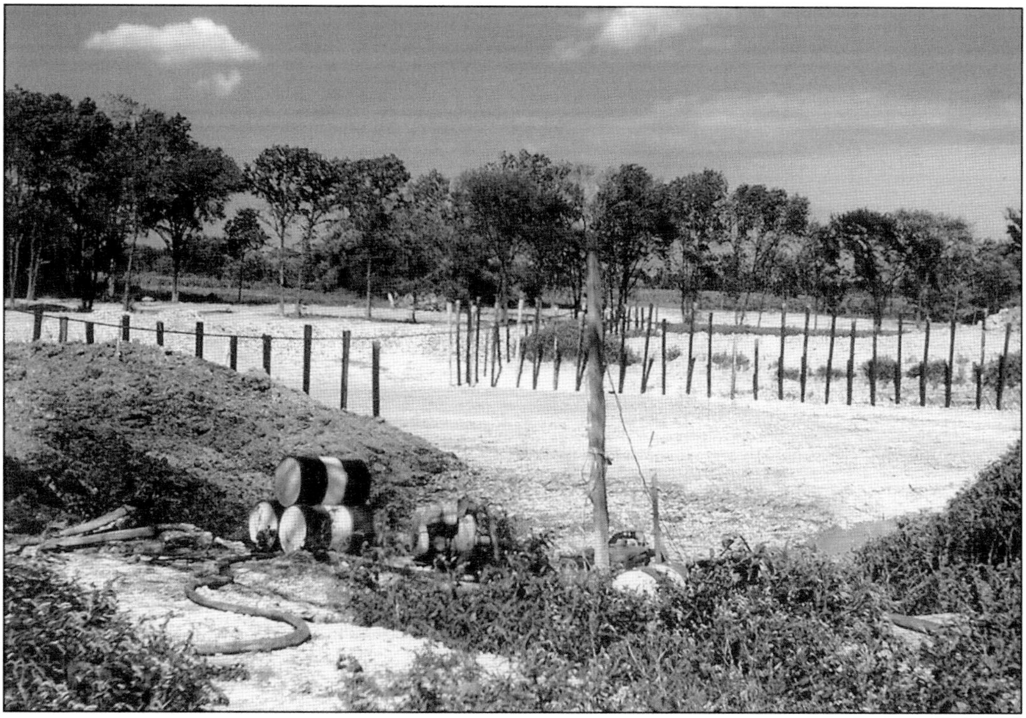

The pond formerly located on the site of the Seaway Marina is staked out, as pumps (at lower left) continue to drain the remnants of the pond in 1958. In the years to follow, the location would overflow with watercraft and be the island terminus of the Kelleys Island Ferry Boat line. (Courtesy of Bob and Carol Schnittker.)

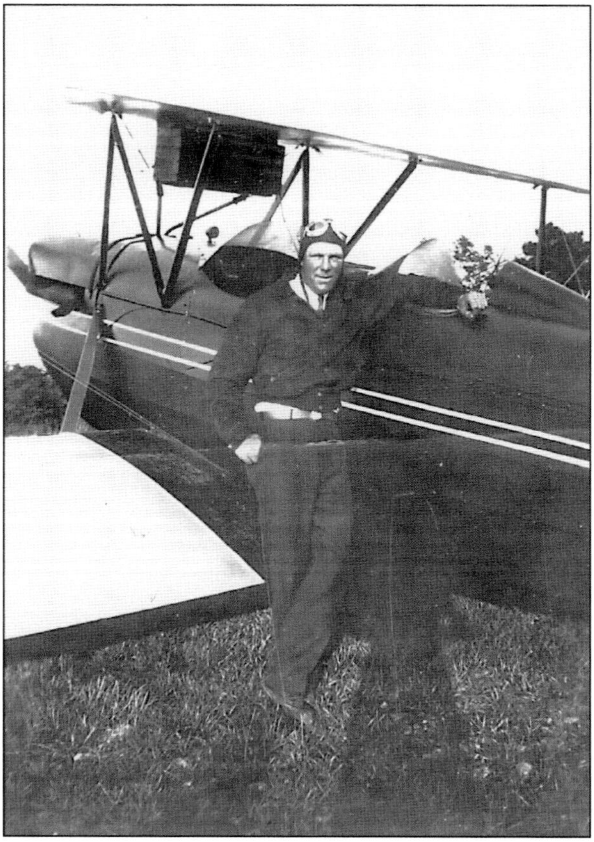

William McKillips, standing next to his Waco 90 biplane, was the first islander to own an airplane and the second to have a pilot's license. McKillips worked for the Post Fish Co. It is believed that up to 25 islanders had pilot's licenses, and many of them had their own landing strips. (Courtesy of Ted Blatt.)

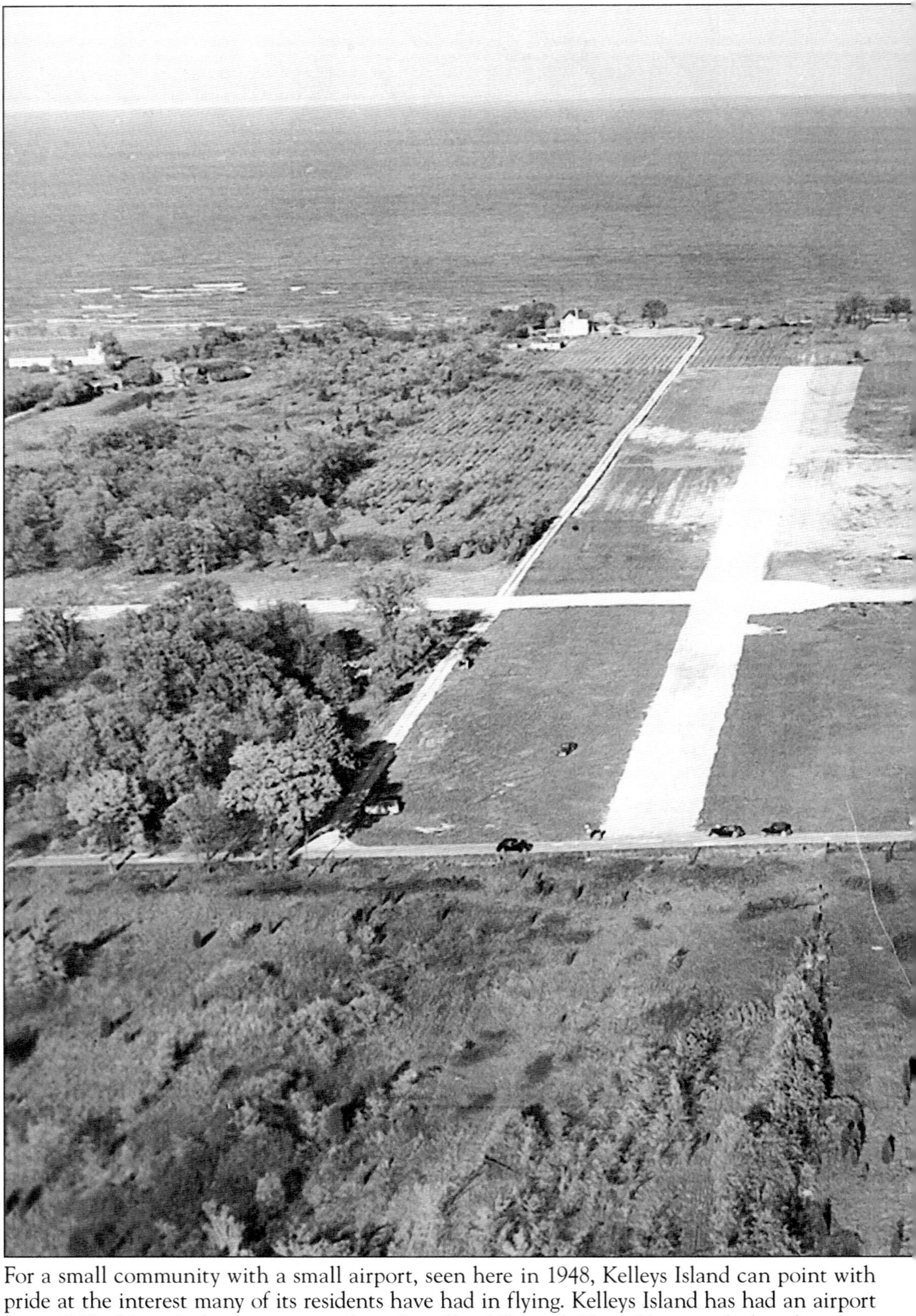

For a small community with a small airport, seen here in 1948, Kelleys Island can point with pride at the interest many of its residents have had in flying. Kelleys Island has had an airport since 1929, although there were a number of unofficial flying fields and hangars before that time.

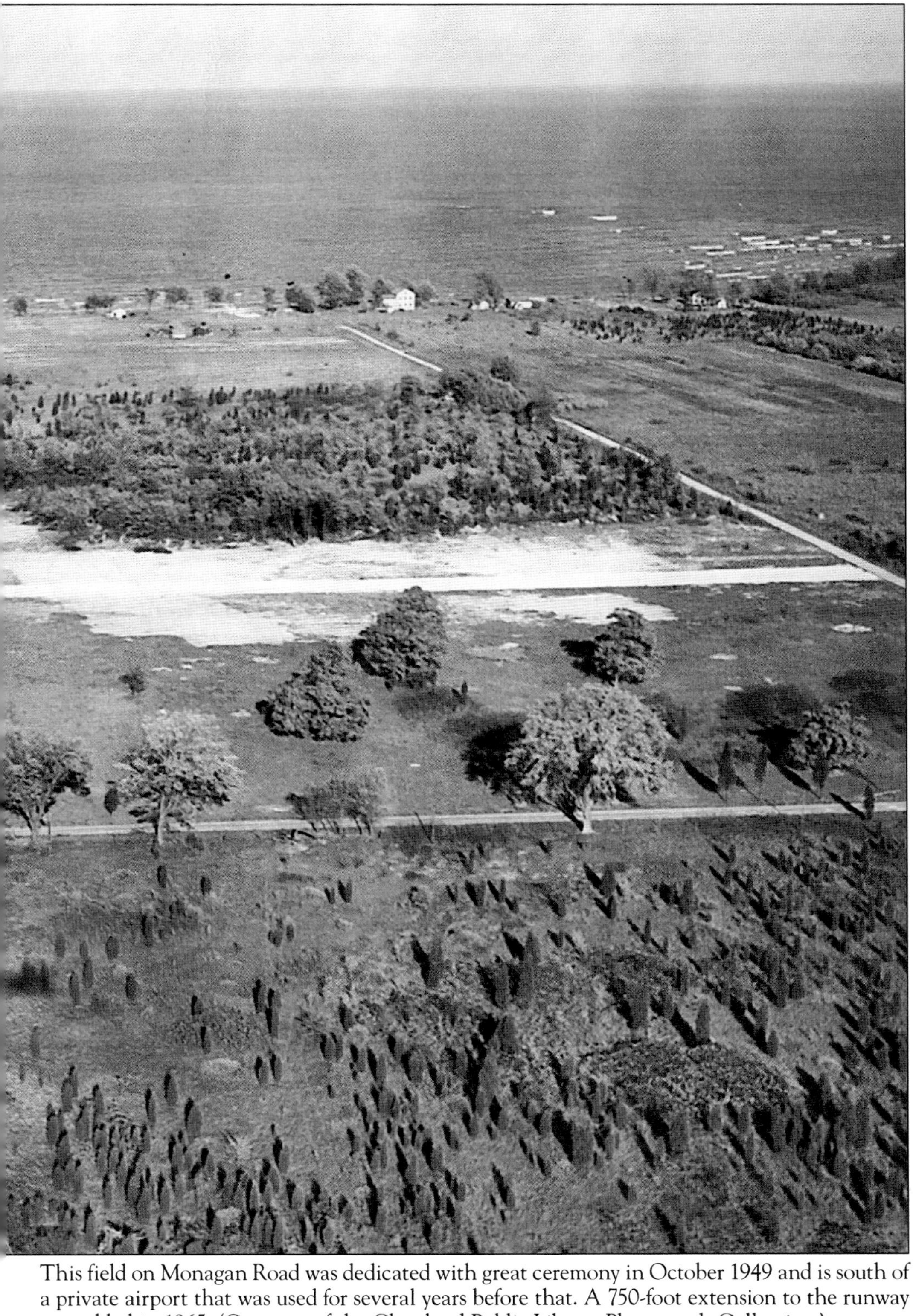

This field on Monagan Road was dedicated with great ceremony in October 1949 and is south of a private airport that was used for several years before that. A 750-foot extension to the runway was added in 1965. (Courtesy of the Cleveland Public Library Photograph Collection.)

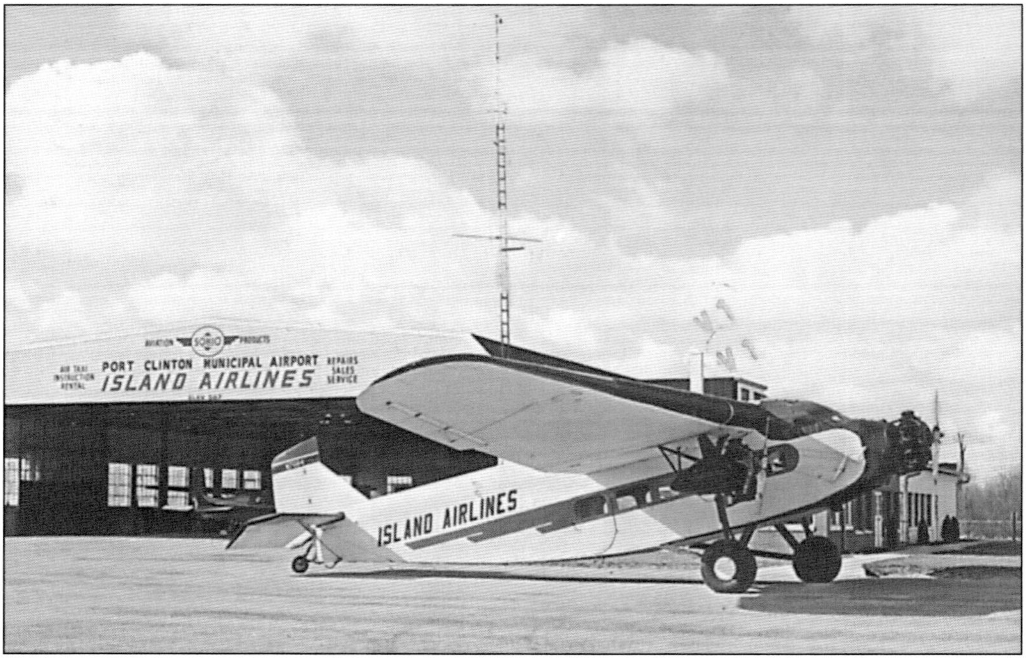

This Ford Tri-Motor, or "Tin Goose," seen here at the Sandusky Airport, was a mainstay for island air travel and shipping from 1930 to 1982. The plane was part of a fleet of Tri-Motors owned by Milton Hersberger, the founder and owner of Island Airlines. These planes carried passengers, mail, medicine, and groceries, and even bales of hay to feed cattle on Kelleys during a storm. Hersberger owned Island Airlines from 1930 to 1953. (Courtesy of Barbara Schock.)

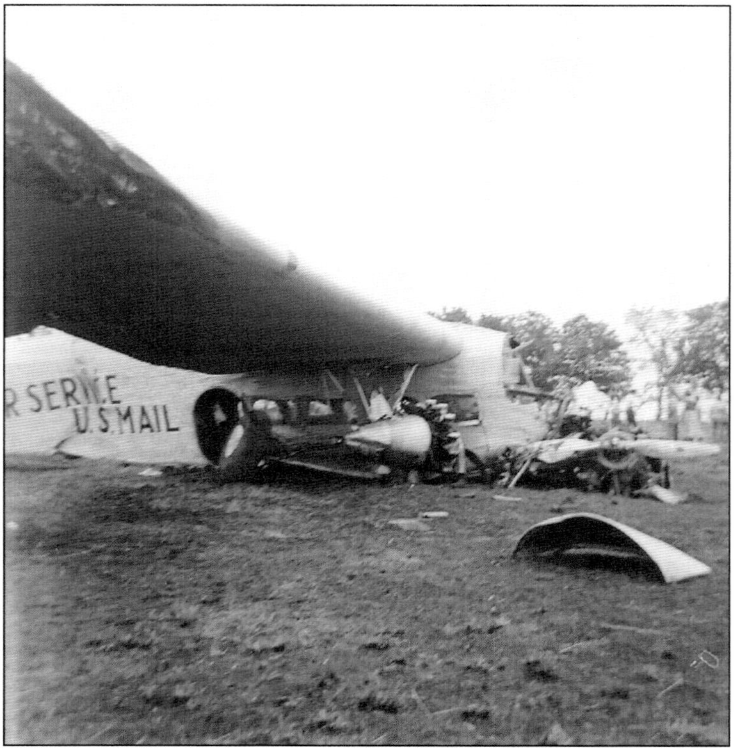

Heroic action by a Put-In-Bay pilot on July 31, 1954, saved the lives of the 12 passengers on this Ford Tri-Motor plane and avoided a disastrous crash into a Scout encampment and a summer residence for Franciscan friars, on Lincoln Road just north of the island airport. The pilot, Hugo Rosendahl, crashed around dusk, shortly after takeoff. This photograph was taken by 13-year-old Richard McMonagle. (Courtesy of Paulette and Richard McMonagle.)

Five

On the Rocks Part II

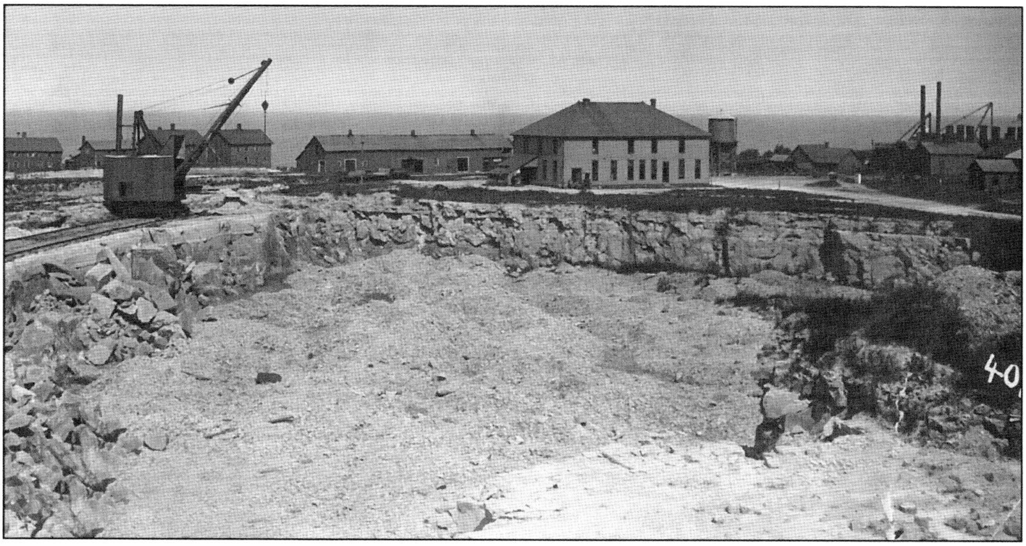

John Clemons and his brother started taking rock out of the North Quarry in the 1830s, before the arrival of the Kelleys, making it one of the first areas to be quarried. Eventually, the north side operation reached a depth of 40 feet and spread out to more than 50 acres. (Courtesy of Bob and Carol Schnittker.)

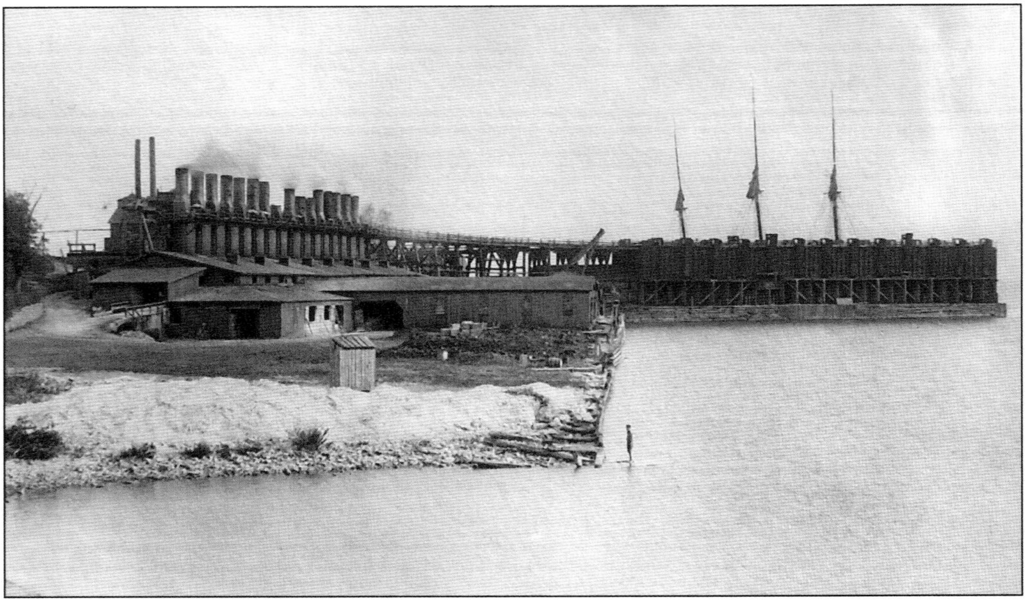

The North Side dock, west of Sandy Beach, was the terminus of a huge quarrying operation. Limekilns are seen on the left, with loading chutes on the right. The building in the front is a storage shed. The dock was elevated, equipped with pockets and chutes, and supplied with stone by a steam locomotive pulling carloads of stone across the top. (Courtesy of the Kelleys Island Historical Association.)

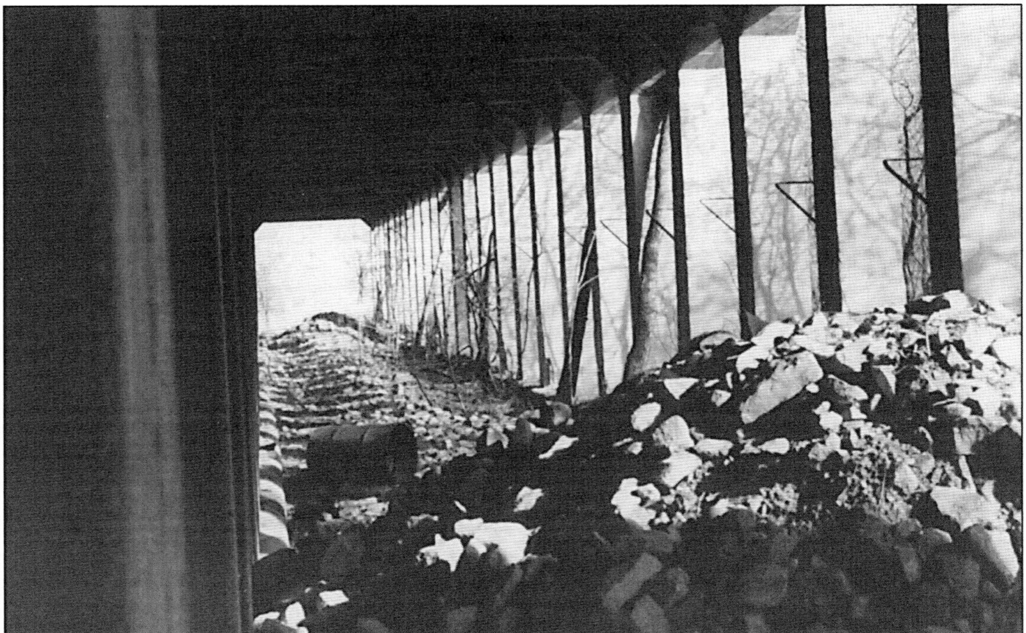

Remains of this limestone loader, built in 1888 north of the Glacial Grooves, still stand today. It can be seen on the North Shore Loop Trail at the northwest end of the island, west of the state park boat-and-trailer parking lot. The Kelley Island Lime & Transport Co. operations created what seemed to be a separate town, with housing, a company store, and quarry machinery. (Courtesy of Frank and Laura Jean Pohorence.)

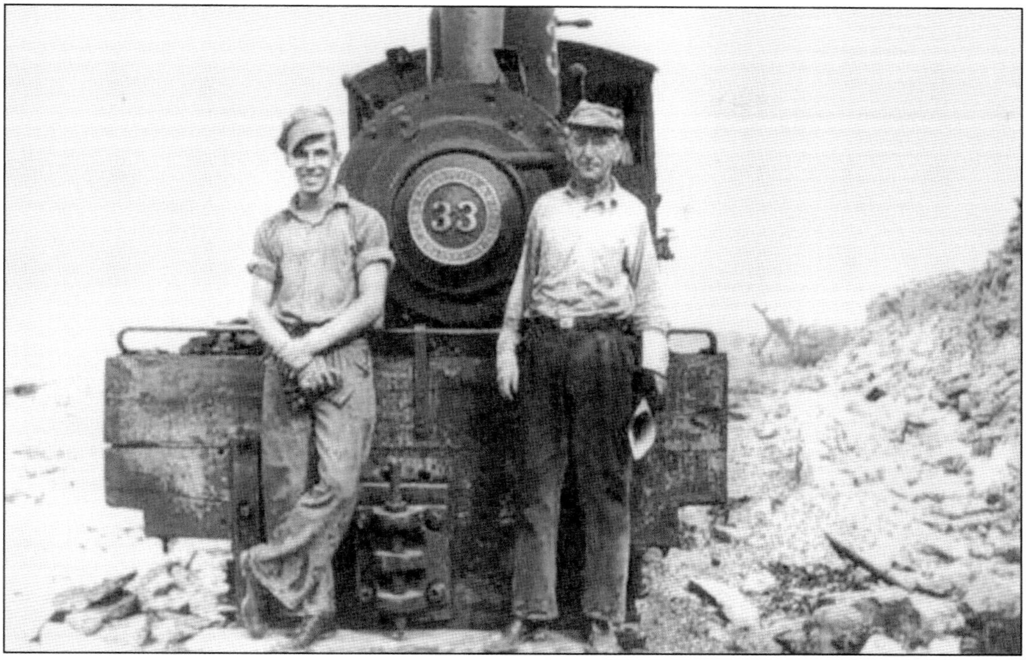

The Shay Engine was a mainstay of quarry operations of the Kelley Island Lime & Transport Co. Specially constructed and operating on movable track, the Shays were purchased between 1898 and 1906 and were used for hauling stone until 1943, when the company ceased its quarrying operations on the island. Seen here in front of one of the island Shays are fireman Kenneth Heckel (left) and engineer Norman Blatt. (Courtesy of Ted Blatt.)

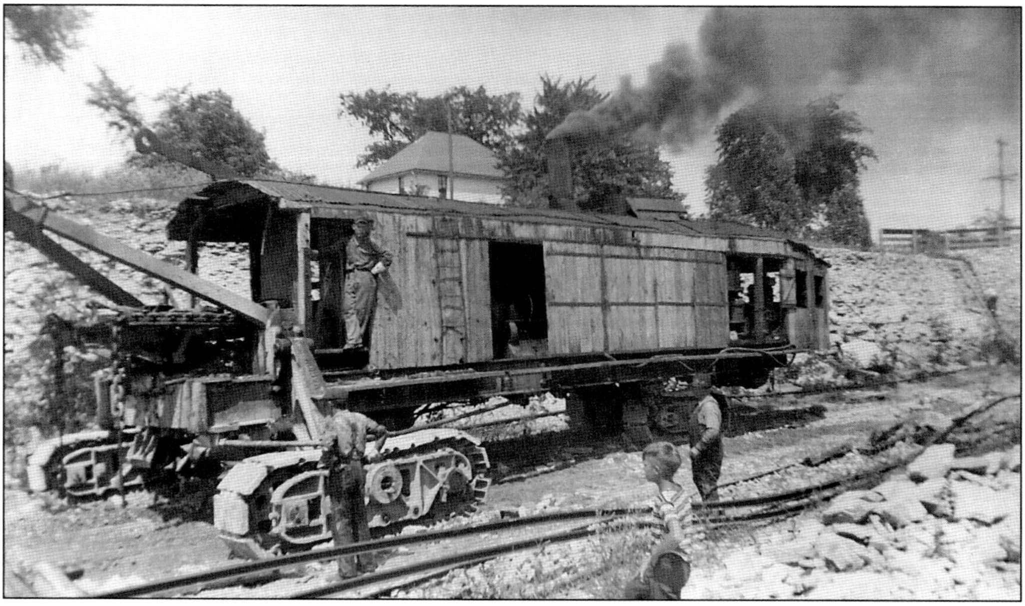

Working in the quarries brought steady income for many islanders who were willing to do the dangerous labor. Seen here on the quarry shovel is George Durket. Standing on the ground are Hugo Seeholzer (left) and George Lenyo. The young boy is Seeholzer's son, Jim. (Courtesy of the Kelleys Island Historical Association.)

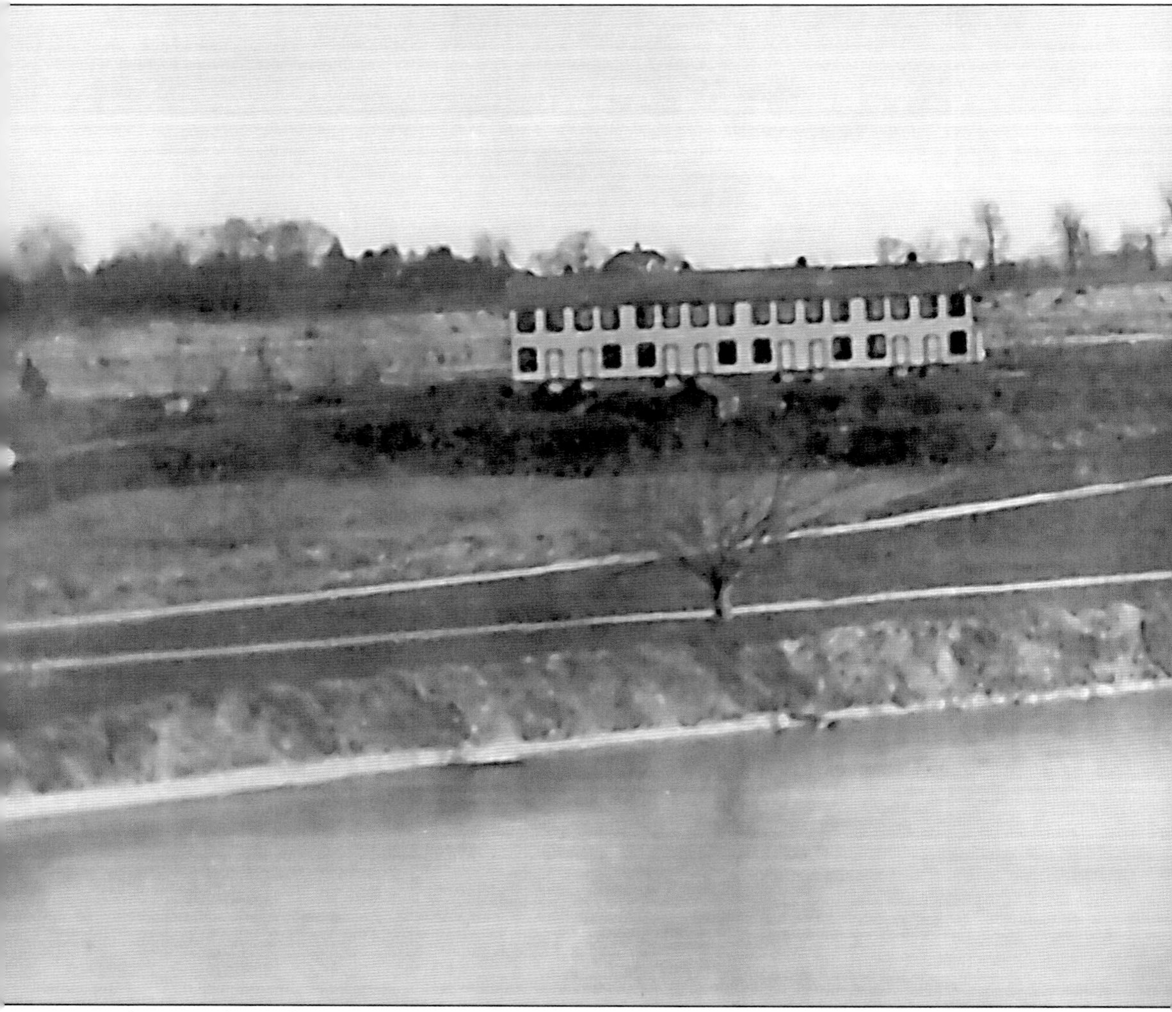

This view from the top of the West Bay dock shows quarry operations there—near the current West Bay Inn—in 1913. The large building on the left was called the Incubator and comprised eight two-level apartments for quarry workers and their wives. The road on the right passes the Kelleys Island Wine Co. and continues to a point near Cameron Road. At this time, West

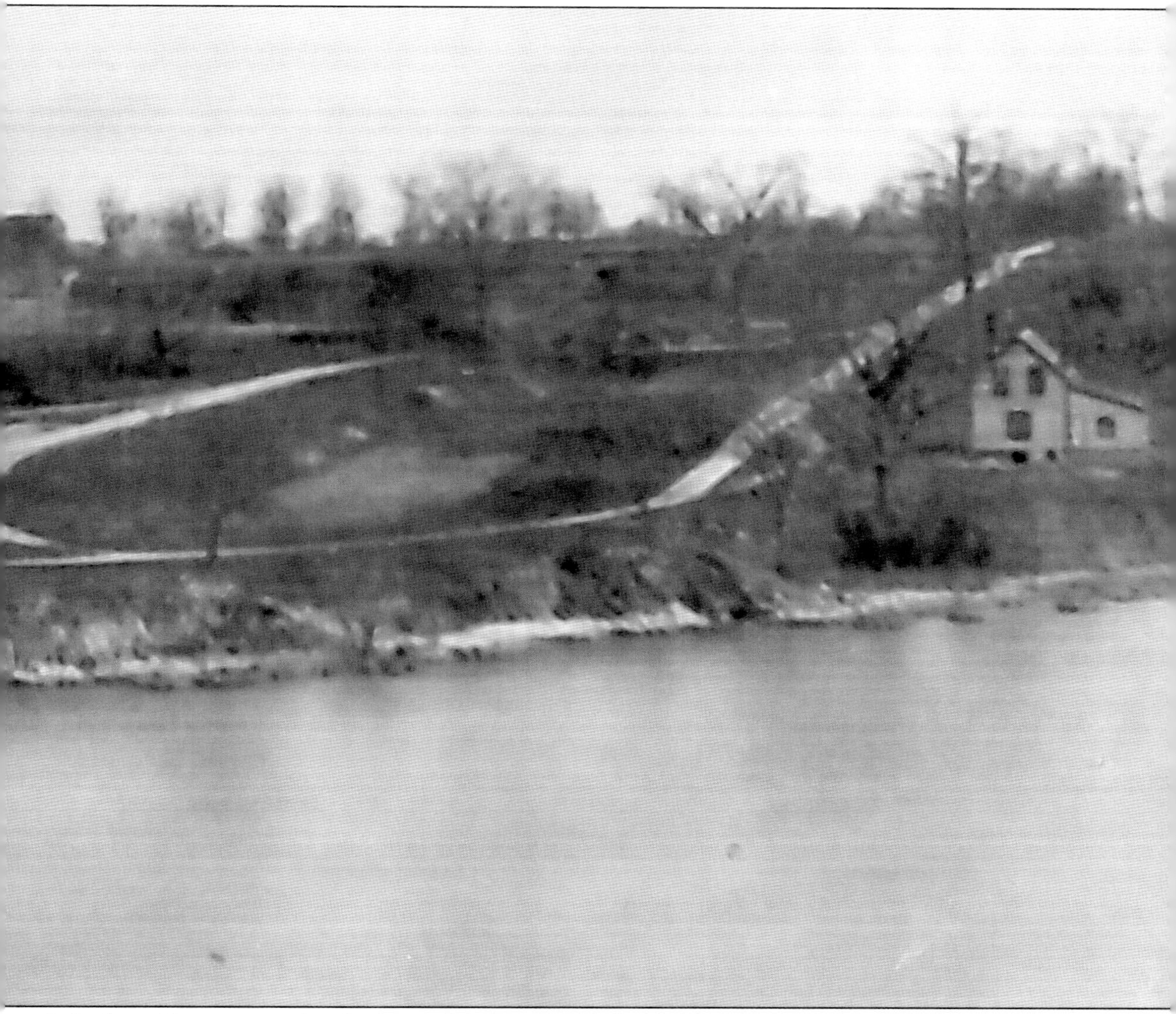

Lakeshore Drive stopped at Carpenter's Point, about a half mile east. Quarrying operations under the Kelley Island Lime & Transport Co. had their best year in 1923, when more than 576,000 tons of stone were shipped. (Courtesy of Gary and Jackie Finger.)

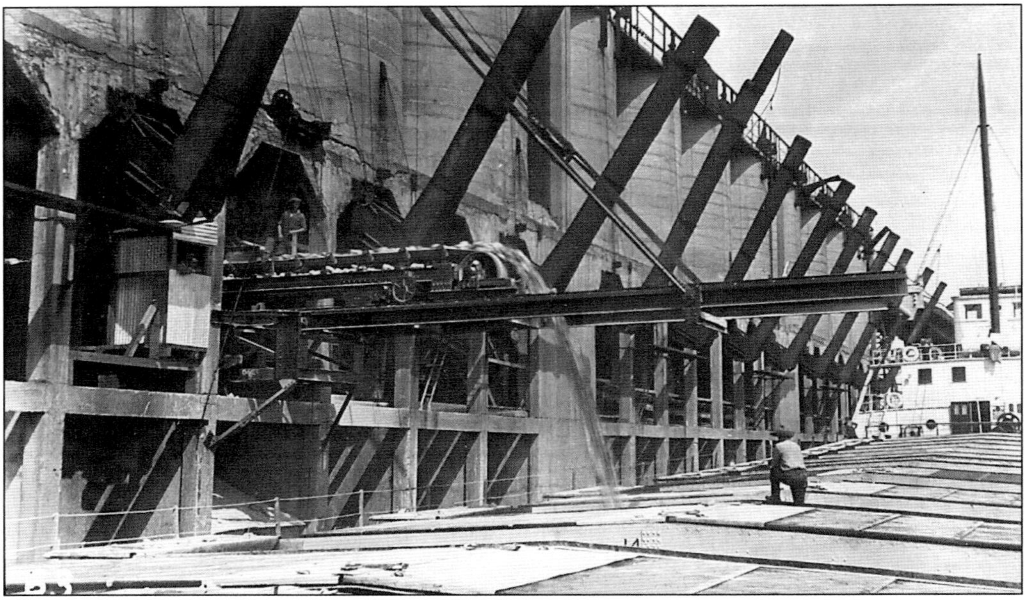

The West Bay dock rivaled the shipping operation at the north end. Modified to a "pocket" structure in 1910, the Kelley Island Lime & Transport loading operation is shown filling the steamer *Tomlinson*. The dock comprised 24 storage bins setting side-by-side and was supplied with stone by elevated tracks. One worker is on the deck and another operates the chute. (Courtesy of the Kelleys Island Historical Association.)

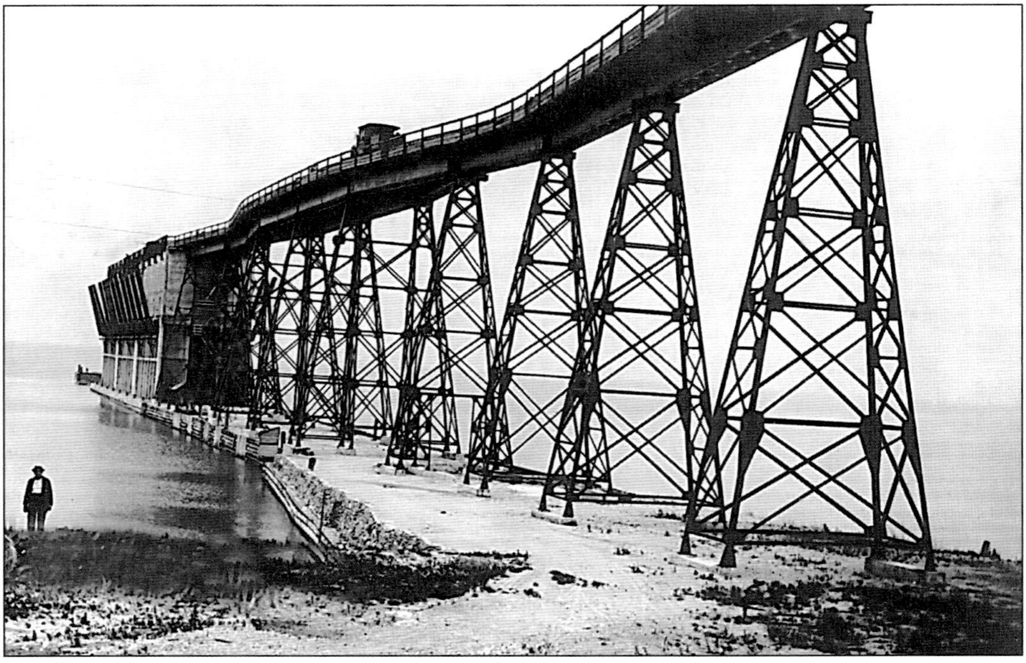

The West Bay dock was a massive sight. At 300 feet, it was constructed as a wooden dock in 1842 and eventually expanded to this reinforced concrete form. One of the Shay engines owned by the Kelley Island Lime & Transport Co. is operating at the top. The dock operated in this fashion until the company closed in 1943. The dock was imploded in 1989. (Courtesy of Frank and Laura Jean Pohorence.)

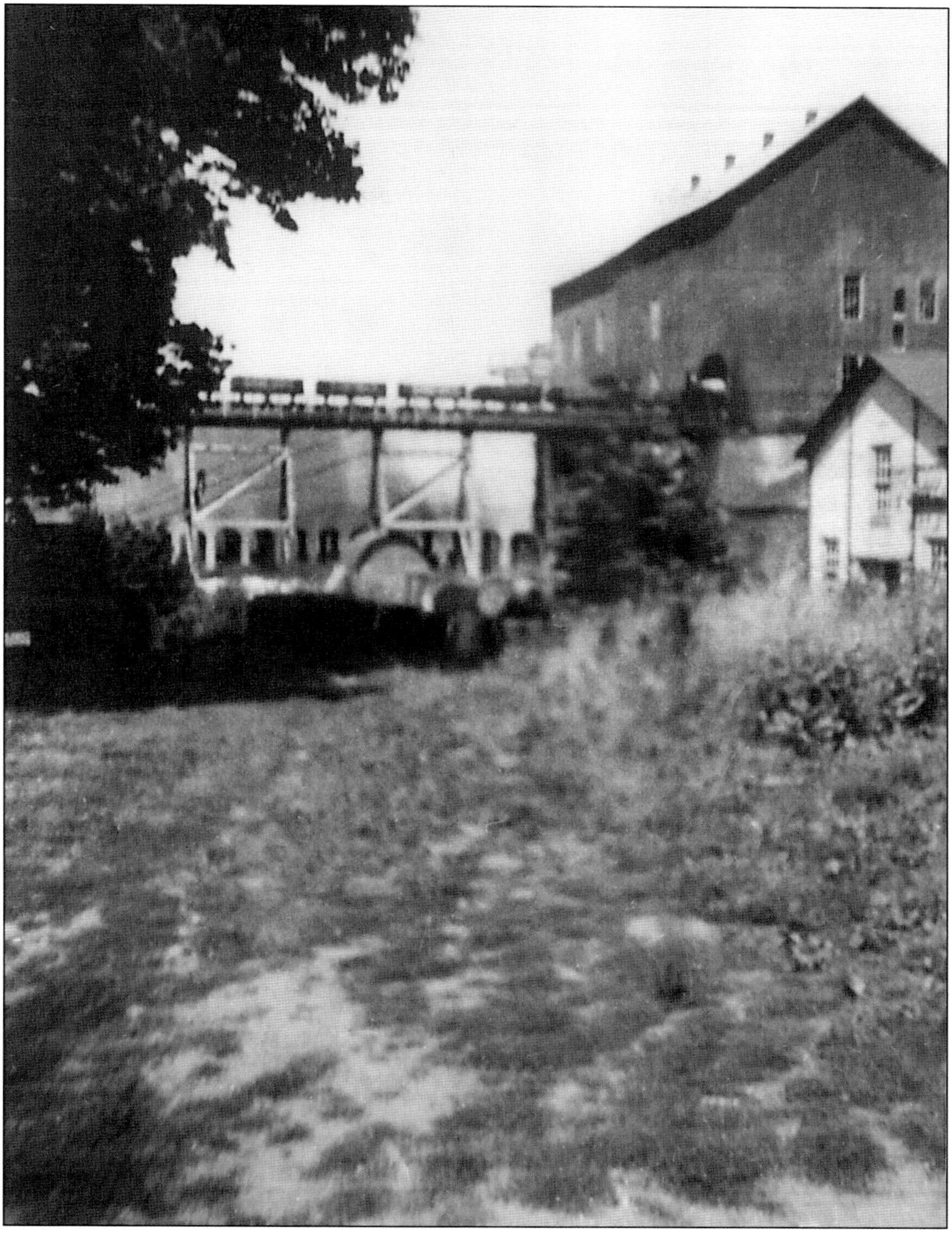

The South Side Crusher, built in 1907 north and east of the post office on West Lakeshore Drive, was part of a complex of south-side quarry buildings that also included offices, a power generating plant, and workers' homes. The railroad on the left is bringing stone from the quarries to be processed into usable-sized aggregate. This facility served the south loading dock, located about three-quarters of a mile west of the center of town. The crusher and a similar operation at the north end of the island were abandoned because it became cheaper to process the stone on the mainland. The power-generating equipment became the basis for the island's electrical system, and was later replaced by underwater cable. (Courtesy of Frank and Laura Jean Pohorence.)

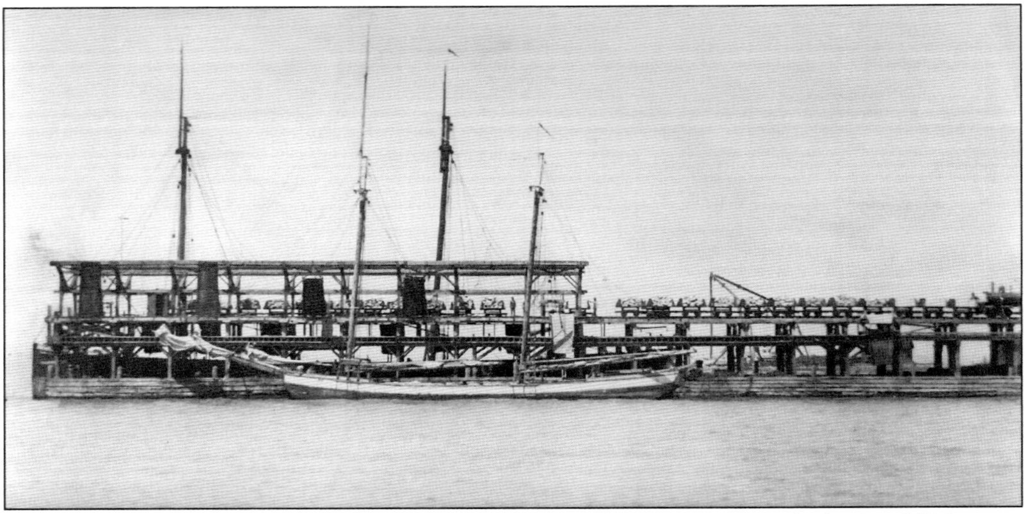

The south loading dock was just east of the Kelleys Island Boat Line's west dock, the old Neuman dock. On the right, one of the Shay locomotives used by the Kelley Island Lime & Transport Co. hauls carloads of stone to be dumped into waiting boats. Both the north and south loading docks were phased out by the loading facilities at the West Bay Dock. (Courtesy of Bob and Carol Schnittker.)

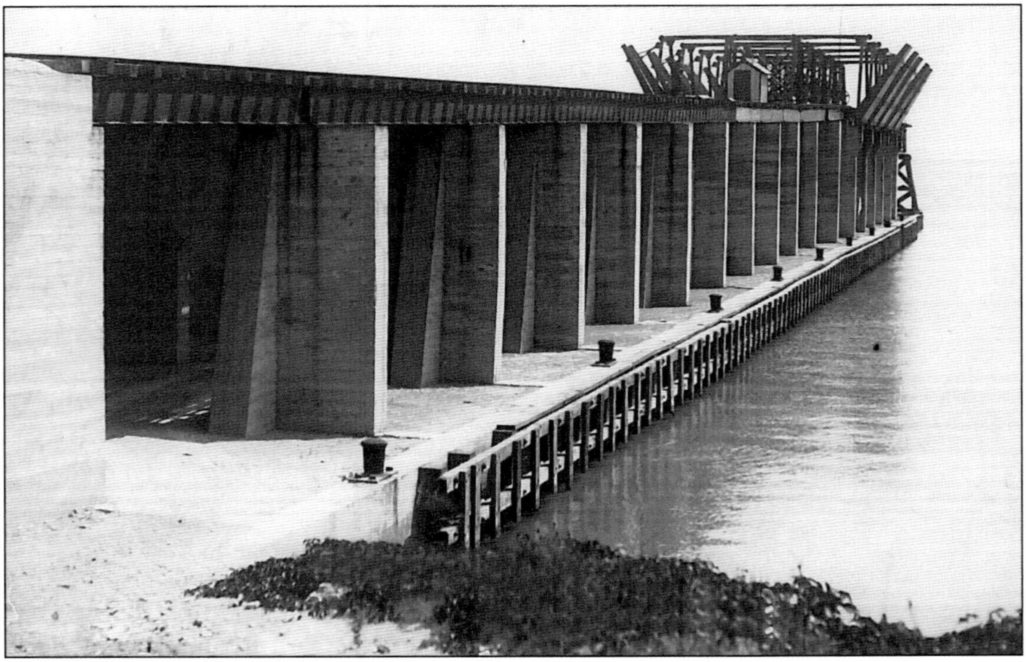

The south loading dock, almost across the street from the current location of the Kelleys Island Post Office, was much smaller than its West Bay counterpart. The south dock was razed in the early 1980s, although parts of the structure stood for many years as a remnant of earlier times. (Courtesy of Bob and Carol Schnittker.)

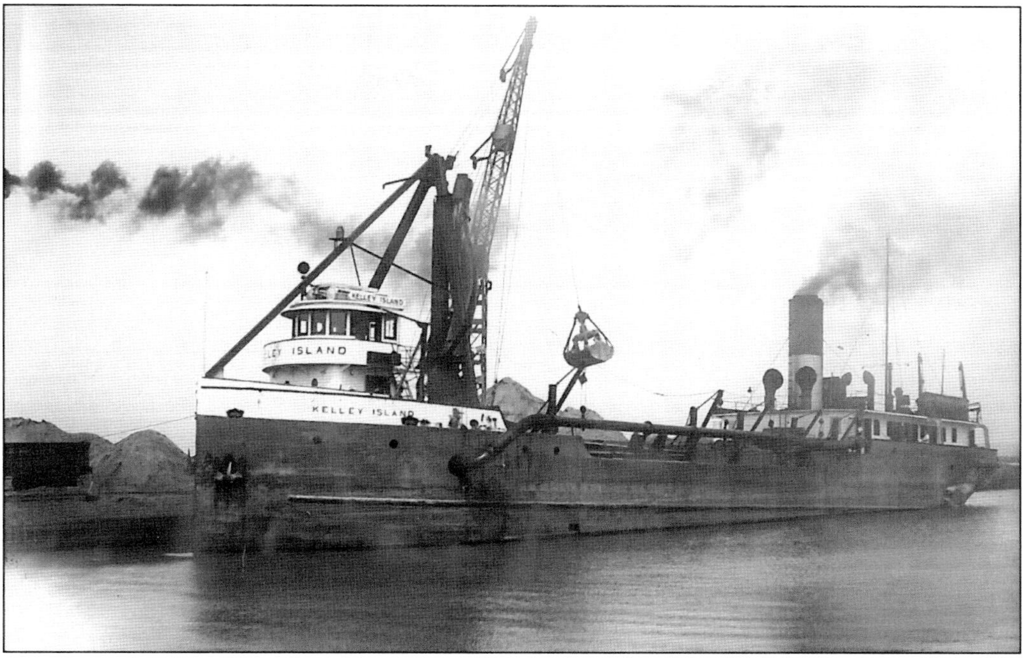

Formed in 1886, the Kelley Island Lime & Transport Co. had its own fleet of ships, including the namesake *Kelley Island* (pictured). With operations at Kelleys and Marblehead and in two other states, KIL&T was the world's largest producer of lime and limestone at the time. (Courtesy of the Sandusky Library Follett House Museum Archives.)

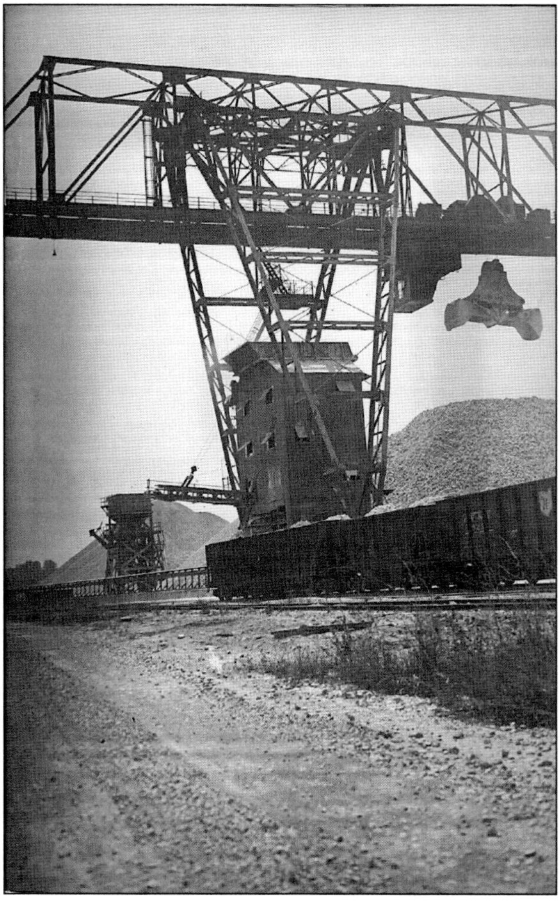

Quarry operations by the Kelley Island Lime & Transport Co. were still active in 1936, although some of the work had been scaled back due to the Great Depression and because it was felt that much of the good stone had been taken. Seven years later, KIL&T closed its quarries on Kelleys Island. (Courtesy of the Cleveland Public Library Photograph Collection.)

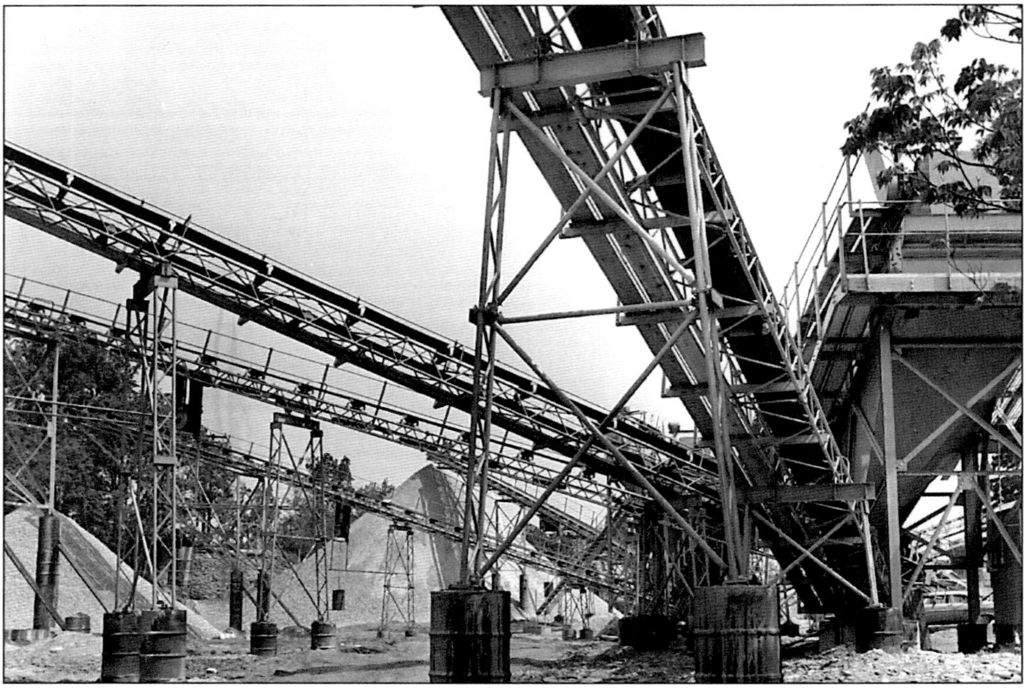

After 20 years of inactivity, the Kelley Island Limestone & Transport Co. quarry on Kelleys Island was purchased by the Breckling Concrete Corp. of Cleveland and reopened in early 1964. Operating through its Kellstone Inc. subsidiary, Breckling invested $1 million in improvements, including a new conveyor system to replace the Shay locomotives that formerly hauled stone to the loading dock. (Courtesy of the Cleveland Press Archives, Cleveland State University Library Special Collections.)

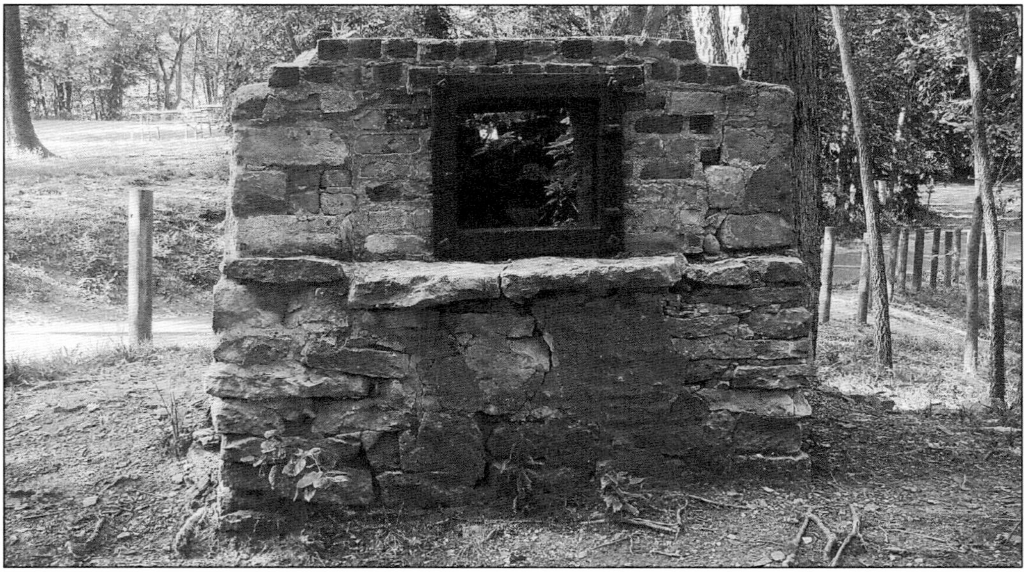

Seeming almost like an invitation to barbecue, this bake oven at the top of the hill descending to Sandy Beach is one of the few visible remnants of the North Quarry community that existed here in the mid-1800s. Built in 1875, this community bake oven would have been used by immigrant quarry workers living nearby, mainly for bread baking. (Courtesy of John T. Sabol.)

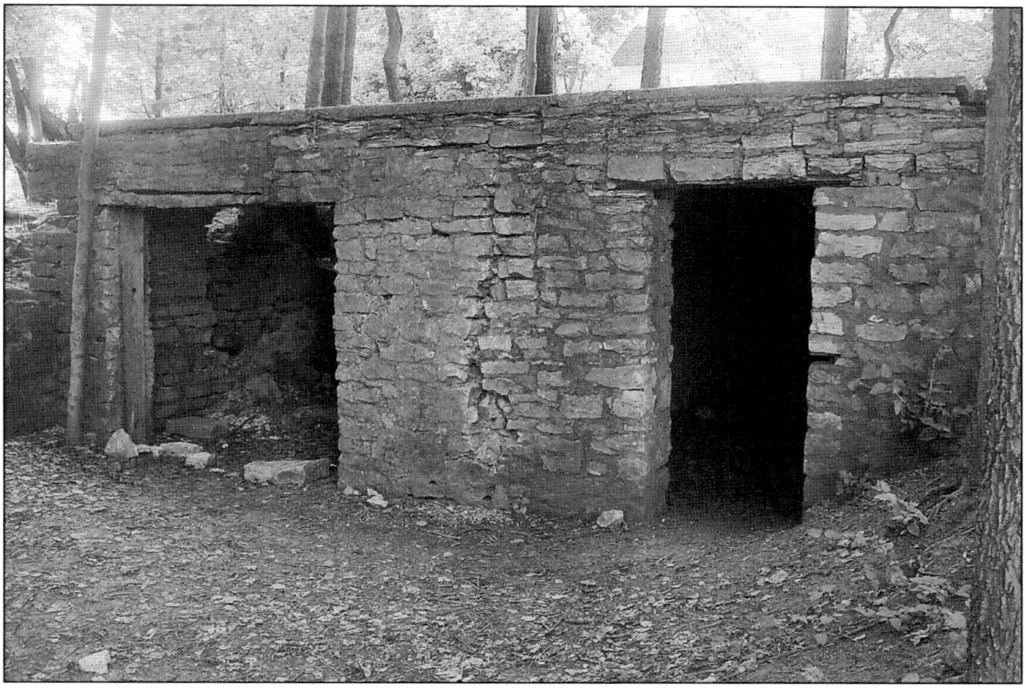

Just across the road from the community bake oven are the remains of the foundation of a quarry workers' boardinghouse. The quarries attracted immigrant labor from a variety of European countries, including Hungary, present-day Slovakia, and Italy. The quarries and vineyards boosted the island population to more than 2,000 by 1900. (Courtesy of John T. Sabol.)

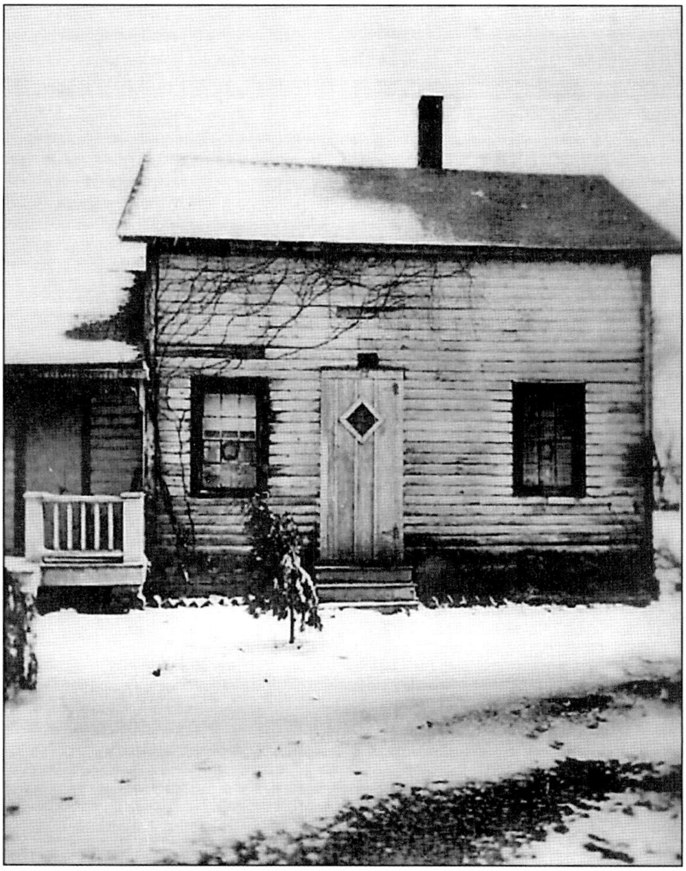

The Andrew Sennish home was a typical quarry worker's house and stood close to the West Bay loading dock. Sennish was born in what is now Slovakia in 1886 and immigrated to the United States in 1902. Many quarry workers' houses are still used on the island. (Courtesy of Larry Sennish.)

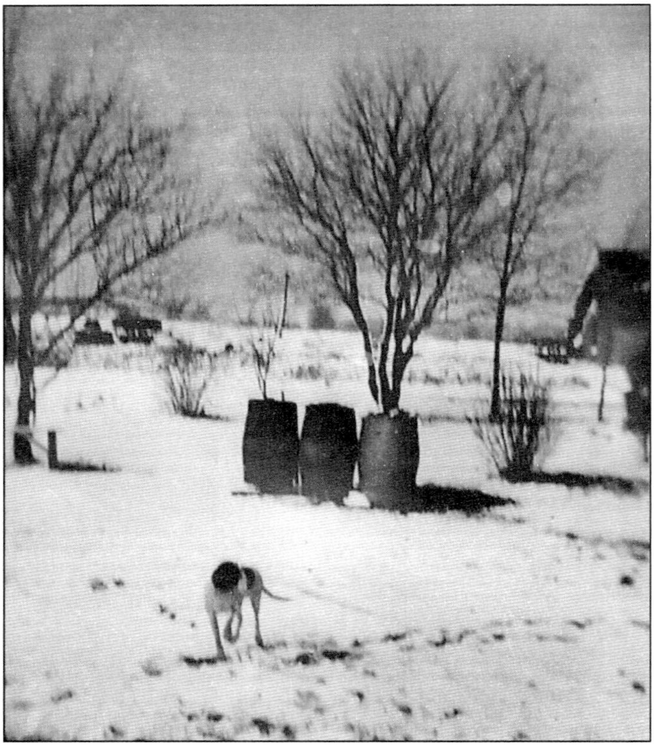

Running water was a rarity and a luxury at quarry workers' homes as well as in other homes on Kelleys Island in the 1930s. Houses kept barrels in their yards that were filled weekly at 25¢ per barrel. Occupations in the West Bay area were mixed, although the 1930 census shows a preponderance of quarry workers. (Courtesy of Larry Sennish.)

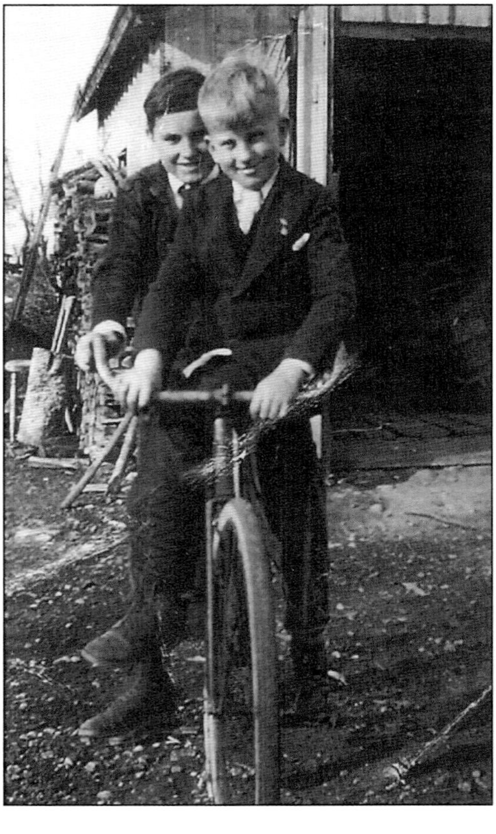

The Sennish and Mervo families lived near each other near Kelleys Island's West Bay. Mike Mervo and Andrew Sennish, both born in what is now Slovakia, eventually found employment on Kelleys as quarry workers. Enjoying a Sunday bike ride in their suits in the 1930s are two of their children, Larry Sennish (left) and Mike Mervo. (Courtesy of Larry Sennish.)

Six

On the Town

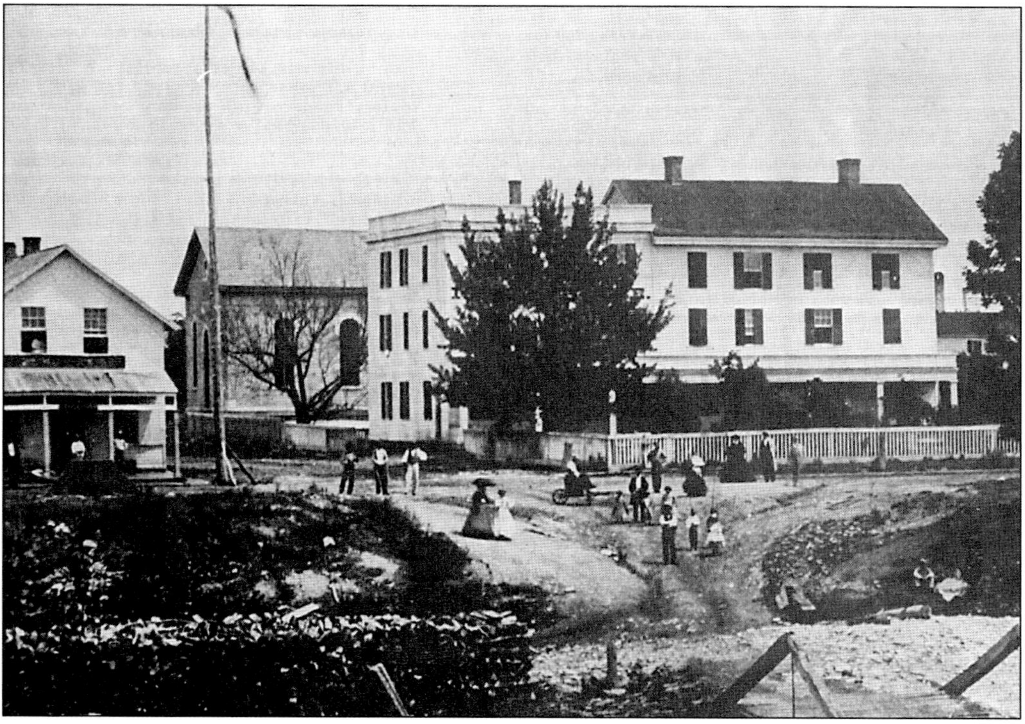

The Kelley family set out to establish their island as a tourist destination with the construction by Addison Kelley of the Island House at the northeast corner of Division Street and East Lakeshore Drive in 1852. The hotel, partially obscured by a tree, and a subsequent structure, the Schardt Hotel, were both destroyed by fire, and the site is now Memorial Park, in the center of town. (Courtesy of Carol Perruchon.)

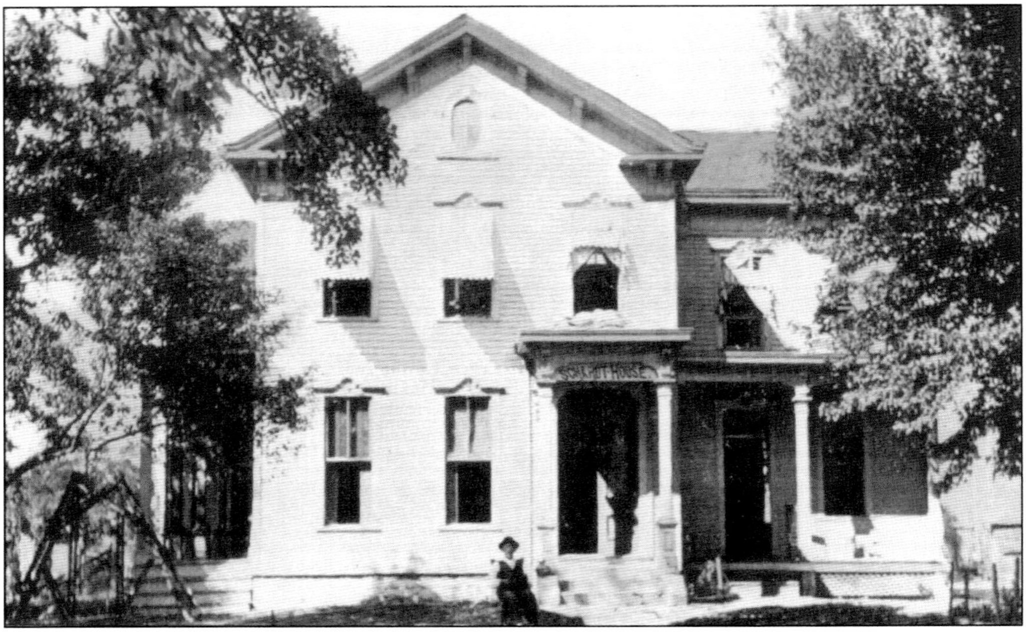

One of the finest hotels on Kelleys Island was in the center of the village on what is now East Lakeshore Drive. The Schardt Hotel was established by Adam Schardt after the Island House, built in the 1850s, was destroyed by fire in 1877. Sadly, Schardt's hotel suffered the same fate as the Island House in June 1912. (Courtesy of the Kelleys Island Historical Association.)

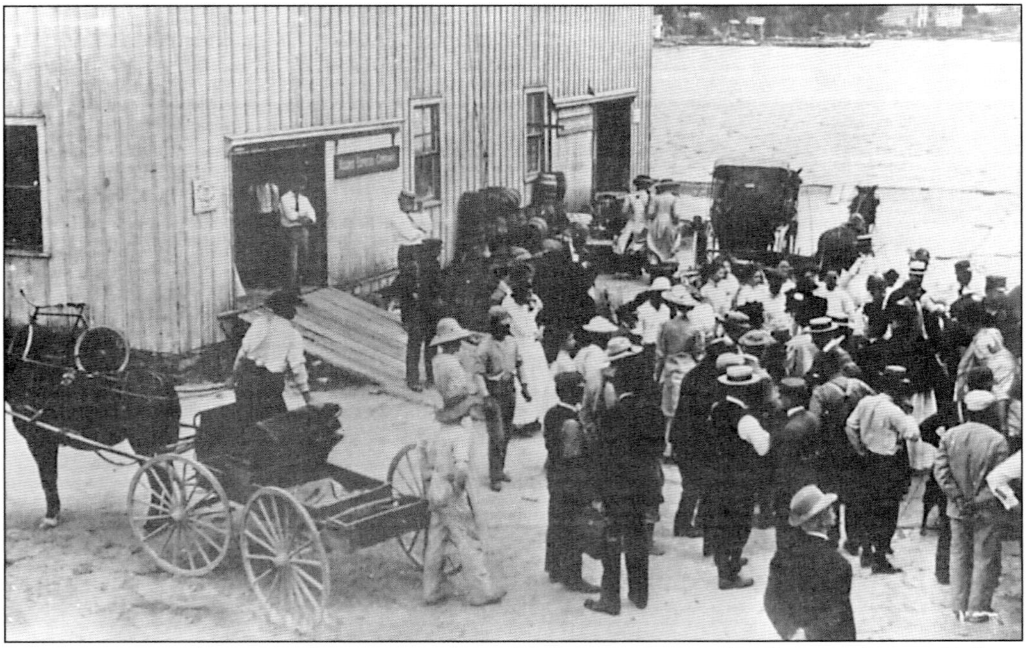

What came to be known as the Store Dock quickly became a central gathering place on Kelleys. Here, islanders—much like the fictional citizens of River City, Iowa, waiting for the Wells Fargo wagon in *The Music Man*—await the arrival of another boat from the mainland. The dock lost its status as the main steamship dock on the island in 1949, but it was revived and is now the dock for the *Jet Express* and the *Goodtime*. (Courtesy of Carol Perruchon.)

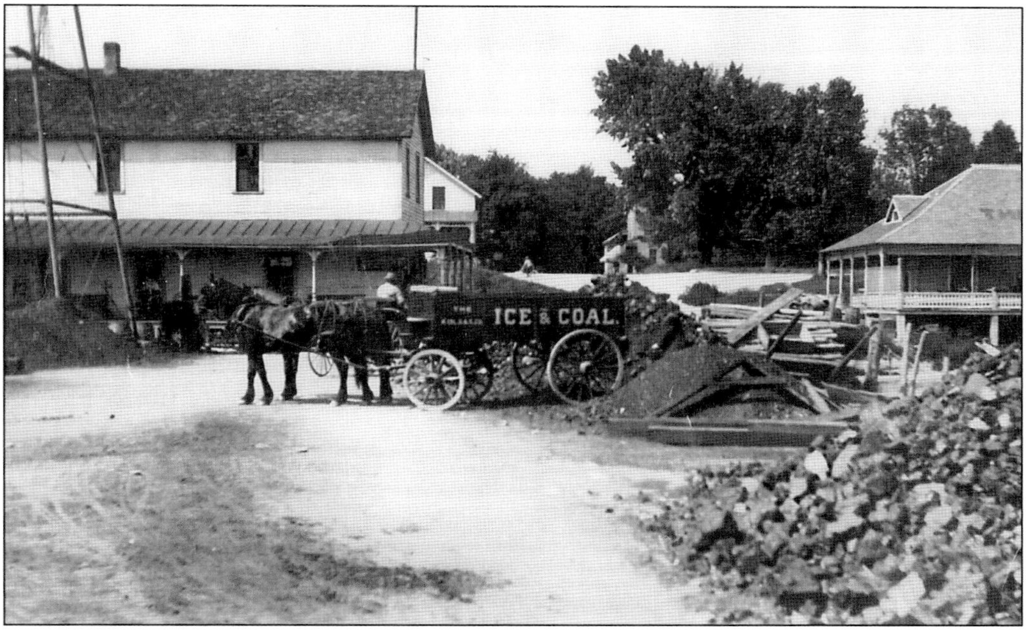

Looking from the Store Dock, at the end of Division Street, the building on the left is Coutcher's Saloon, which was built in 1894 and destroyed by fire in 1915. On the right is the Casino. Preparing a load of coal for delivery is a crew from the Kelleys Island Dock & Steamboat Co. On the bluff overlooking the dock, part of the Store on the Corner is visible. (Courtesy of Gary and Jackie Finger.)

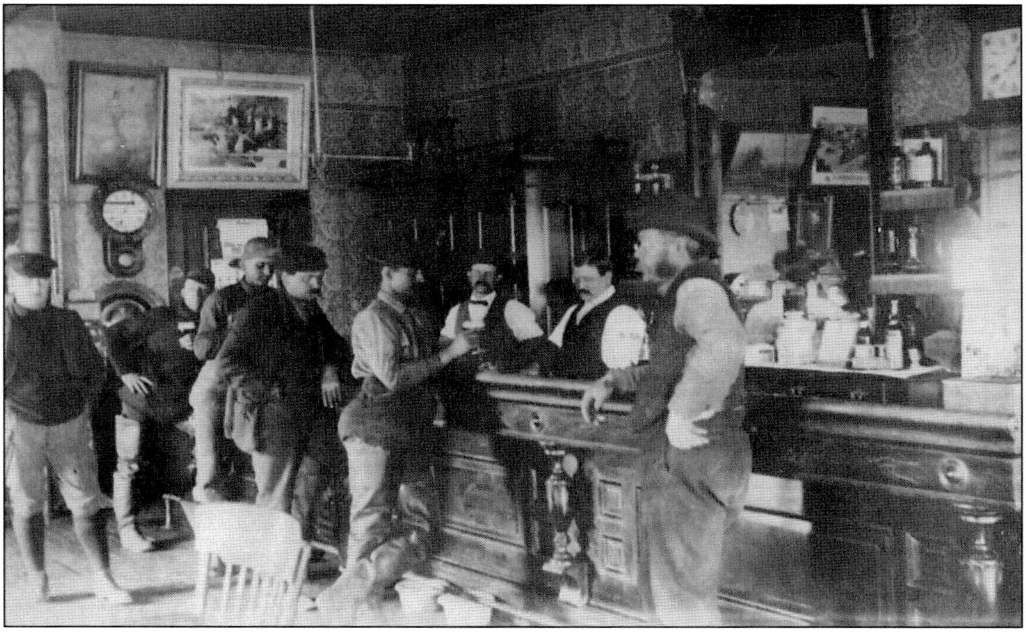

Coutcher's Saloon, below the bluff marking the south end of Division Street, was built in 1894. In front of the stove in this 1901 photograph is Clifford Seaton. Standing from left to right at the bar are Nelson Dwelle, unidentified, Fred Dischinger Sr., Bill "Jumpsey" Voight, and Dan Magg. Behind the bar are saloon owner January Coutcher (left) and Fred Elminger. (Courtesy of Gary and Jackie Finger.)

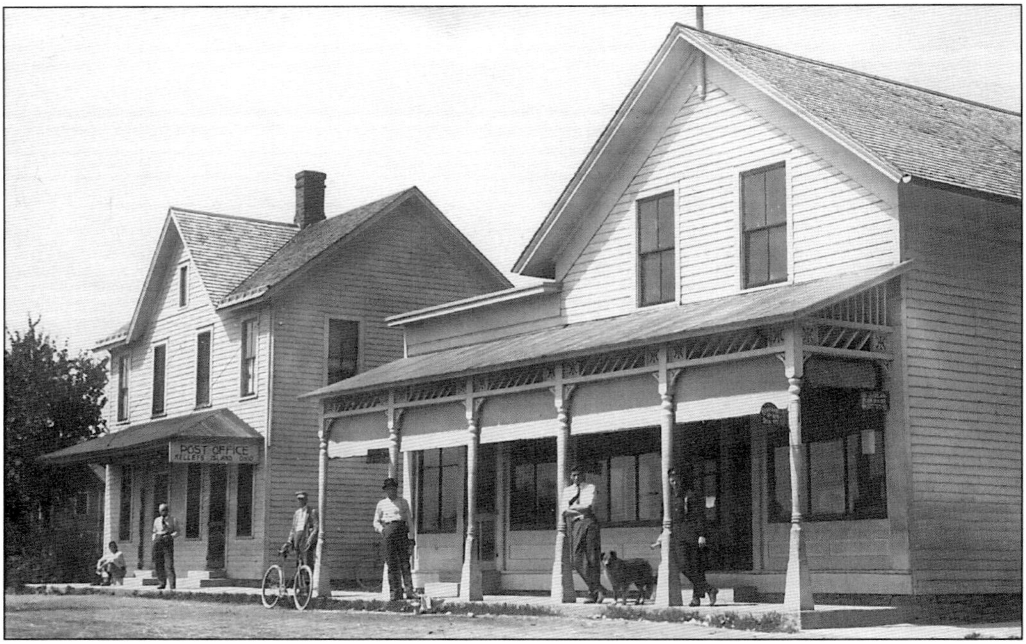

This scene at the corner of Division Street and West Lakeshore Drive seems quite different from the center of town today. However, the actual buildings are the same. On the right, the Store on the Corner, formerly the Lodge, became Matso's Place and is now the Captain's Corner. Just to the west, the post office transformed into Martin's Ice Cream Parlor, then Martin's Bar, and is now the Village Pump. (Courtesy of the Kelleys Island Historical Association.)

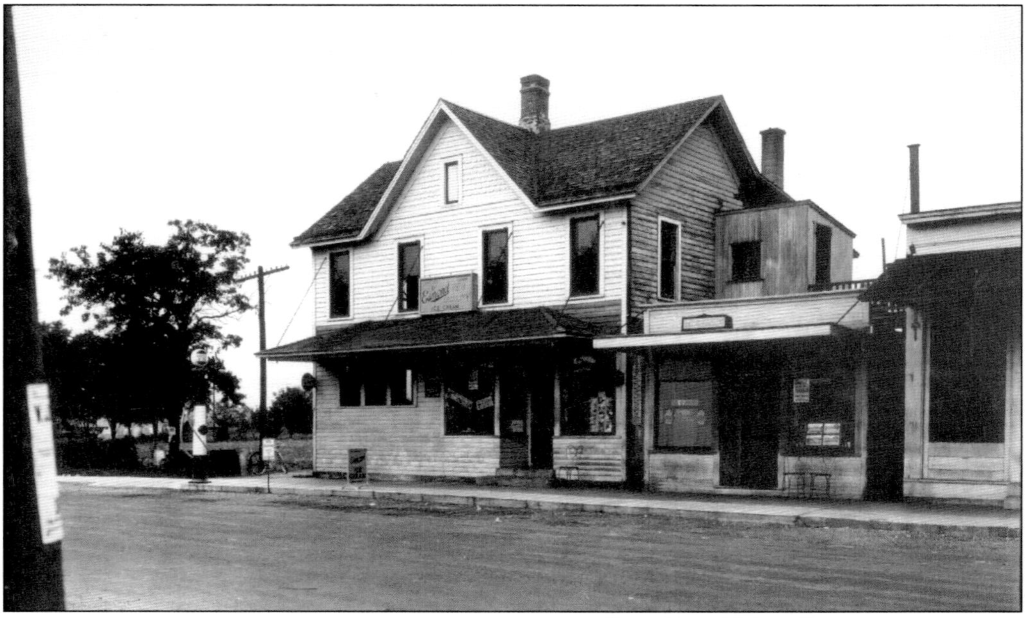

This 1934 view of the north side of West Lakeshore Drive shows what is now the Village Pump on the left. The current entrance to the Village Pump was once the entrance to Martin's Ice Cream Parlor, but the sign over the entrance indicates it is the "Casino." The Martins moved the structure, formerly a quarry building, into the space. (Courtesy of the Frohman Collection, Rutherford B. Hayes Presidential Center.)

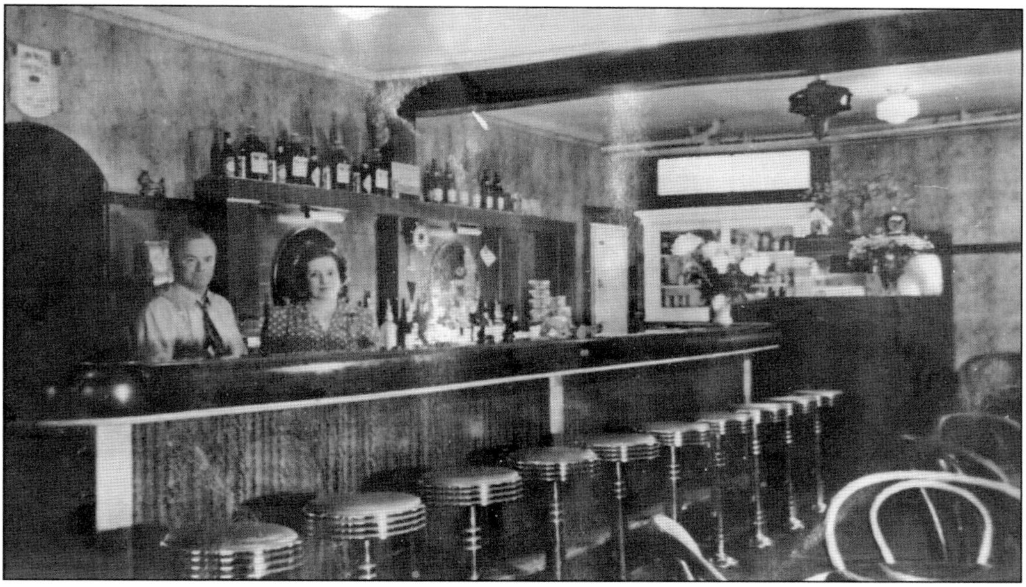

The Village Pump was formerly Martin's Bar, run by Charles and Elizabeth Martin (seen here) from the 1930s until the 1960s. The bar itself was the island post office until 1921, when Emmett Martin established a confectionery in the space. His brother Charles later took over and converted the building into a bar. (Courtesy of Gary and Jackie Finger.)

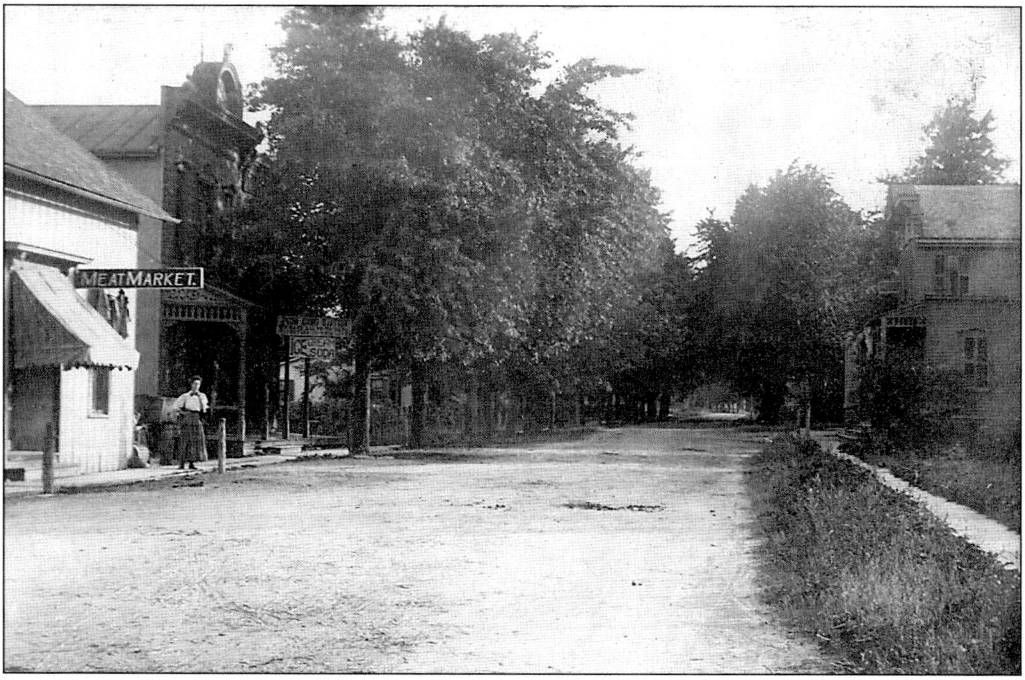

As borne out by this scene from the early 1900s, Division Street looking north from the downtown area has always been a business center. Trieschmann's Meat Market is on the left. Now known as the Island Market, it is one of the oldest continuously operated retail establishments on the island. (Courtesy of John T. Sabol.)

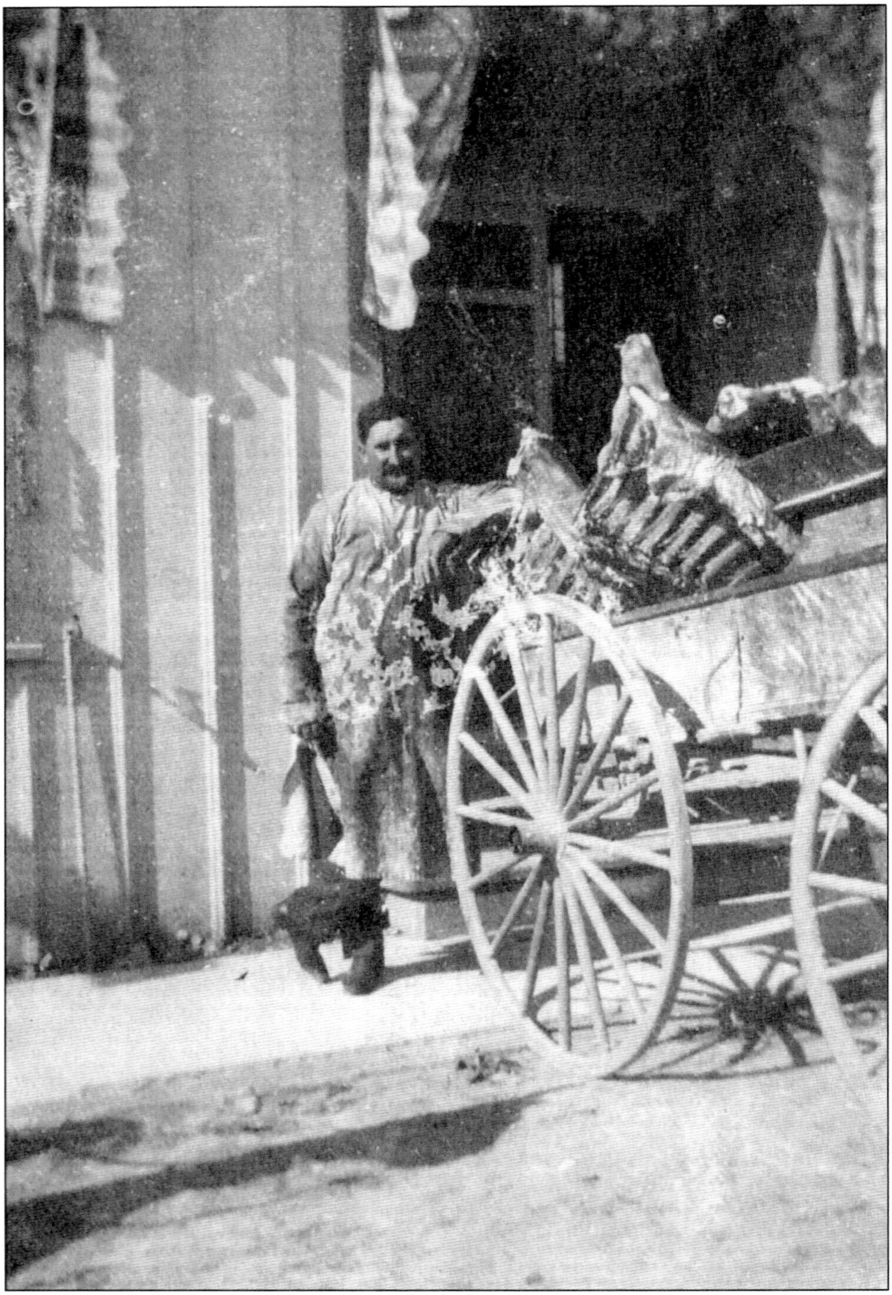

Henry Trieschmann, the island butcher, stands outside his meat market (now the Island Market) on Division Street around 1900. A native of Hesse, Germany, he immigrated to the United States in 1866 and arrived on Kelleys Island in 1870. Trieschmann owned a slaughterhouse near Woodford and Monagan Roads and provided fresh meat to island residents. He also served on the board of the Sweet Valley Wine Co., eventually becoming president. His house, just up the street from the market, is today's Island House Restaurant. The store was built in 1866 and operated by Trieschman until 1915, when his son, Henry Jr., took over. A succession of owners operated it from 1942 until 1946, when it was purchased by Frank Pohorence. (Courtesy of Fritz Pape's photo album, Pape family collection.)

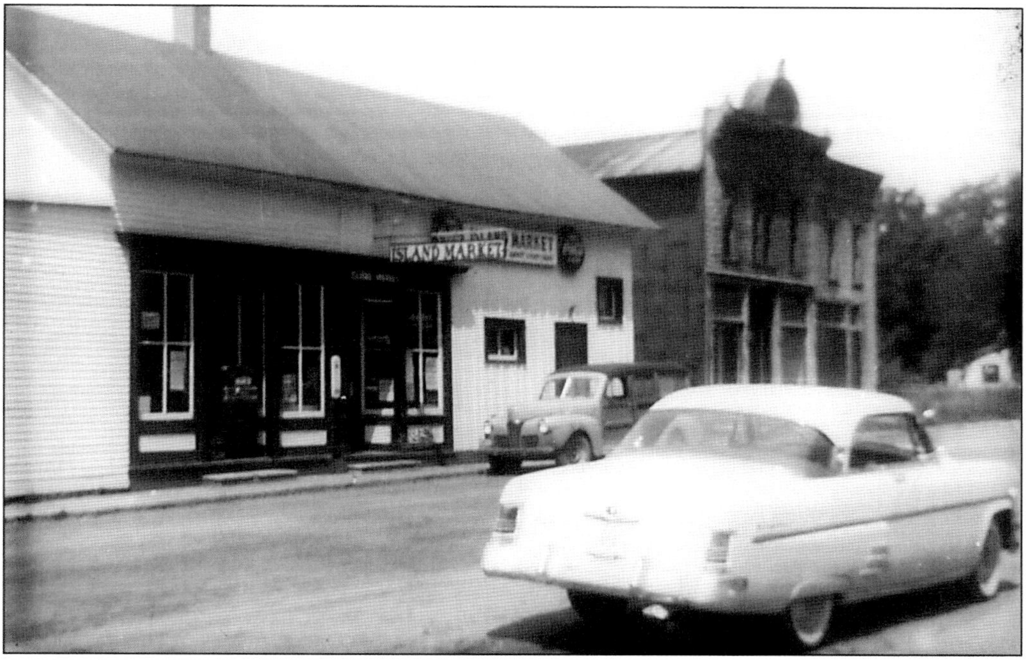

Frank Pohorence purchased the Island Market in 1946 and made extensive changes to the interior. His wife, Laura Jean, also ran the market, which was purchased by Rob and Kim Watkins in October 1983. They also made extensive changes to the interior. (Courtesy of Frank and Laura Jean Pohorence.)

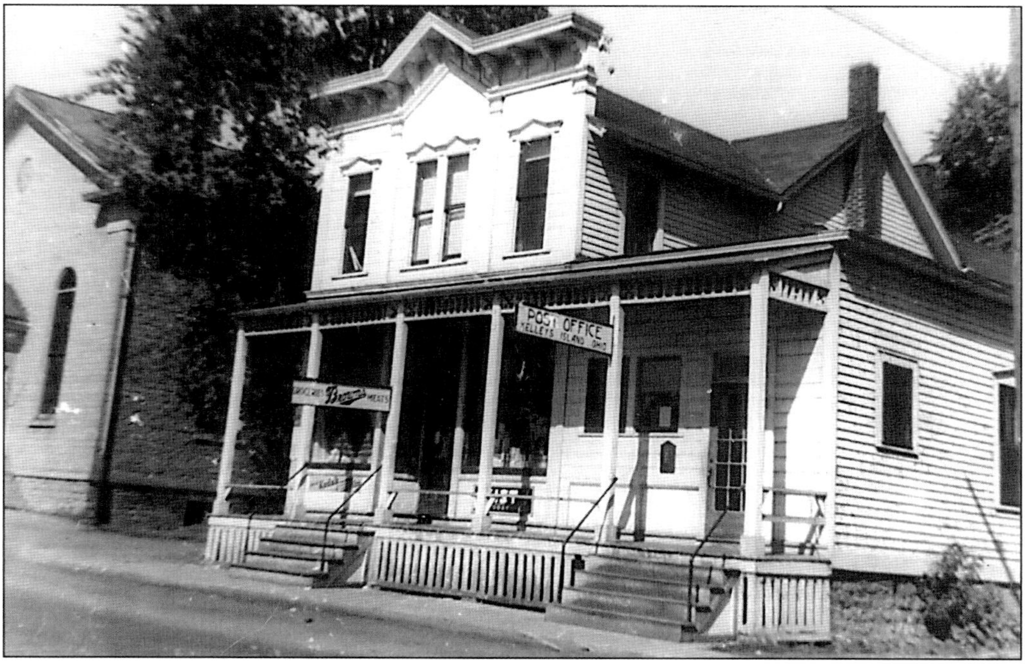

A longtime anchor in Kelleys Island's commercial district on the east side of Division Street, the two-story wing of what is now the General Store was built in 1885, with the one-story wing on the south added later to serve as the island's post office, twice, until 1974. The first floor of the northern wing still serves its original purpose as a general store. (Courtesy of Bill and Sis Bradburn.)

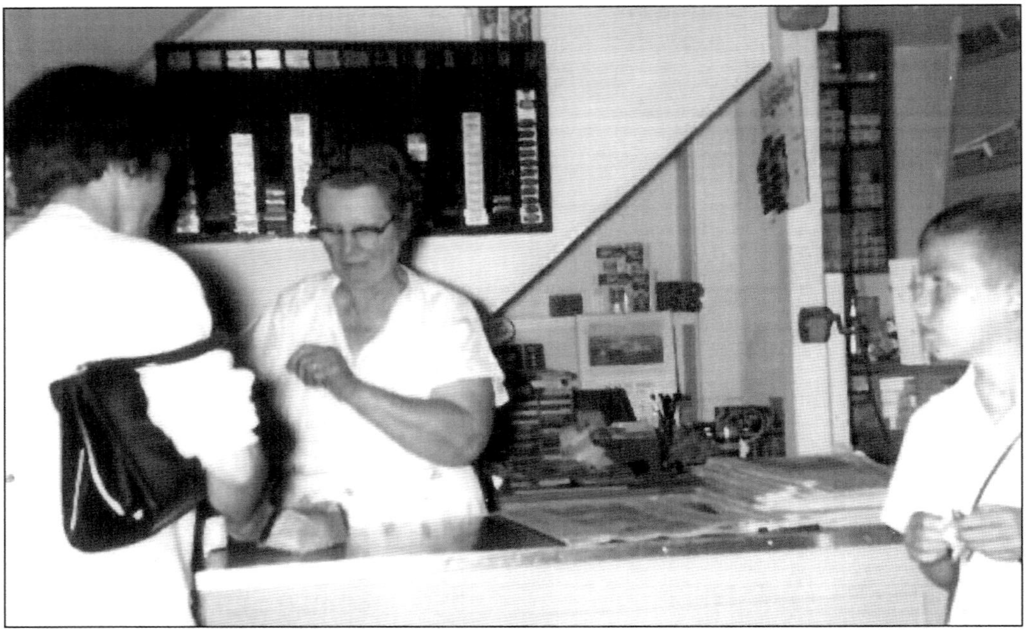

Until the 1960s, the general store on Division Street was widely known as Brown's. Walter and Mamie Brown (center) and Frank Lange purchased the store from the Reinheimer family, probably in the 1930s. After Walter's death, his wife ran the store with her two sons, Howard and Clifford, until the 1960s, according to the Kelleys Island Historic District National Register Nomination, 1987. (Courtesy of Claudia Brown and the Kelleys Island Historical Association.)

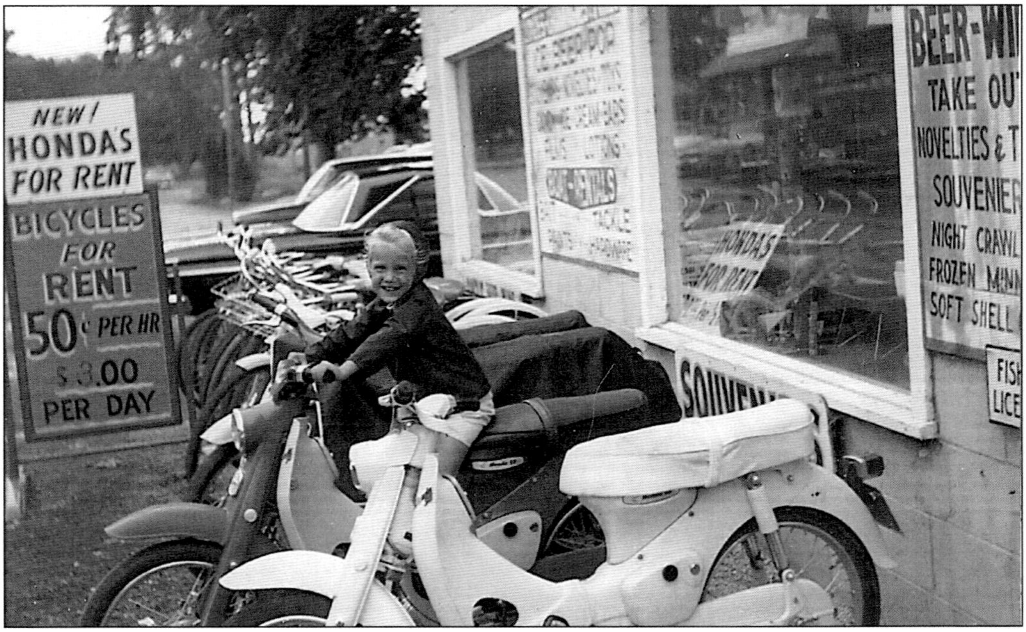

Miller Marine Service—a multifunctional business renting boats, mopeds, and bicycles—was owned and operated by Burt Miller. It was also the first business on the island to rent golf carts. Today, golf carts are so popular on the island they sometimes seem to be the only means of transportation. Sitting on one of Miller's mopeds in August 1968 is his granddaughter Becky Miller. (Courtesy of Jim Miller.)

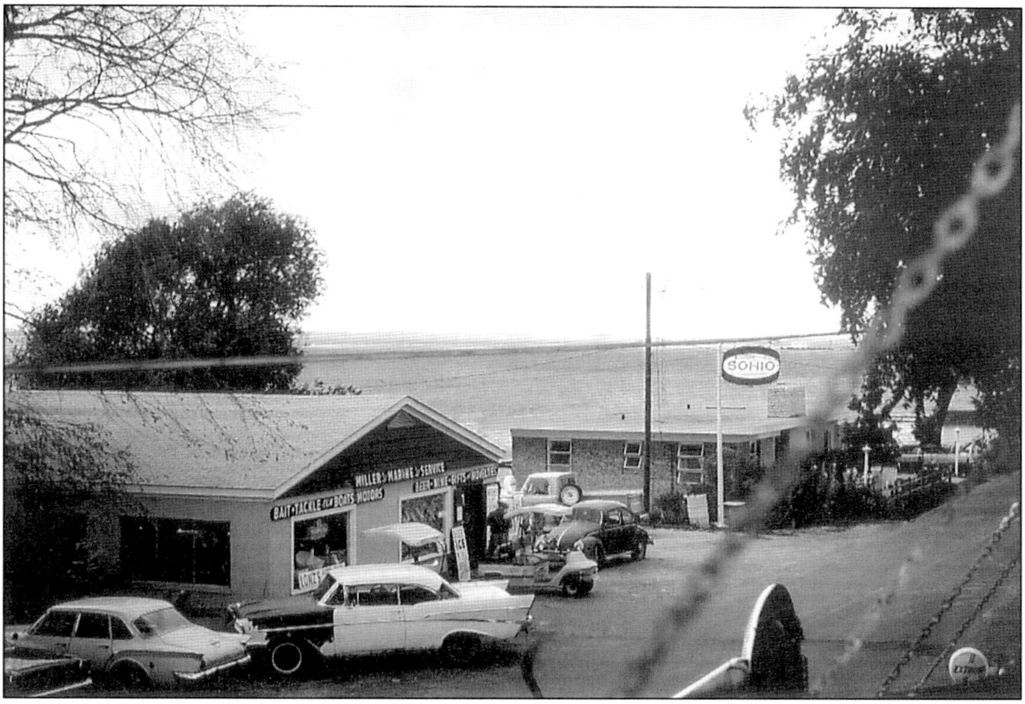

This view of Miller Marine in the 1960s is from the second floor of what is now the Village Pump. For several years, Miller Marine was the only place on the island where boats could stop for gas. Today, the building houses the Kelleys Landing gift shop. (Courtesy of Jim Miller.)

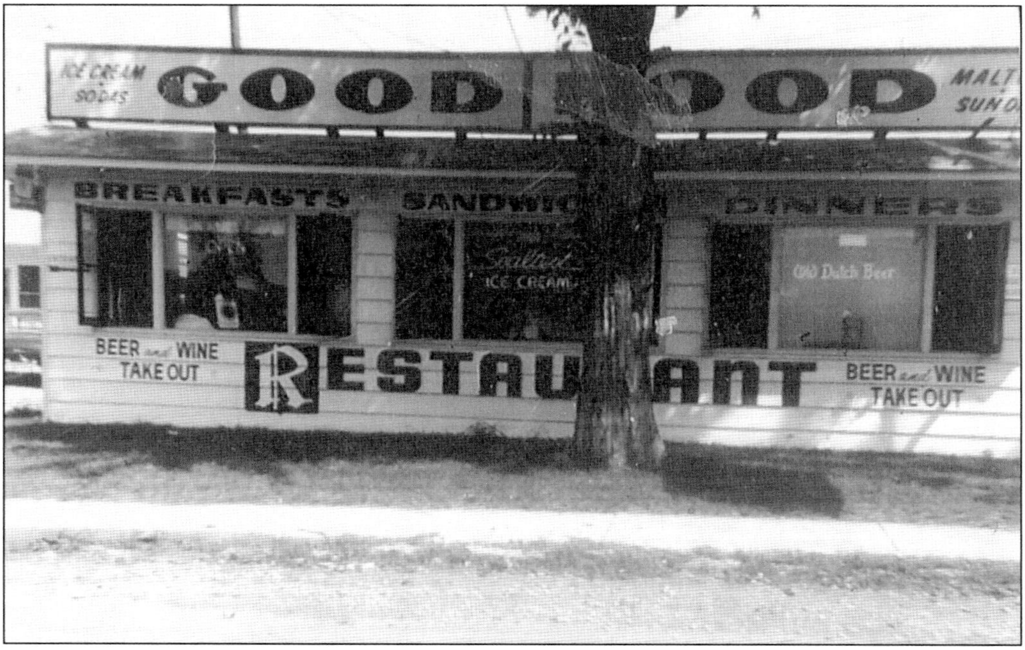

The Marine Grille, seen here, almost directly across West Lakeshore Drive from Miller Marine Service, is now occupied by Bag The Moon Saloon. The Marine Grille also included motel units separated from the restaurant by a driveway. The motel was approximately where the Bag The Moon bar area is today. (Courtesy of Jim Miller.)

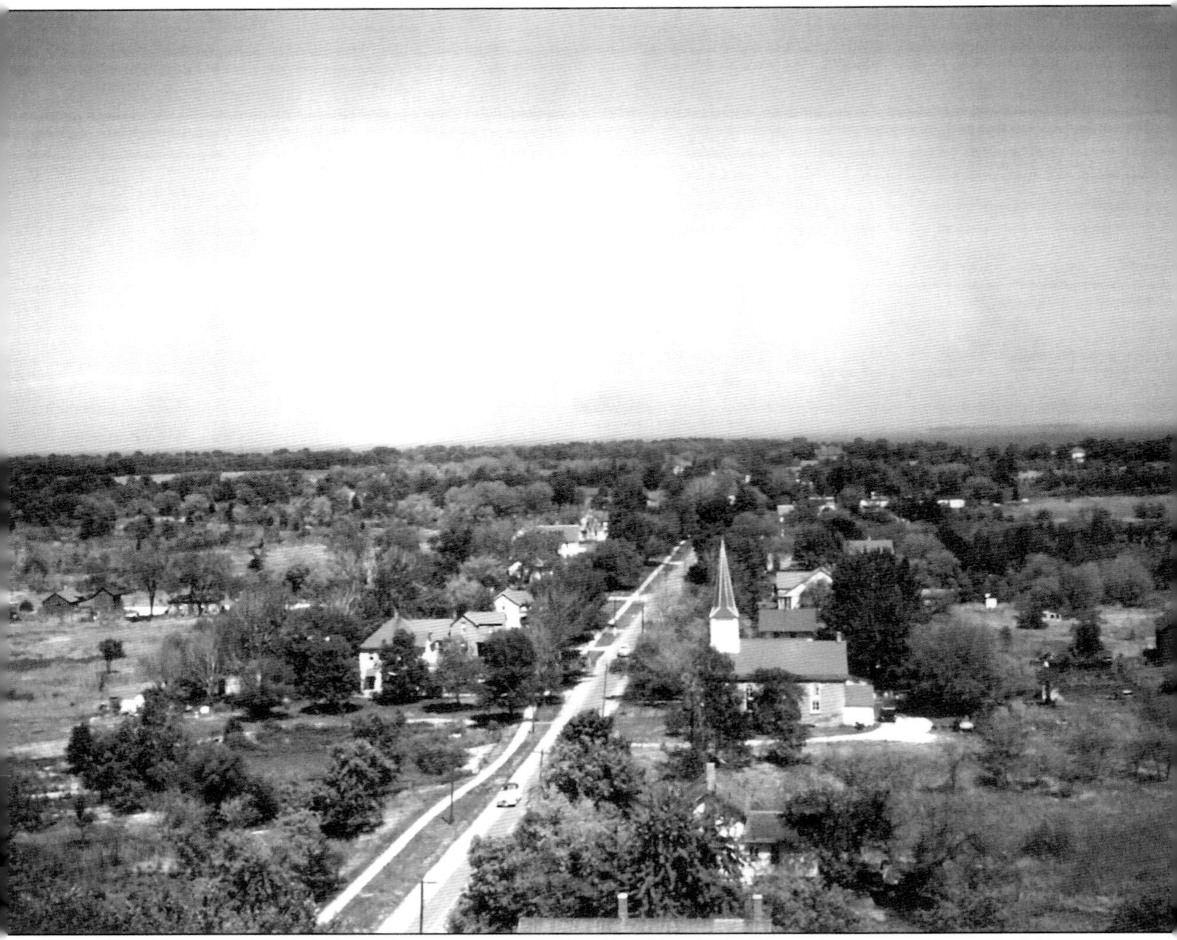

This aerial view north along Division Street on Kelleys Island was taken in the mid-1950s in an unconventional manner. Ed Frindt, the youthful photographer, climbed to the top of the water tower at the southeast corner of Chappel and Division Streets to take the photograph with a simple Kodak Brownie camera. He was later caught by legendary Kelleys Island police chief Norbert McKillips and luckily got off with a lecture. Known as Norby, McKillips was respected but often had a big heart, sometimes allowing young folks on the island for the weekend to sleep in the village jail. McKillips died in January 1984 after suffering a heart attack in December 1983. The incident resulted in a tragic rescue attempt in which four people died. A medical flight from Put-In-Bay to Kelleys in heavy fog resulted in a plane crash that killed medical technician Bruce Mettler, Put-In-Bay township trustee Duane Dress, medical technician Mike Sweeney, and pilot Robert Rigoni. (Courtesy of Ed and Carol Frindt.)

Seven

Island Education

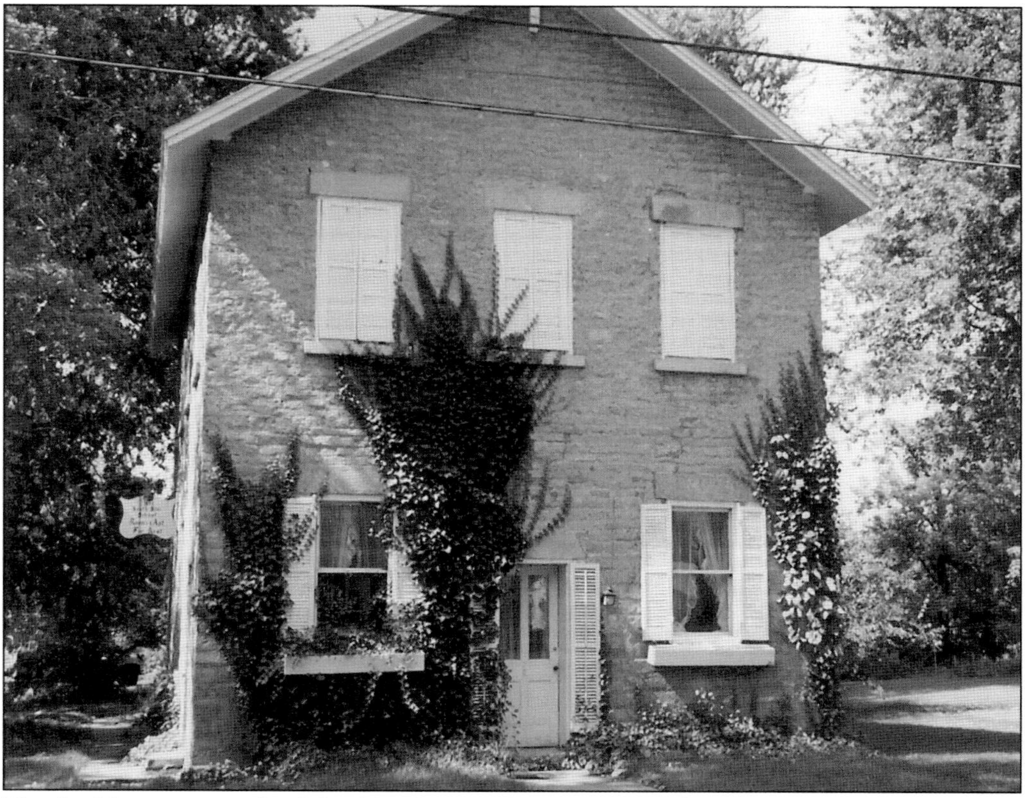

This building, just north of the Island House Restaurant on the west side of Division Street, formerly housed the Kelleys Island School District No. 1 primary school. It was erected in 1853 and housed grades one through eight. After Estes School was built, this structure became a private residence and then served as a station of the Sandusky Public Library. (Courtesy of Jack and Linda Hostal.)

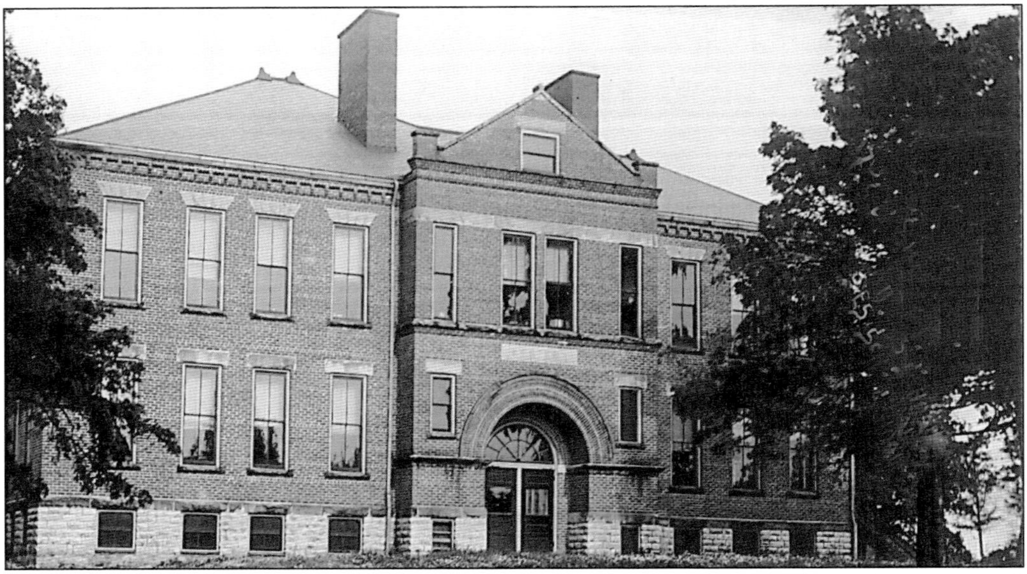

Estes School, at Division Street and Ward Road, was built in 1902 for $14,000. The school consolidated into one building classes that had been conducted in four other schools. In addition, some island children attended classes at a Catholic and a Lutheran school, according to the Kelleys Island Historical Association. Because of dwindling enrollment, students currently attend school on the mainland. As soon as the student population increases, Estes will reopen. The rear of this building now houses the island's public library. (Courtesy of Frank and Laura Jean Pohorence.)

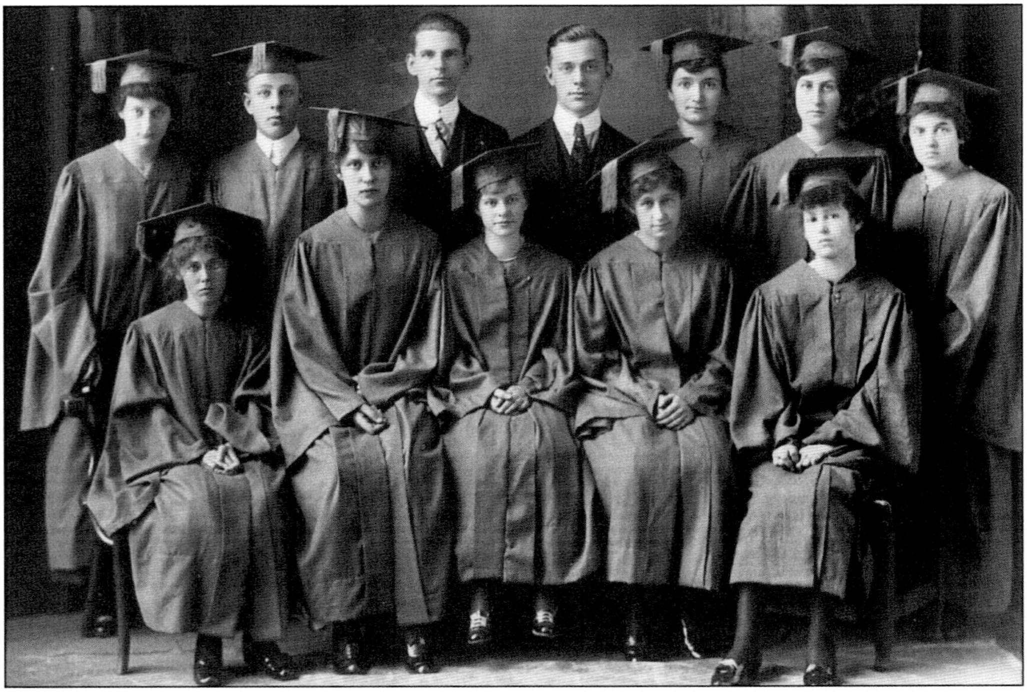

The 1916 graduating class of Estes School includes Marguerite Dwelle (first row, far left), Harriet Martin (first row, third from left), and Laura Martin (second row, far right). Also in the class are, in no particular order, Meda Lincoln Brown, Margaret Himmelein, Orville Lange, Marcella Myers, Marion Roswurm, and Gertrude Suhr. (Courtesy of Frank and Laura Jean Pohorence.)

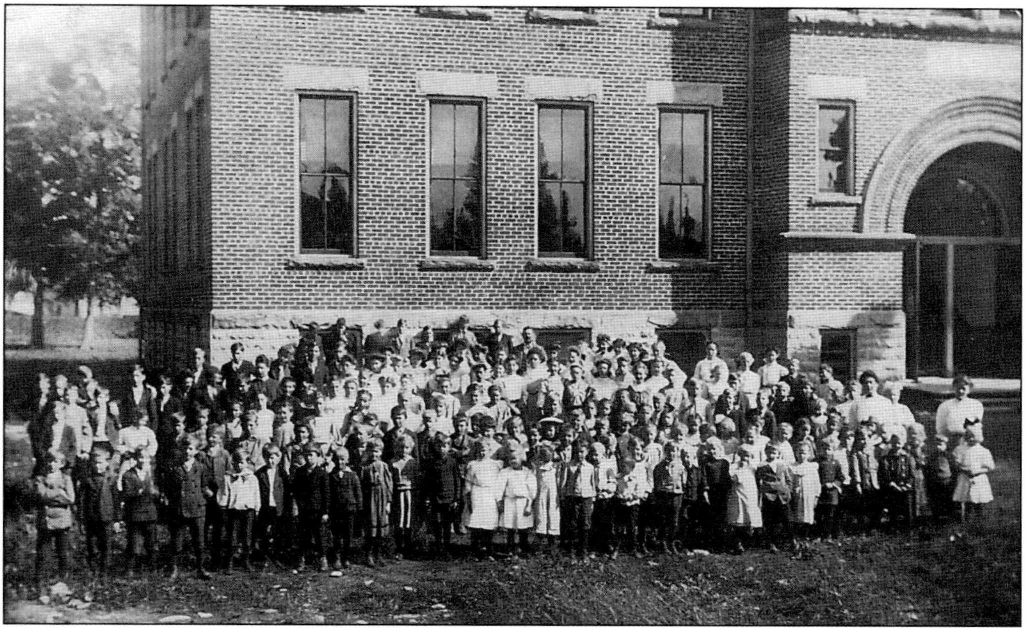

Peak enrollment at Estes School was 200 pupils, giving a good idea of the island population in the school's early days. Once housing all 12 grades plus kindergarten, the school is currently closed because school-age population has decreased. Island students currently attend classes in Danbury Township. When the school-age population increases, Estes will reopen. (Courtesy of Bob and Carol Schnittker.)

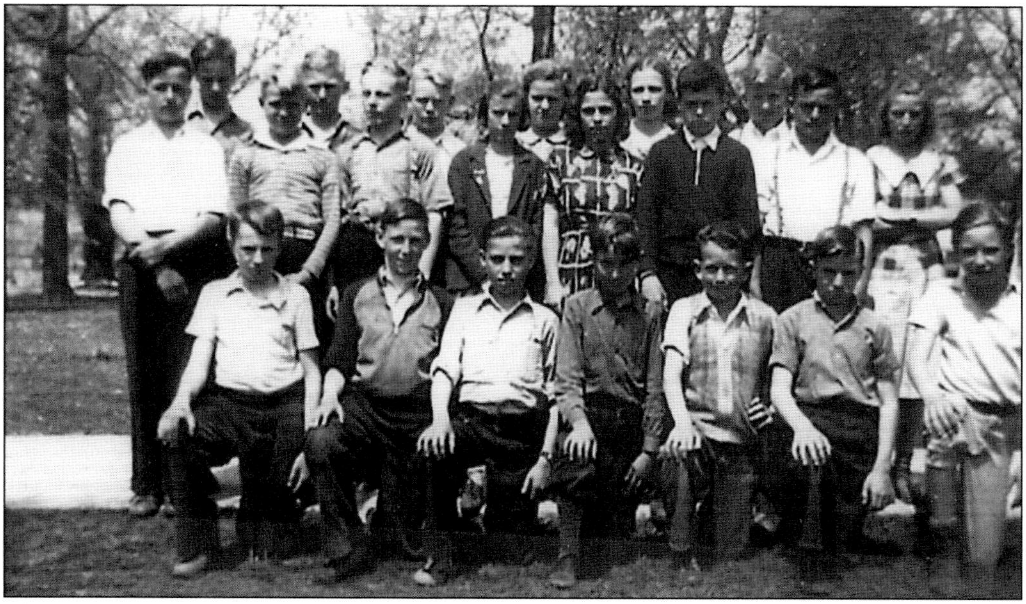

The seventh- and eighth-graders at Estes School in 1938 are, from left to right, (first row) Frank Yazombeck, Ted Blatt, Logan Bickley, Lester Colbert, James Volz, Jake Martin, and Wallace Murphy; (second row) Louie Rudolph, Max Schnittker, Clyde Beatty, Alice Jean Kurtz, Betty McKillips, Tony Capiccioni, and Frank Rudolph; (third row) Bobby Walland, Donald Haig, Billy Schnittker, Margaret Mazur, Florence McKillips, Lawrence Sennish, and Dawn Seeholzer. (Courtesy of Ted Blatt.)

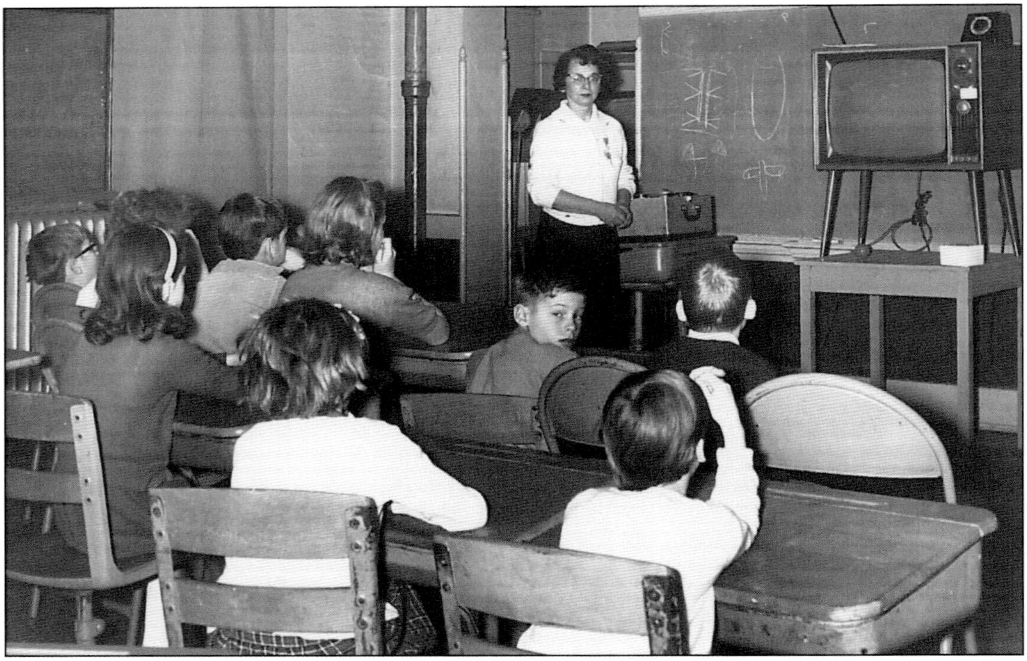

Helen Baker supervised instruction for the lower grades. The console television played a prominent role as a teaching tool in 1962. "It's much better than our movie projector," Baker said at the time, "because films are limited and many of them are commercial." (Courtesy of the Cleveland Press Archives, Cleveland State University Library Special Collections.)

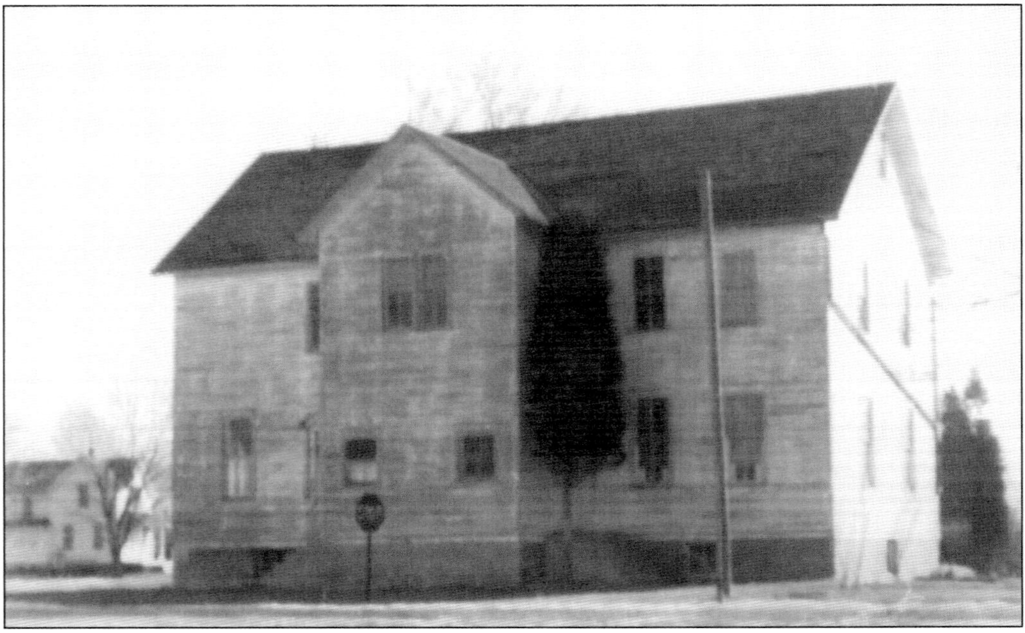

This building, at Addison and Woodford Roads, once housed the St. Michael Parish School. Built in 1905, the school featured two classrooms on the first floor and an auditorium on the second floor. When it opened, about 60 students attended the school. The structure was renamed Marquette Hall after the school closed and was used as a social hall until it was razed in 1968 . (Courtesy of the Kelleys Island Historical Association.)

Eight

Camping Memories

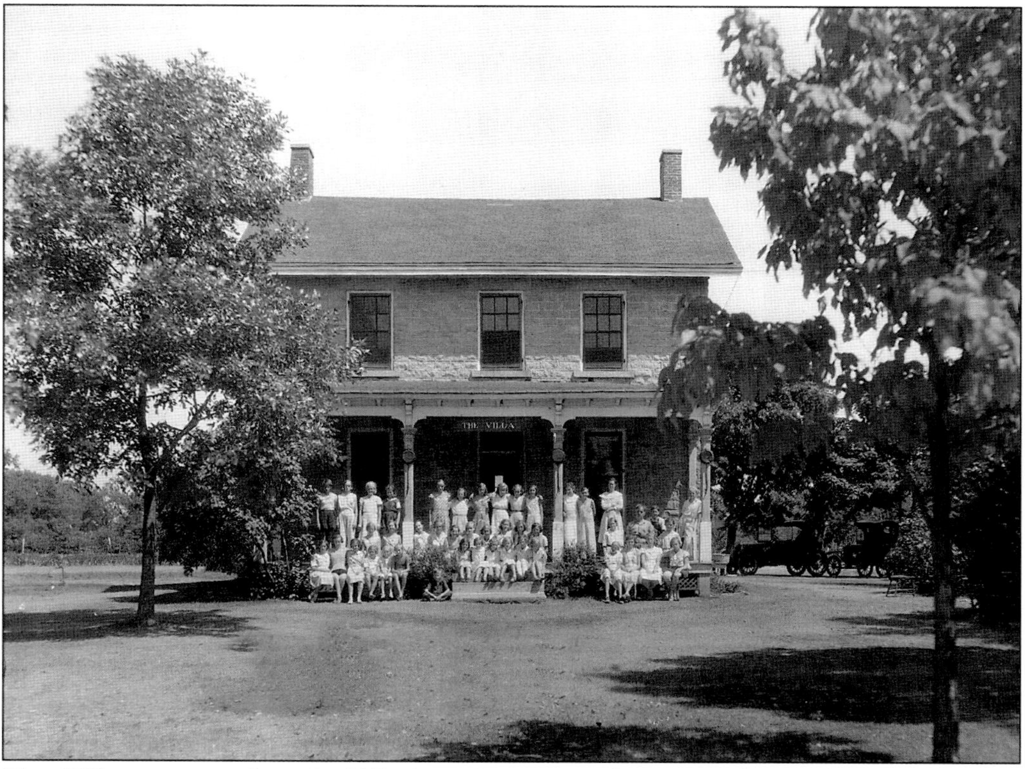

This 1933 camp group from the Villa (now Camp Patmos) was one of many that came out on a weekly basis from about 1921 until the Catholic camp closed in 1944. It was owned by Fr. Vaclav Chaloupka of Nativity of the Blessed Virgin Mary Church in Cleveland, who first visited Kelleys Island in 1907 to hear the confessions of Slovak quarry workers. (Courtesy of the Frohman Collection, Rutherford B. Hayes Presidential Center.)

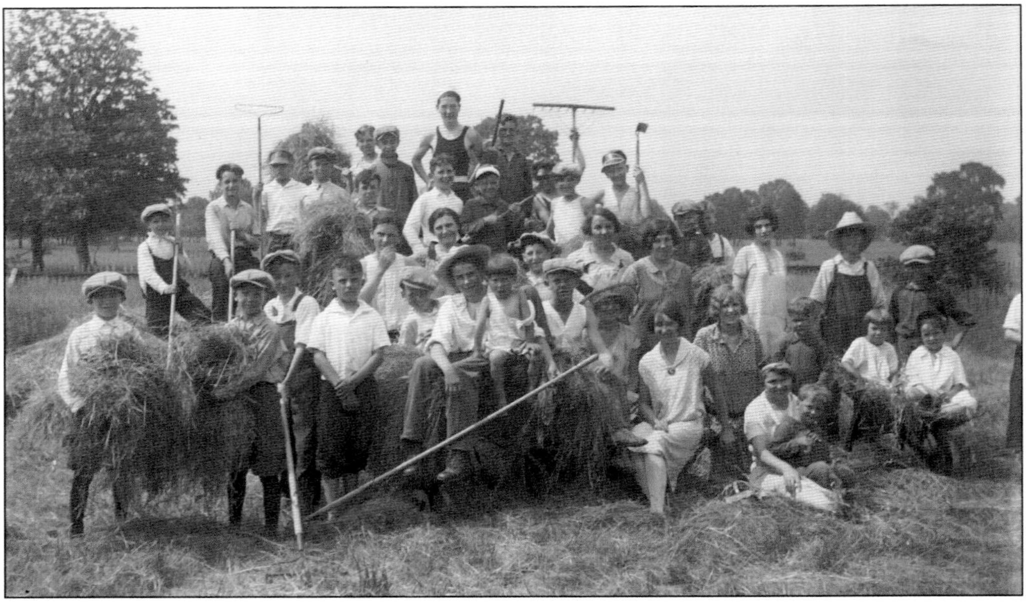

Time spent on Kelleys Island with Fr. Vaclav Chaloupka, the pastor of Nativity of the Blessed Virgin Mary Parish in Cleveland, was not without its share of work. Besides fun in the sun and water, children and even adults helped with the various chores, including harvesting some hay. Their Slovak parents, used to an agrarian lifestyle, would have approved. (Courtesy of Slovak Institute and Library.)

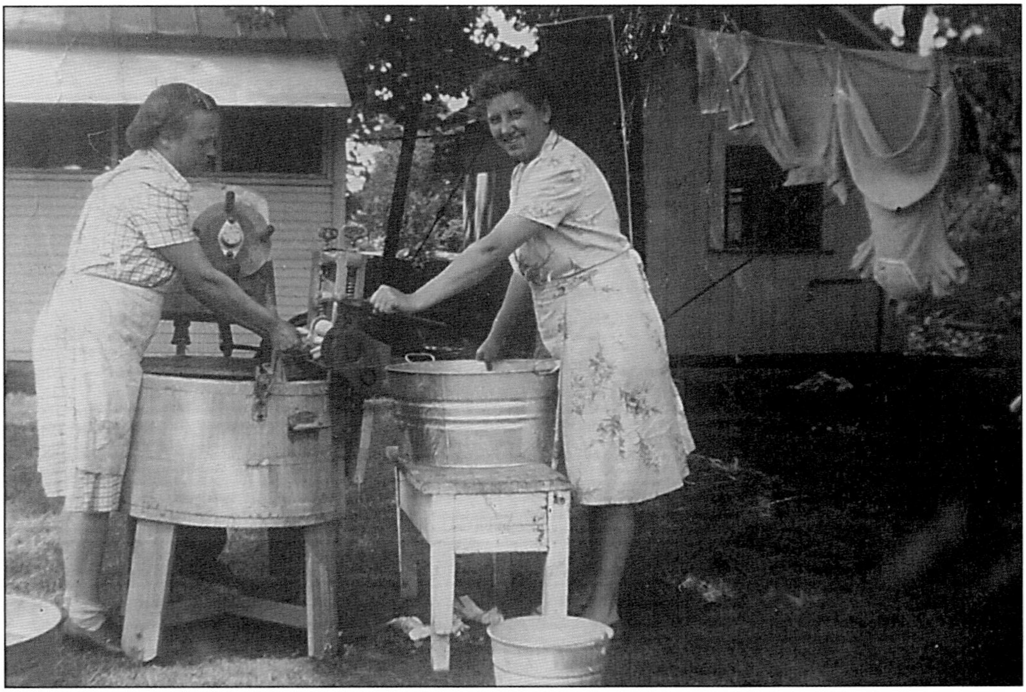

Fr. Vaclav Chaloupka's camp, the Villa, ran almost entirely on volunteer help, mainly from parishioners at Nativity of the Blessed Virgin Mary Parish. Many stayed the summer and were able to watch their children enjoy the island environment. Seen here doing the laundry in 1938 are Nativity parishioners Florence Sabol (left) and Agnes Cech. (Courtesy of John T. Sabol.)

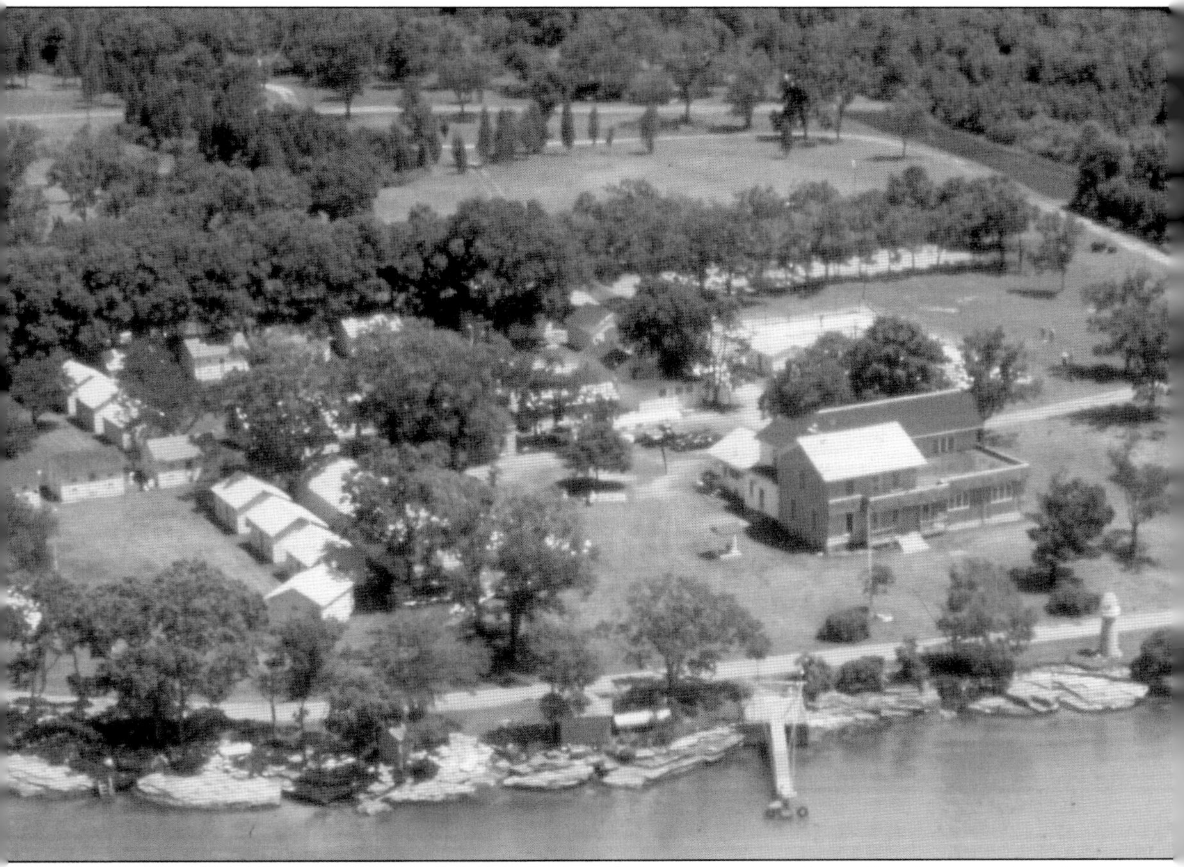

In 1921, Fr. Vaclav Chaloupka of Nativity of the Blessed Virgin Mary Parish in Cleveland purchased the land for his camp, the Villa, on Long Point, which at the time was a farm owned by Samuel Hamilton, the father of Frank Hamilton and one of the original landowners on Kelleys Island. Father Chaloupka expanded this building at least twice and built several other buildings and a roller-skating rink on the property. He closed the camp in 1944, and in 1952 sold the Villa to the Ohio Regular Baptist Home and Camp, which renamed the site Camp Patmos and also expanded it. This view of Camp Patmos shows the front of the camp, facing the west shore of Long Point along Monagan Road. At the right is the original Hamilton house, later known as the Villa, which has now been expanded several times. (Courtesy of Camp Patmos.)

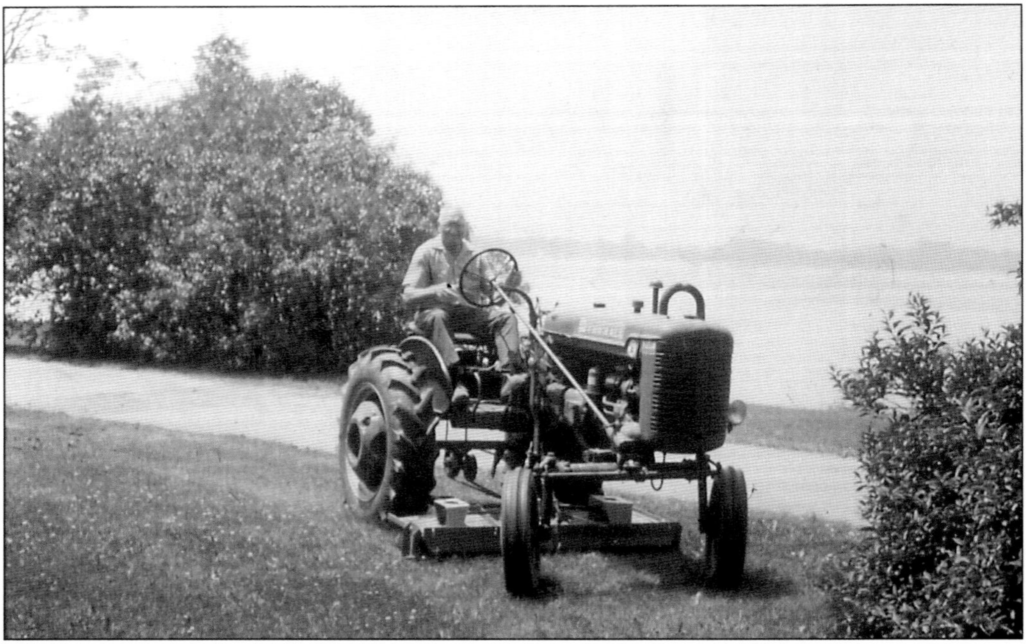

John Morse, seen here in 1976, was a great benefactor to Camp Patmos. His gift in 1963 of more than 21 acres allowed the camp to expand from one shore of Long Point to the other. It created the addition of a softball diamond, a basketball court, and two volleyball courts—regulation and sand. It also gave the camp access to the flat-rock beach on the east shore. (Courtesy of Camp Patmos.)

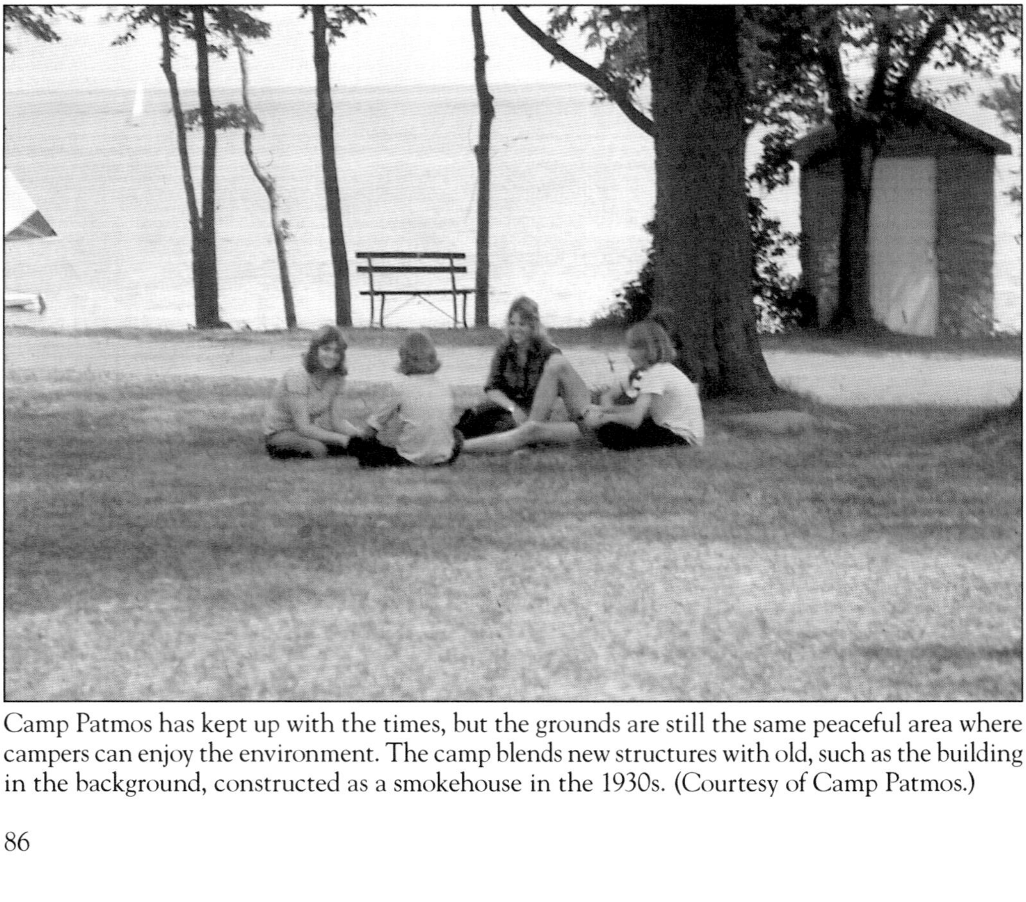

Camp Patmos has kept up with the times, but the grounds are still the same peaceful area where campers can enjoy the environment. The camp blends new structures with old, such as the building in the background, constructed as a smokehouse in the 1930s. (Courtesy of Camp Patmos.)

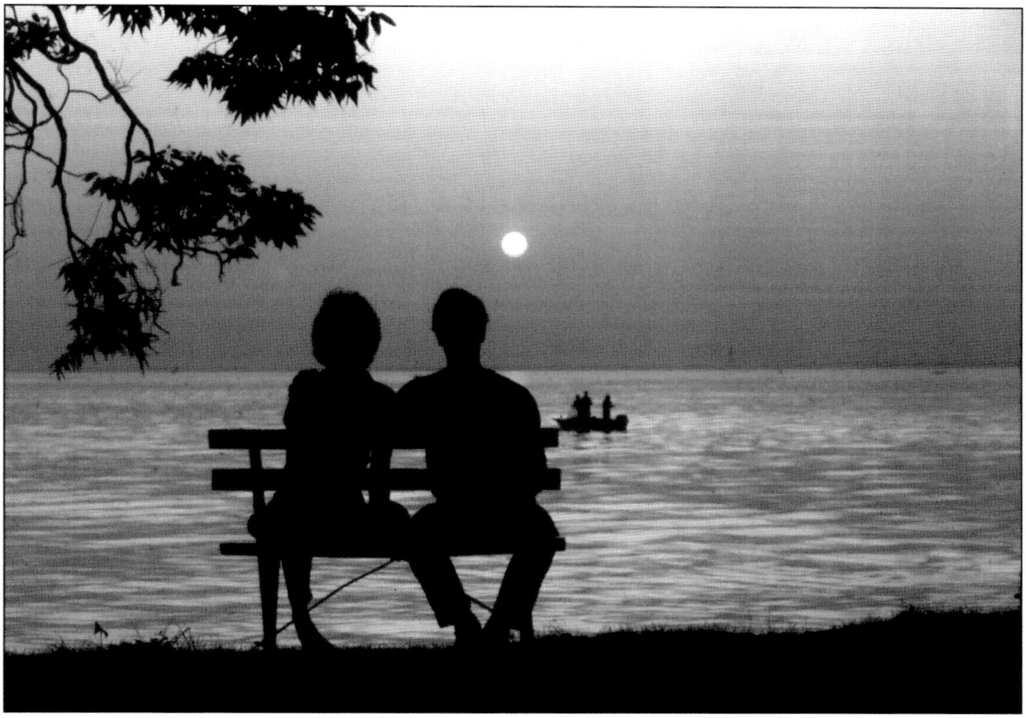

Facing the west shore of Long Point, Camp Patmos is an ideal place to enjoy a Kelleys Island sunset. In 2012, Camp Patmos celebrated its 60th year of operation on Kelleys Island. Expansion has included a large chapel, a dock, a swimming pool, and numerous smaller dormitories. (Courtesy of Camp Patmos.)

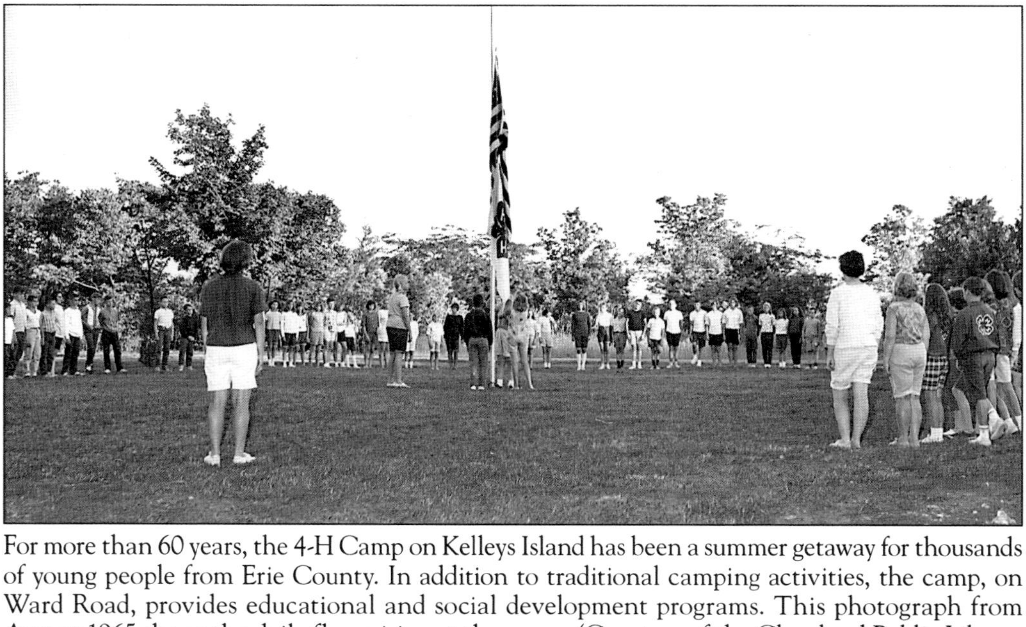

For more than 60 years, the 4-H Camp on Kelleys Island has been a summer getaway for thousands of young people from Erie County. In addition to traditional camping activities, the camp, on Ward Road, provides educational and social development programs. This photograph from August 1965 shows the daily flag-raising at the camp. (Courtesy of the Cleveland Public Library Photograph Collection.)

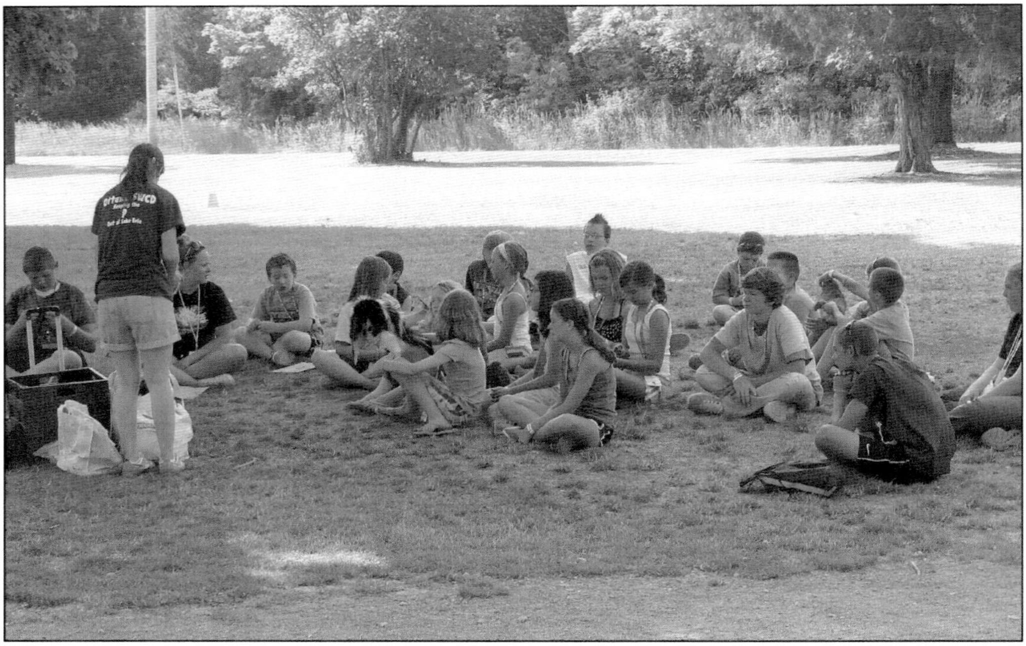

Formerly a farm and vineyard operated by James Seton, what is now the 4-H Camp property was sold to Wilson Hamilton after 1915. The camp purchased the 23 acres more than 60 years ago. Besides the main buildings and 13 campers' cottages, the grounds have open spaces for nature study and other classes. (Courtesy of the Erie County 4-H Camp Inc.)

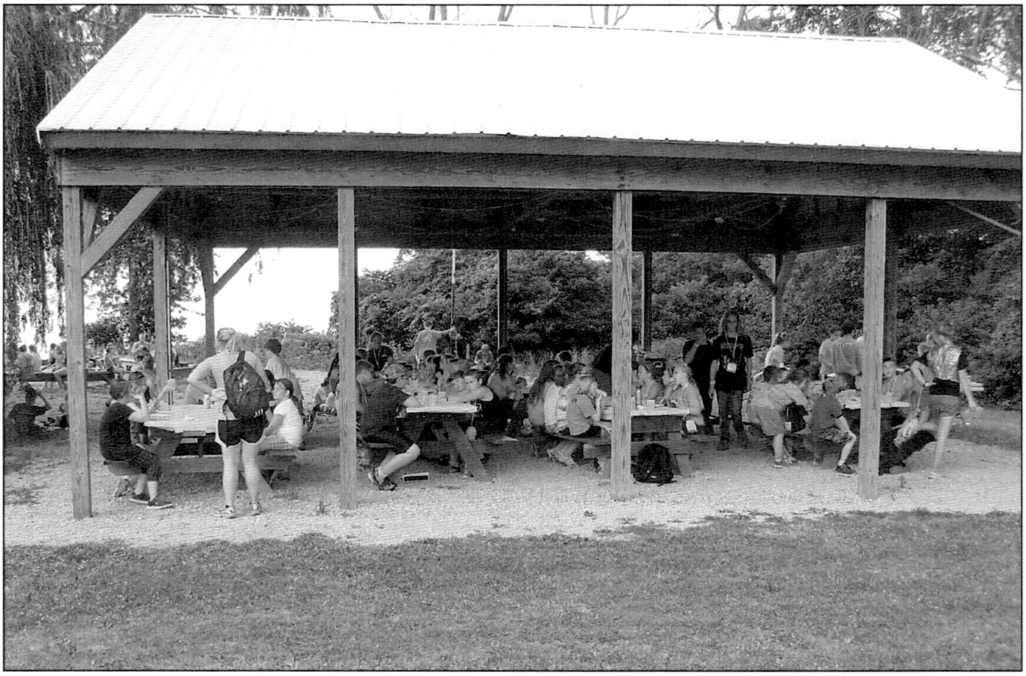

Besides 4-H members, the camp also hosts high school bands, Boy Scouts, Girl Scouts, church groups, and inner-city youth groups. The camp currently handles groups ranging in size from 75 to 200. This group enjoys an outdoor snack at the camp's pavilion. (Courtesy of the Erie County 4-H Camp Inc.)

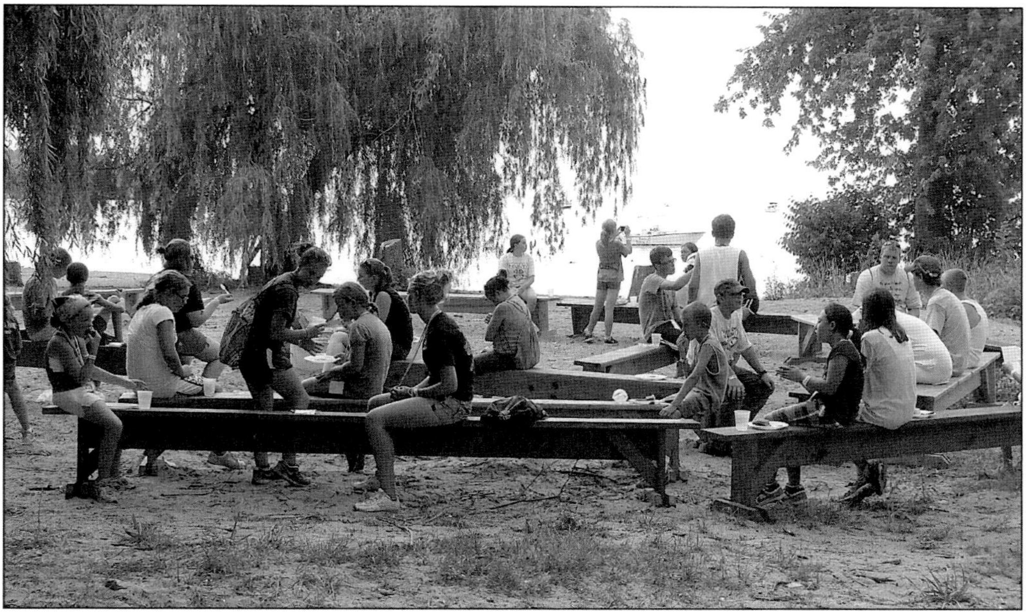

The 4-H Camp is in the North Bay of Kelleys Island northeast of Sandy Beach and has one of the two sand beaches on the Island. The camp's beach is a great place to just hang out, but campers can choose from a variety of activities in and out of the water. (Courtesy of the Erie County 4-H Camp Inc.)

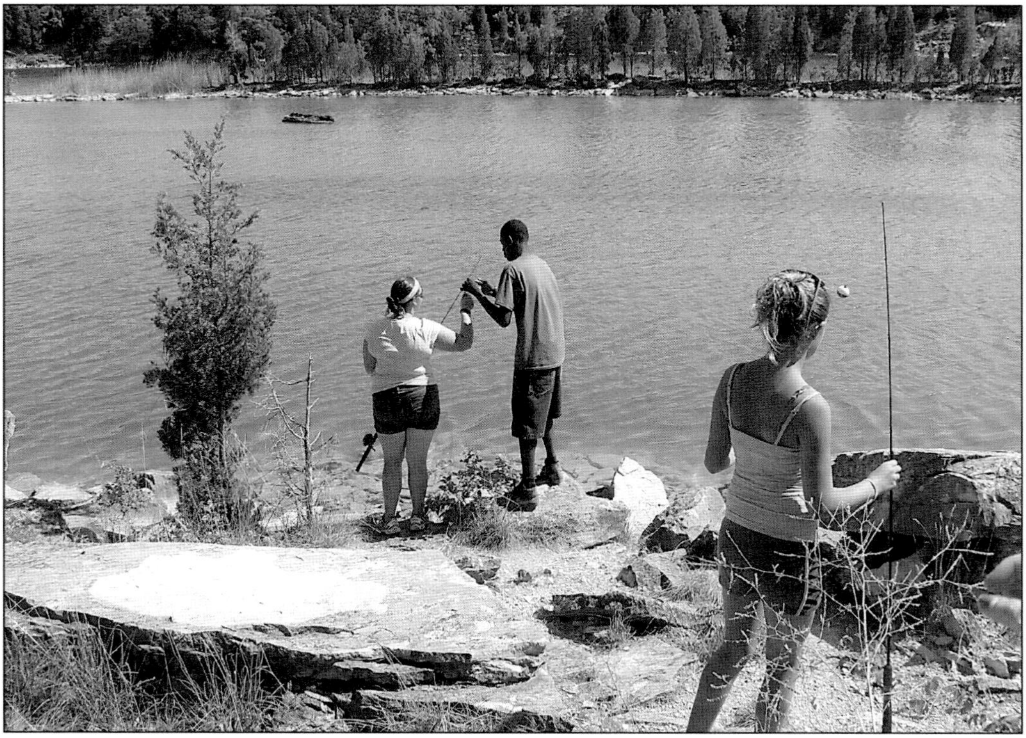

Almost directly across Ward Road from the camp is the East Quarry Nature Trail, featuring a horseshoe lake in the abandoned quarry. These campers are getting instruction on the fundamentals of fishing. (Courtesy of the Erie County 4-H Camp Inc.)

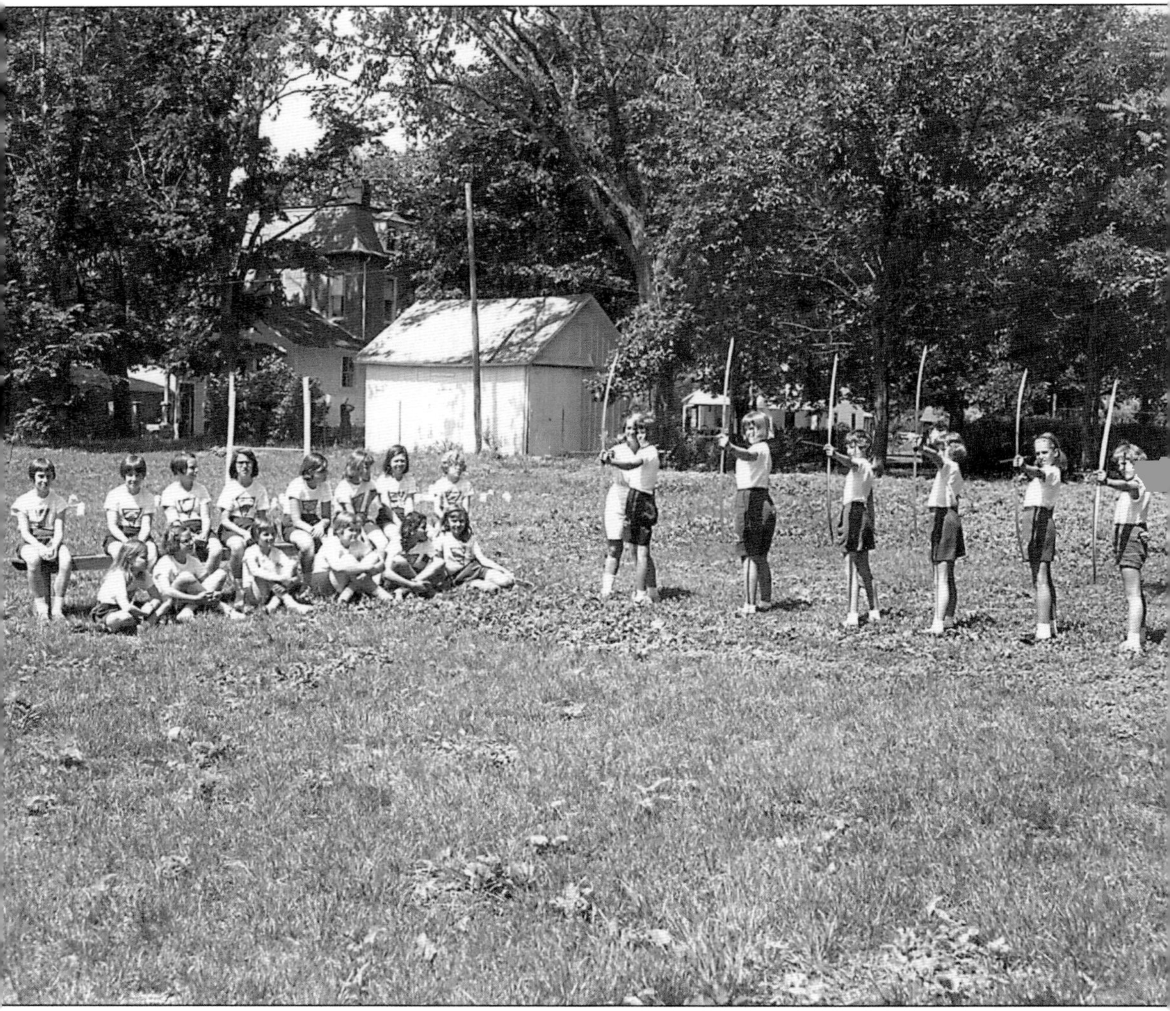

In 1933, the Dominican Sisters of Adrian, Michigan, purchased the Addison Kelley Mansion as a retreat center for the order, similar to other properties on the island owned by Franciscan friars and the Congregation of the Blessed Sacrament. In 1947, the Sisters opened the Dominican Camp for Girls, giving campers a full agenda of activities during the four weeks they spent there. The grounds adjoining the mansion had enough room to conduct an archery class, along with many other pursuits. Two camping terms were available to girls aged 8 to 16. In the camp's first year, the fee for four weeks was $75. (From the archives of the Adrian Dominican Sisters, Adrian, Michigan; courtesy of Alden Photographers, Sandusky, Ohio, 1965.)

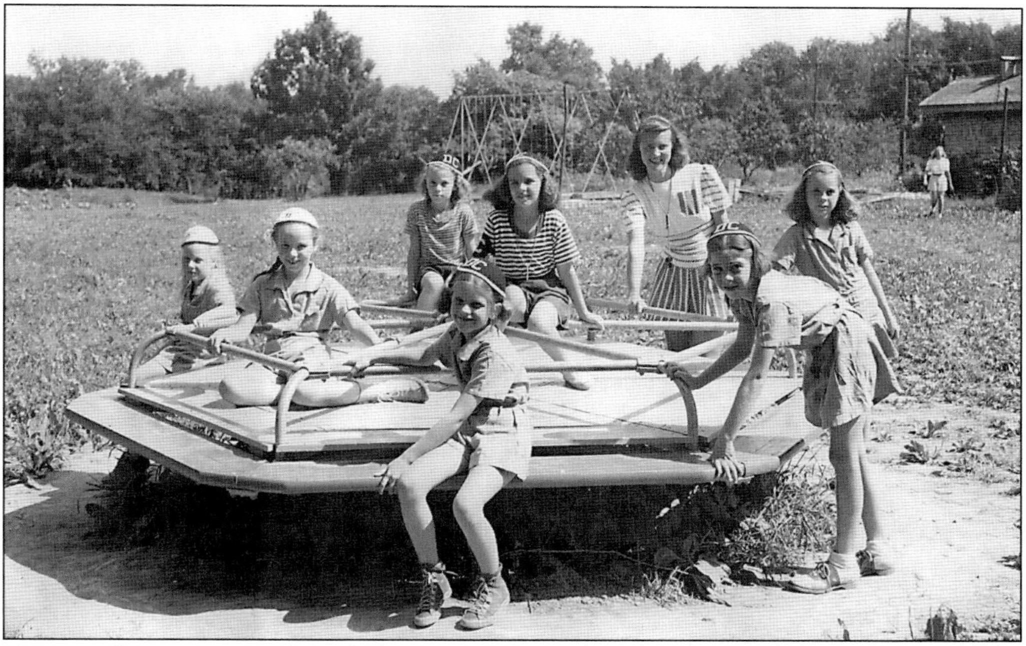

Playground equipment, such as the merry-go-round seen here in 1948, was self-contained at the Dominican camp. When the Dominican Order purchased the mansion in 1933, the sisters envisioned it as a summer retreat house similar to other religious retreats on Kelleys Island owned by the Blessed Sacrament Fathers and the Franciscan order. (From the archives of the Adrian Dominican Sisters, Adrian, Michigan; courtesy of Mound Photographers, Sandusky, Ohio, 1948.)

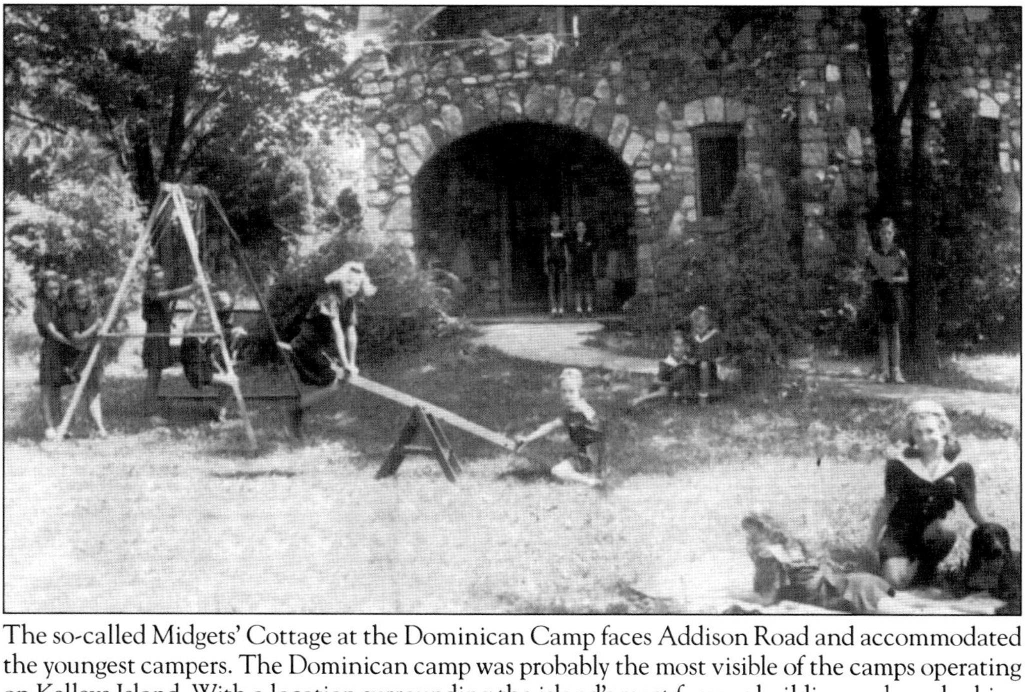

The so-called Midgets' Cottage at the Dominican Camp faces Addison Road and accommodated the youngest campers. The Dominican camp was probably the most visible of the camps operating on Kelleys Island. With a location surrounding the island's most famous building and overlooking Inscription Rock, the camp attracted the attention of tourists. (Courtesy of the Kelleys Island Historical Association.)

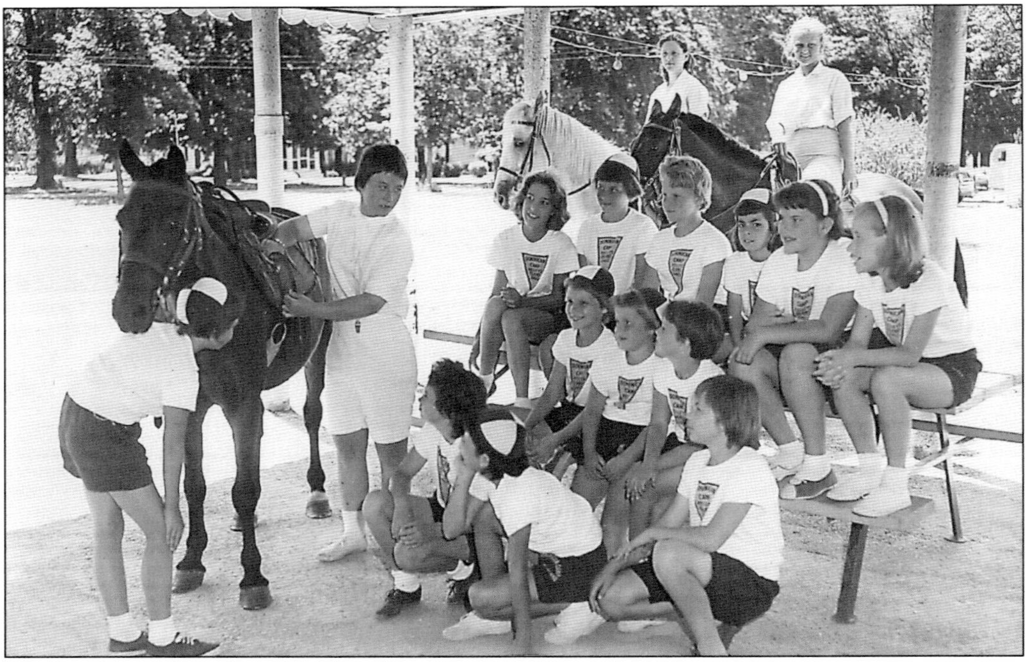

These girls learn the art of saddling a horse at the Dominican Camp for Girls in 1962. The girls also took boat trips on Lake Erie, held beach parties, and participated in other worthwhile projects, according to the camp's brochure at the time. (From the archives of the Adrian Dominican Sisters, Adrian, Michigan; courtesy of Alden Photographers, Sandusky, Ohio, 1962.)

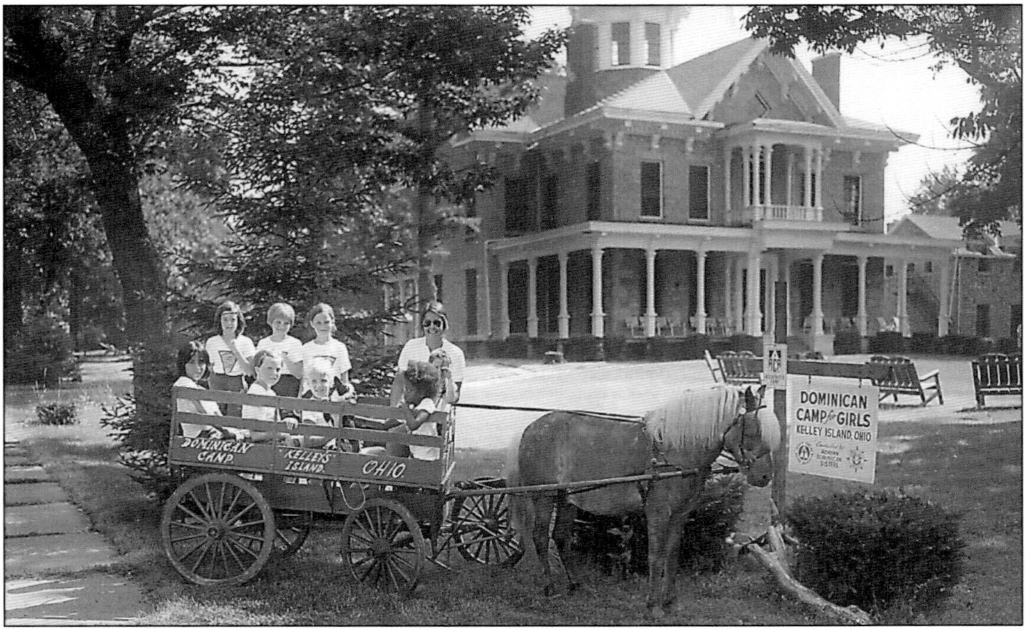

The Dominican Camp program had a full mix of educational and fun activities, including the horse cart seen here in 1971. The Adrian Dominican order closed the camp in 1972, citing rising costs and enrollment decline, according to a *Toledo Blade* account at the time. (From the archives of the Adrian Dominican Sisters, Adrian, Michigan; courtesy of Alden Photographers, Sandusky, Ohio, 1971.)

Nine

WINTER TALES

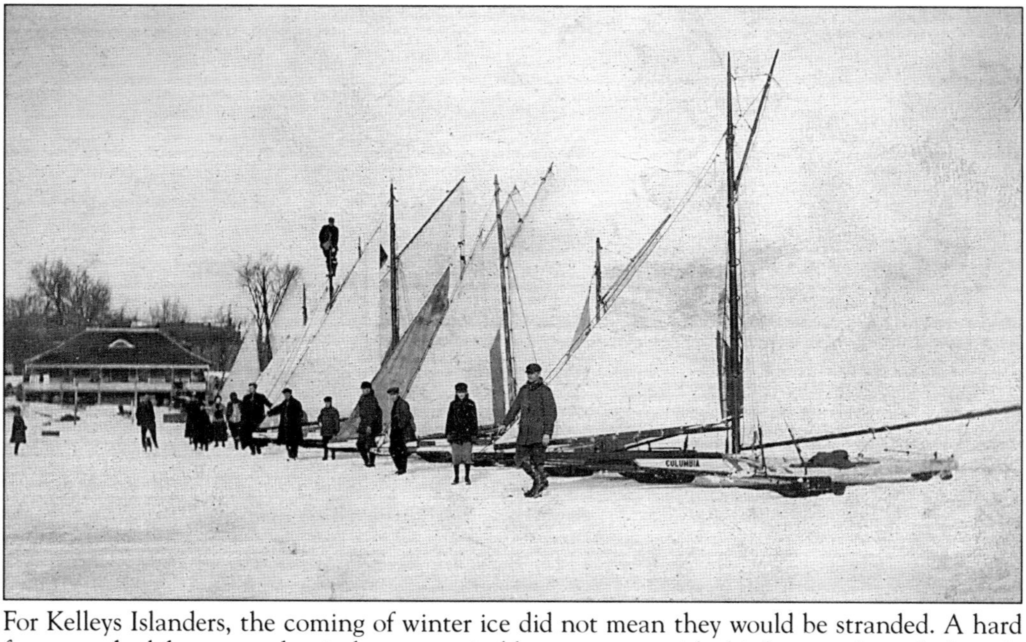

For Kelleys Islanders, the coming of winter ice did not mean they would be stranded. A hard freeze on the lake meant that iceboats were in bloom, as seen with this lineup of vessels directly opposite the Casino in Lake Erie. With a good wind, an iceboat trip across the lake on good ice was quite speedy. (Courtesy of Judy Du Shane.)

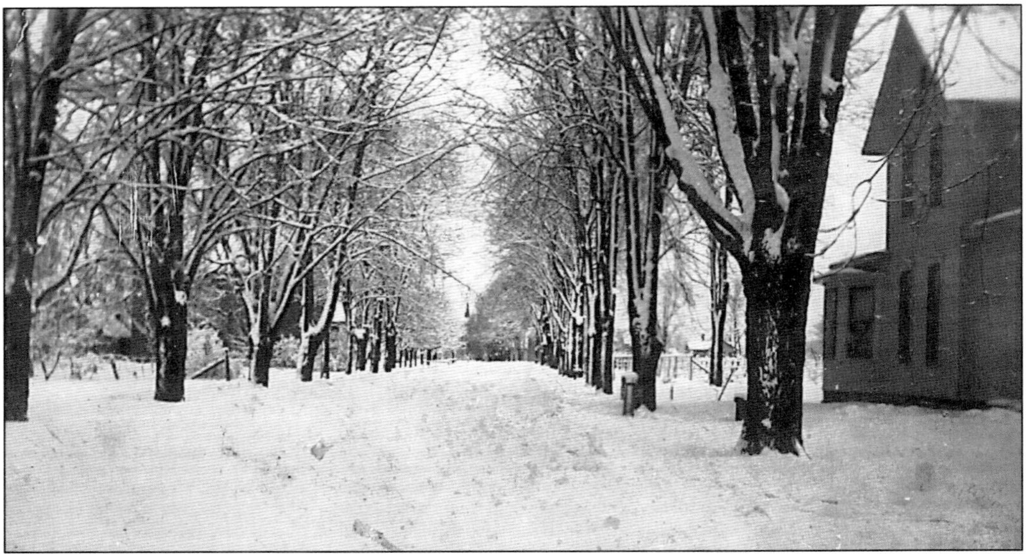

In winter, most island roads lose the luster of summer, as snow obstructs travel at times. This view shows Division Street looking north with the so-called Doctor's House on the right. Located two doors from Kelley's Hall, this house was purchased by the village and the Kelley Island Lime & Transport Co. in 1930 to provide a residence for the island doctor. (Courtesy of Frank and Laura Jean Pohorence.)

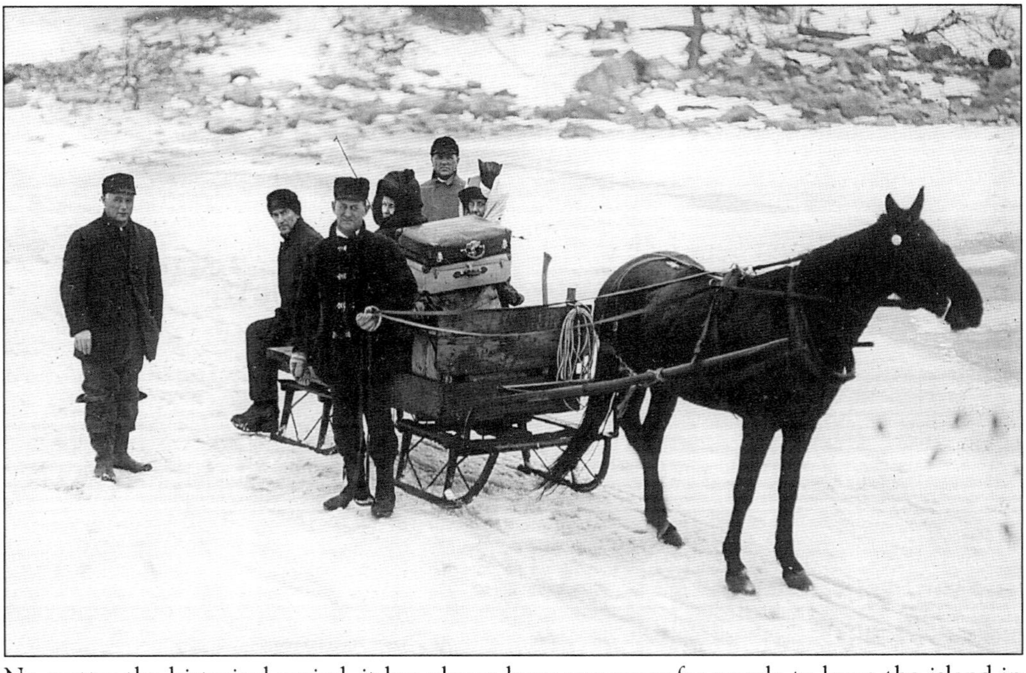

No matter the historical period, it has always been necessary for people to leave the island in midwinter. Seen here going for a sleigh ride in the early 1900s are, from left to right, Alphonso Erne, George Gerlach, January Coutcher, Sarah Hamilton, William Burger, and Mary Burger. The horse is Queenie. (Courtesy of the Kelleys Island Historical Association.)

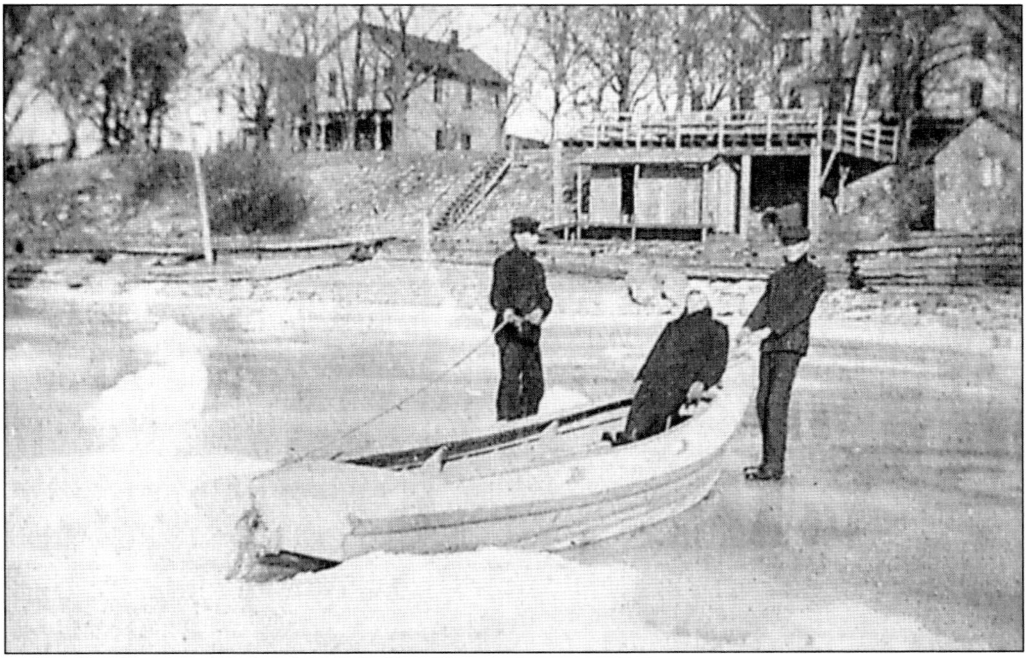

This trio brings a rowboat onshore through the ice in front of the Himmelein Hotel in the late 1890s. The hotel's wooden dance and viewing platform sits at the top of the bluff adjacent to the road. Wooden steps descend to the beach, featuring a bathhouse. To the left of the Himmelein Hotel is the Schardt House, a hotel that was originally Addison Kelley's first house. (Courtesy of Fritz Pape's photo album, Pape family collection.)

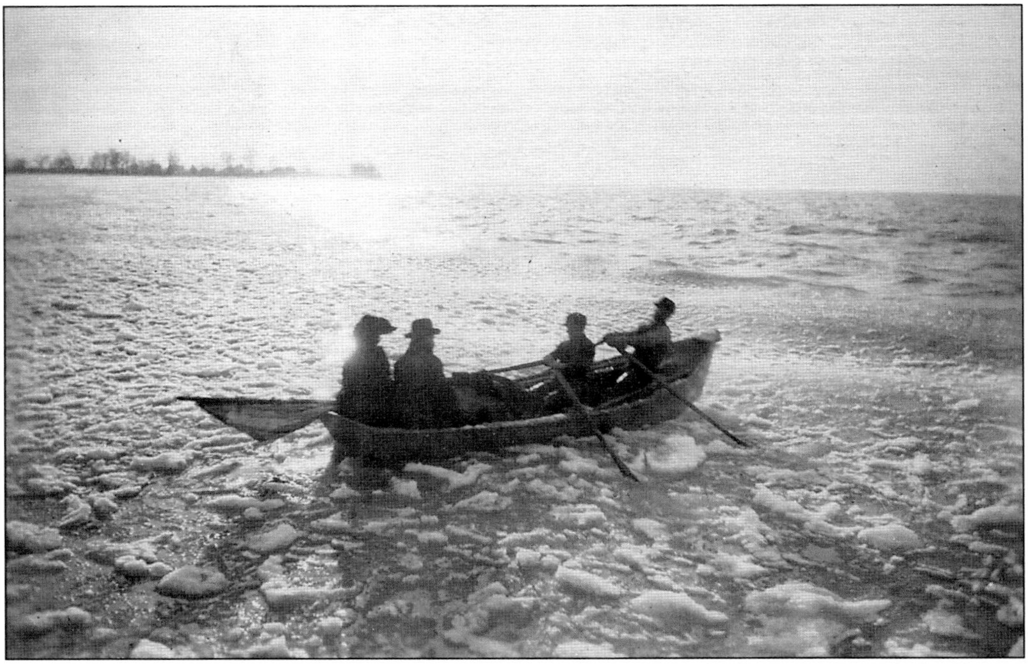

Trips across Lake Erie during the winter are always treacherous challenges, particularly if ice is too thin or cracking. These unidentified travelers row through the broken ice and into seemingly clear water. (Courtesy of the Kelleys Island Historical Association.)

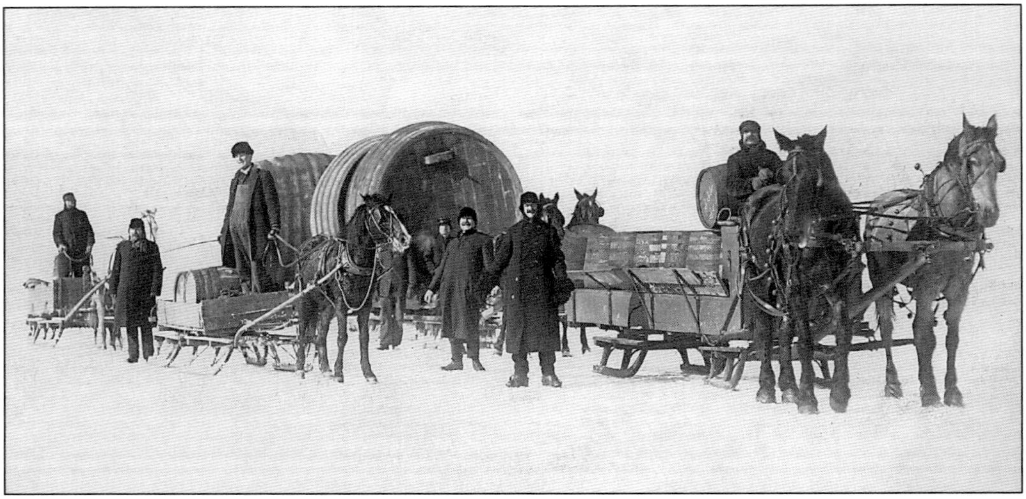

Kelleys Island's wine industry shipped during all seasons, and even giant wine casks were transported during the winter, giving an earlier meaning to the term *ice wine*. Trips like this were probably made only when the ice was at its thickest. (Courtesy of the Kelleys Island Historical Association.)

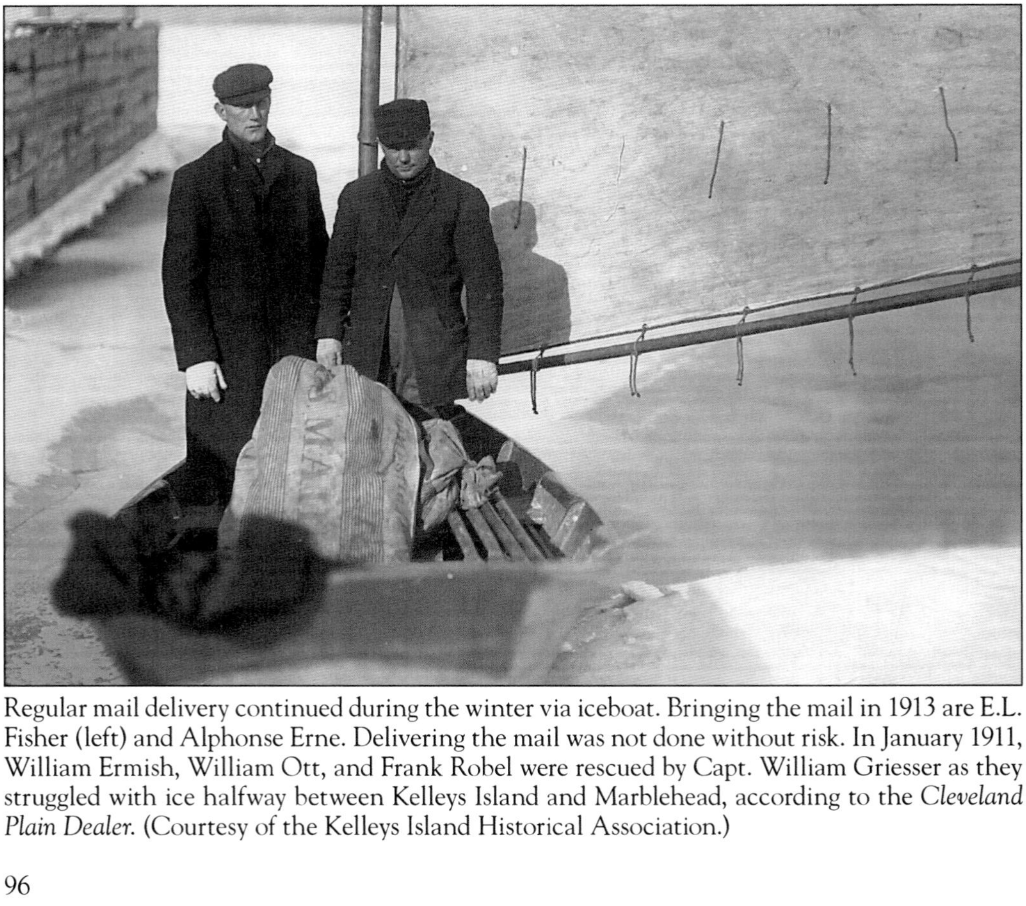

Regular mail delivery continued during the winter via iceboat. Bringing the mail in 1913 are E.L. Fisher (left) and Alphonse Erne. Delivering the mail was not done without risk. In January 1911, William Ermish, William Ott, and Frank Robel were rescued by Capt. William Griesser as they struggled with ice halfway between Kelleys Island and Marblehead, according to the *Cleveland Plain Dealer*. (Courtesy of the Kelleys Island Historical Association.)

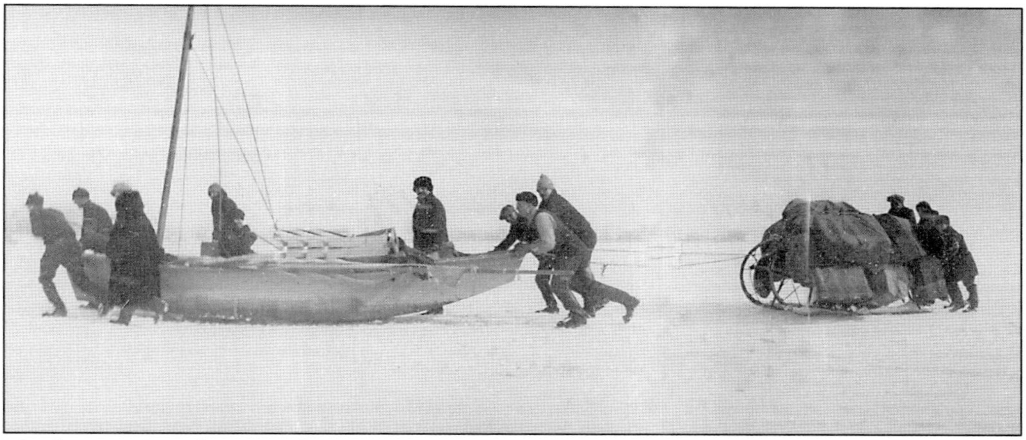

Until 1929, when the post office started flying the mail to Kelleys Island, mail boats skimmed over the icy lake during the winter. Here, Bill Schnittker and others pull the bow of the iceboat while Henry Schlesselman and others push the stern. (Courtesy of Bob and Carol Schnittker.)

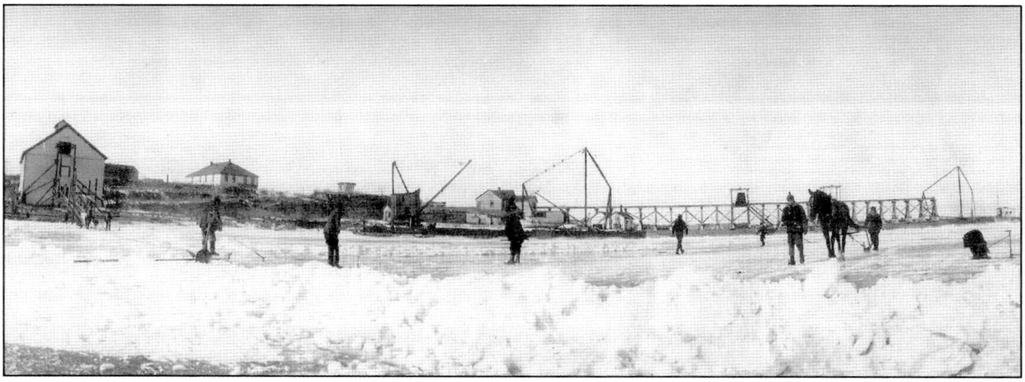

In earlier years, winter activity on Kelleys Island included ice harvesting, such as this work being done in the North Bay off of Sandy Beach. Workers cut the ice and brought it in to be stored in warehouses until it was needed for a variety of purposes, including home refrigeration. (Courtesy of Bob and Carol Schnittker.)

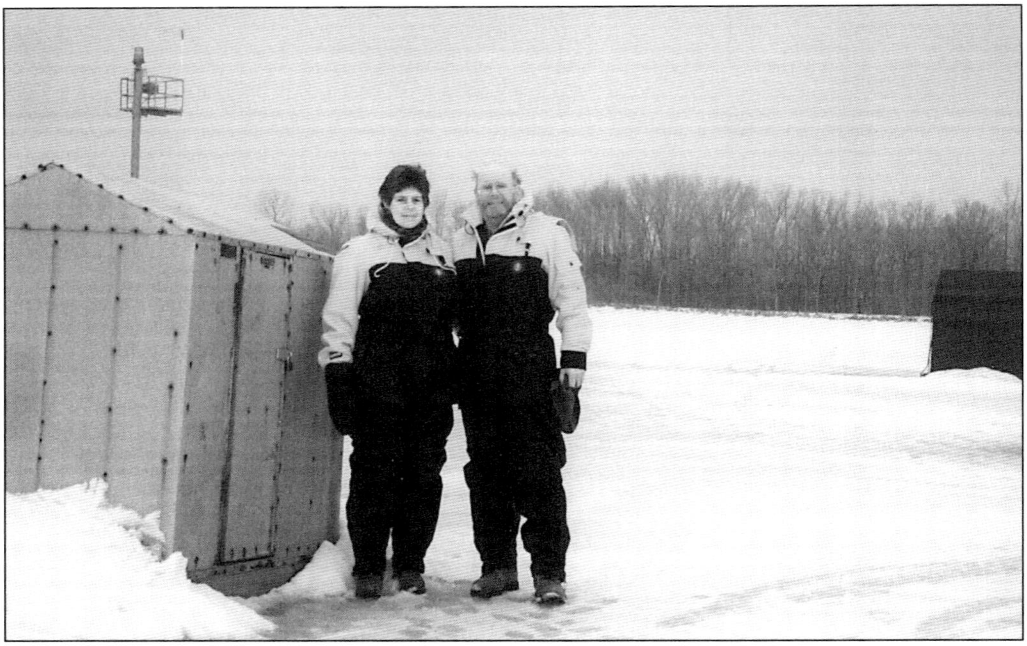

When the winters get cold enough and Lake Erie freezes to a reasonable thickness, it is time to haul the ice shanty onto the lake for ice fishing season. Besides residents such as Linda and Jack Hostal, seen here, this winter sport attracts anglers from off of the island, who can fly in and rent a heated shanty. (Courtesy of Jack and Linda Hostal.)

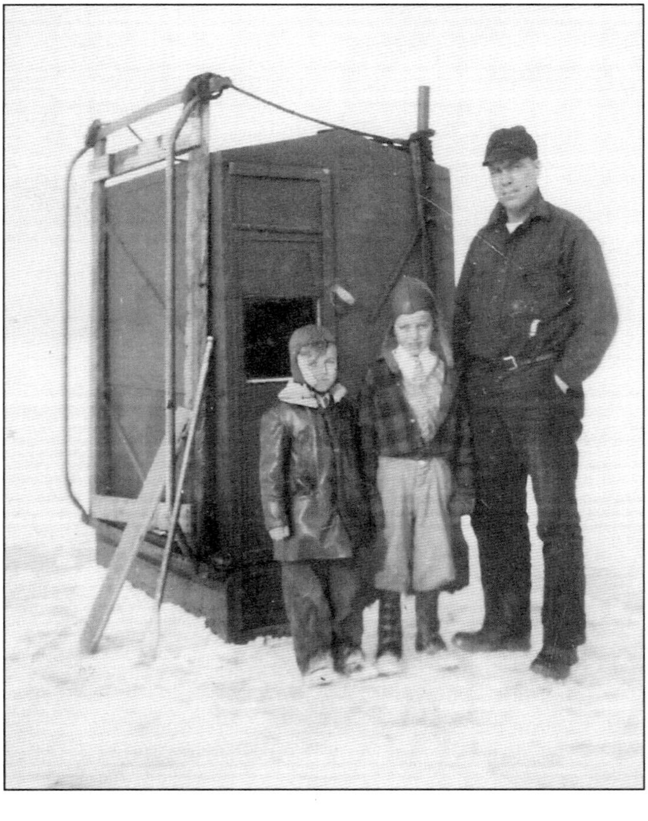

During ice fishing season, everyone gets into the act. Seen here from left to right are Lyle Bickley, Logan Bickley, and their father, Bob Bickley. Most of the island's ice fishing is done in the North Bay, which is easily accessible off of Sandy Beach, giving rise to a colony of shanties. (Courtesy of Ted Blatt.)

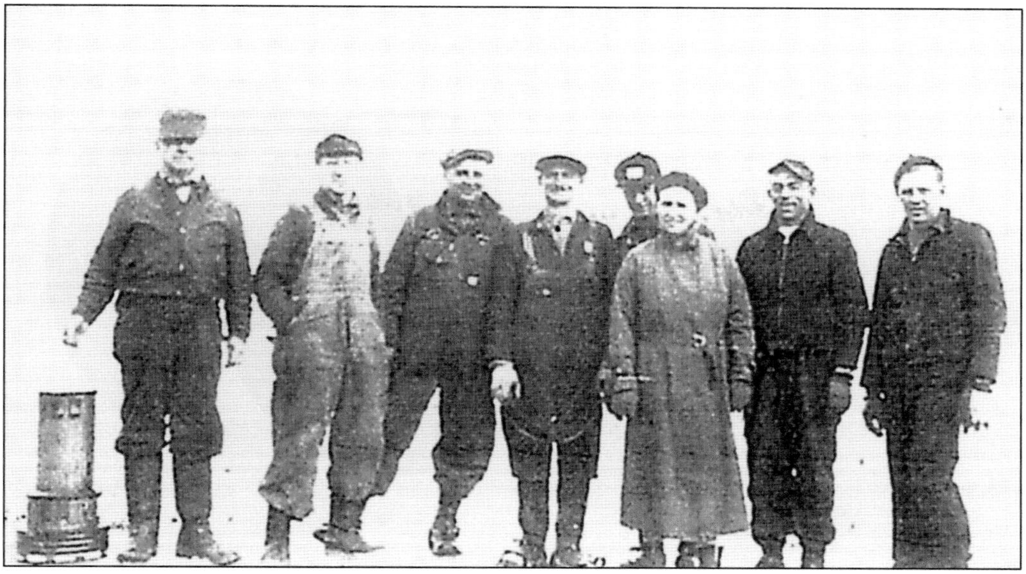

Out on the ice in the 1930s are hardy anglers, from left to right, George Sennish, Norman Blatt, George Lenyo, Fred Moeck, Herman Geisberger, Emily Geisberger, Paul Perruchon, and Ray Kiefer. They are wearing "creepers" on their feet to maintain traction. (Courtesy of Ted Blatt.)

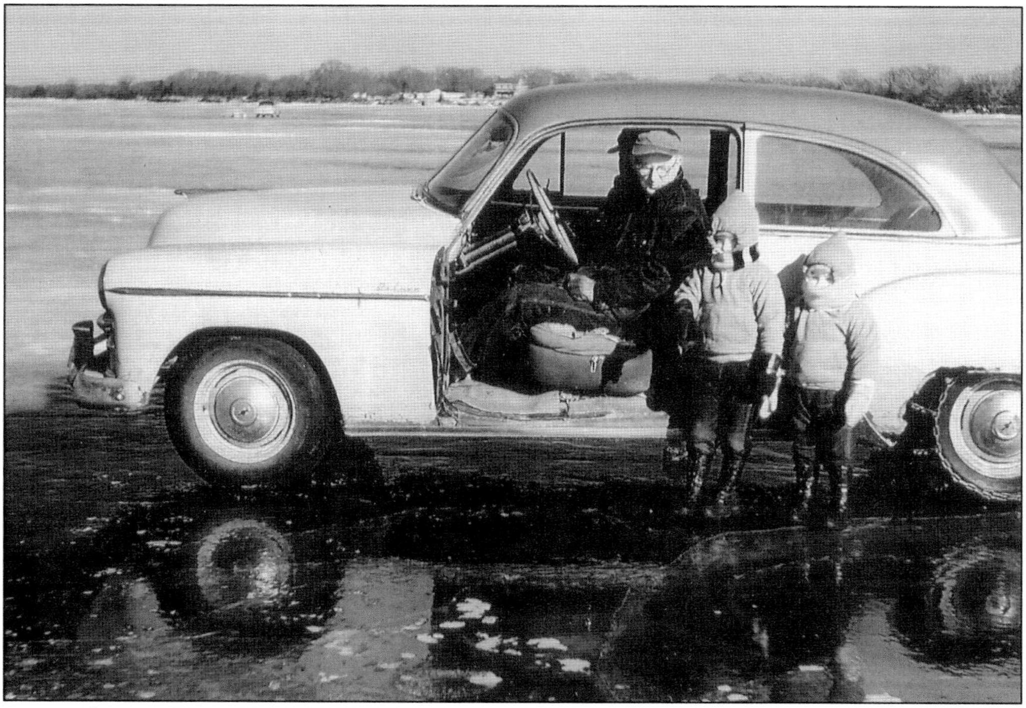

Ice can be tough—sometimes. Posing offshore in Kelleys Islands' North Bay outside of a 1951 Chevrolet driven by Dick Sennish are Paul (left) and Dale Schnittker. Islanders who took their cars on the lake usually removed the doors. This served a dual purpose: making the car lighter and making it easier to escape if the ice cracked. They also used older cars. (Courtesy of Bob and Carol Schnittker.)

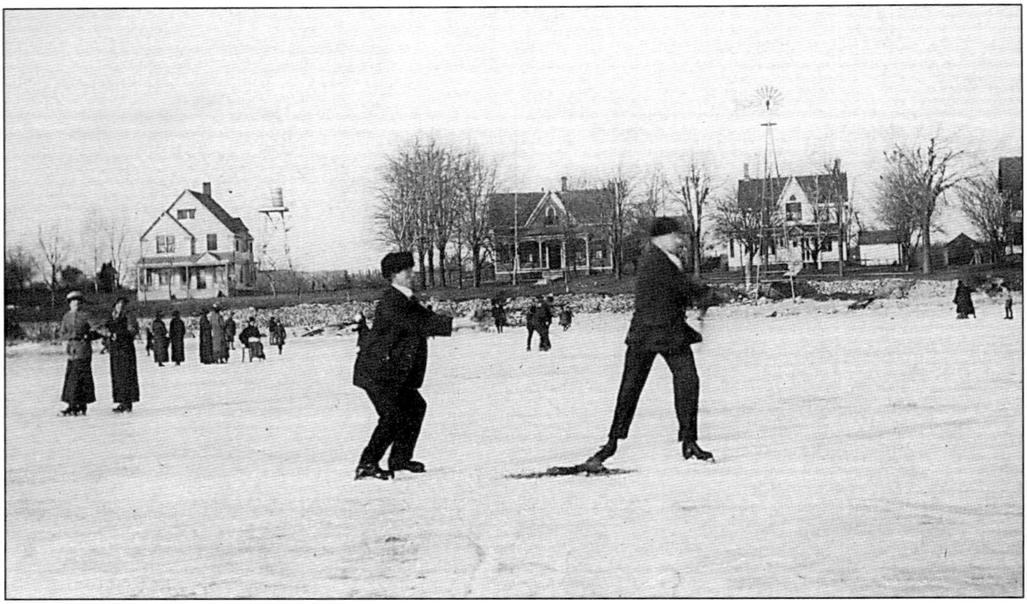

Although the ice baseball game seen here was probably played in the 1930s, the first recorded game of ice baseball on Kelleys Island took place on January 22, 1911, according to the *Cleveland Plain Dealer*. About 700 spectators, including 150 women, witnessed the game, played on a field staked out on the frozen surface of the south shore of Lake Erie. The sport gave a new meaning to the term *slide*. (Courtesy of Judy Du Shane.)

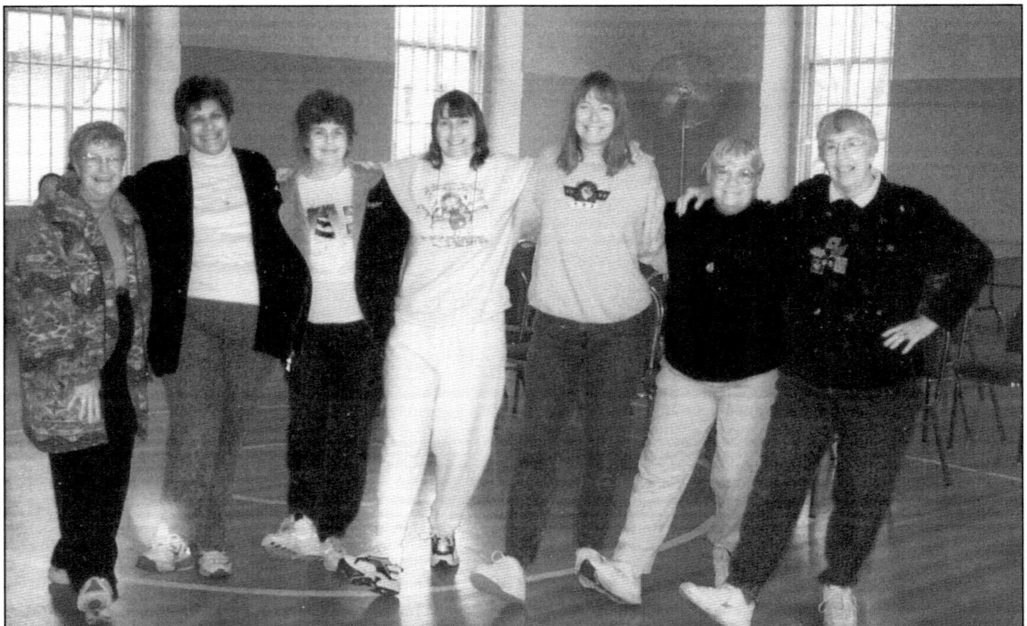

With a decrease in outside activities in the winter, some year-round residents kick up their heels at Kelley's Hall on Division Street. Seen here, from left to right, are Sally Hiller, Chris Yako, Linda Hostal, Lori Hayes, Leslie Korenko, Judy Du Shane, and June Campbell. Year-round residents can also take art classes during the winter months. (Courtesy of Jack and Linda Hostal.)

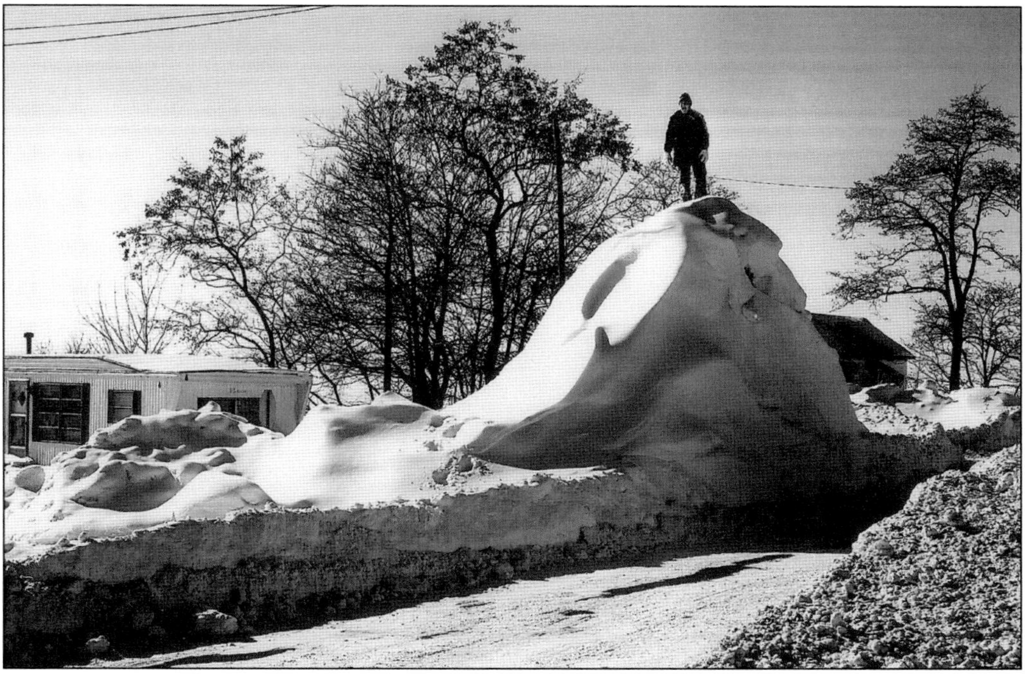

A youthful Ron Schnittker stands at the top of a seemingly high drift following a winter storm in the 1970s. It is possible that snow blowing across the lake drifted around a tree at the Neuman Boat Line dock (now the west dock of the Kelleys Island Ferry Boat Line). (Courtesy of Bob and Carol Schnittker.)

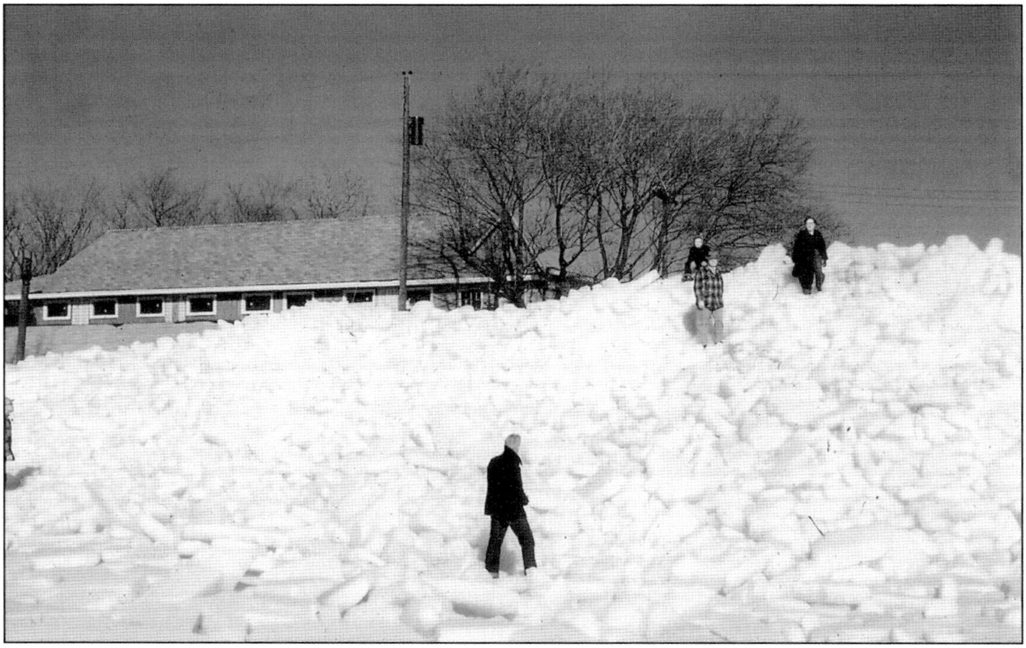

Charles Schnittker stands at the bottom of this giant ice mountain just east of what is now the Seaway Marina as his grandsons Paul and Dale try to climb to the top in the mid-1950s. The icy Everest almost dwarfs the twine house in the background. Today, that twine house is Sunrise Point. (Courtesy of Bob and Carol Schnittker.)

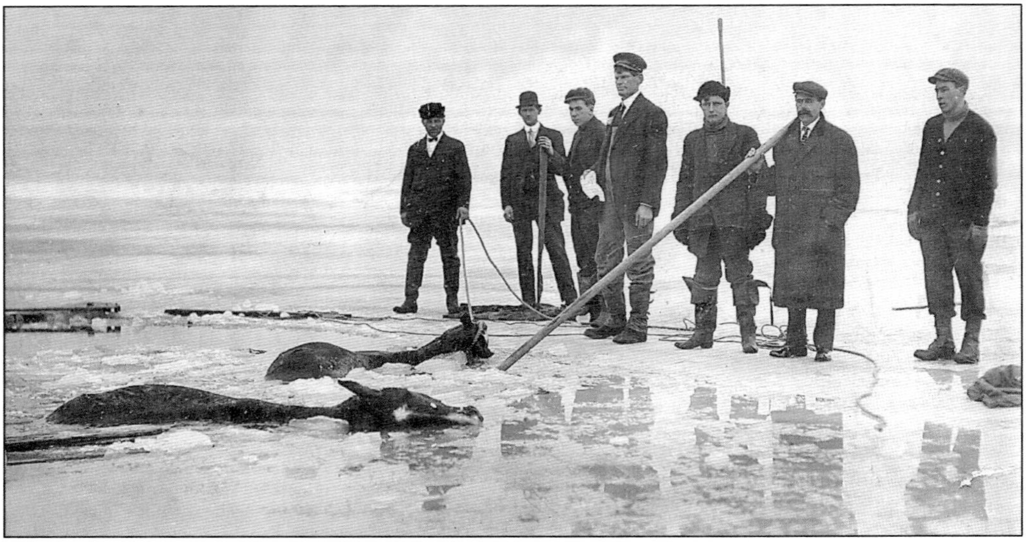

If the ice is starting to melt or if lake currents do not cooperate, this safe trip can become treacherous, as this 1912 photograph shows. Accounts of horses, sleds, and iceboats falling through the ice go back to 1856, so this was not an uncommon occurrence. A February 1888 account in the *Cleveland Plain Dealer* tells of a mail carrier who was carried "quite a distance" by floating ice. (Courtesy of the Kelleys Island Historical Association.)

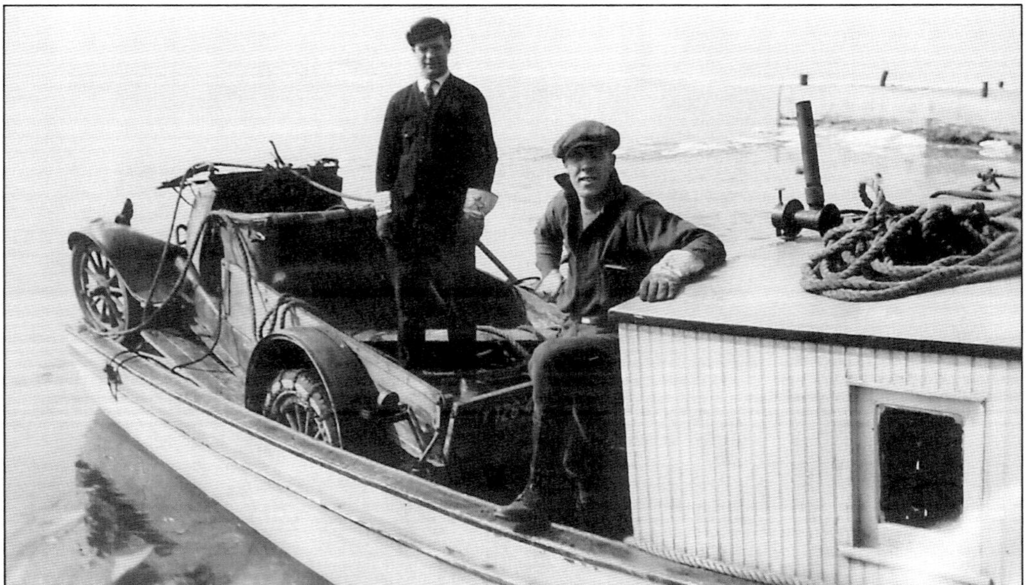

When Lake Erie ice gets thin, anything can happen. And when folks try to drive over the ice, the problems are only compounded. Rescuing this Ford Model T following the spring thaw are Ollie Schlesselman (left) and Bill Schnittker. (Courtesy of Bob and Carol Schnittker.)

Ten

Fun, Sun, and Plain Folks

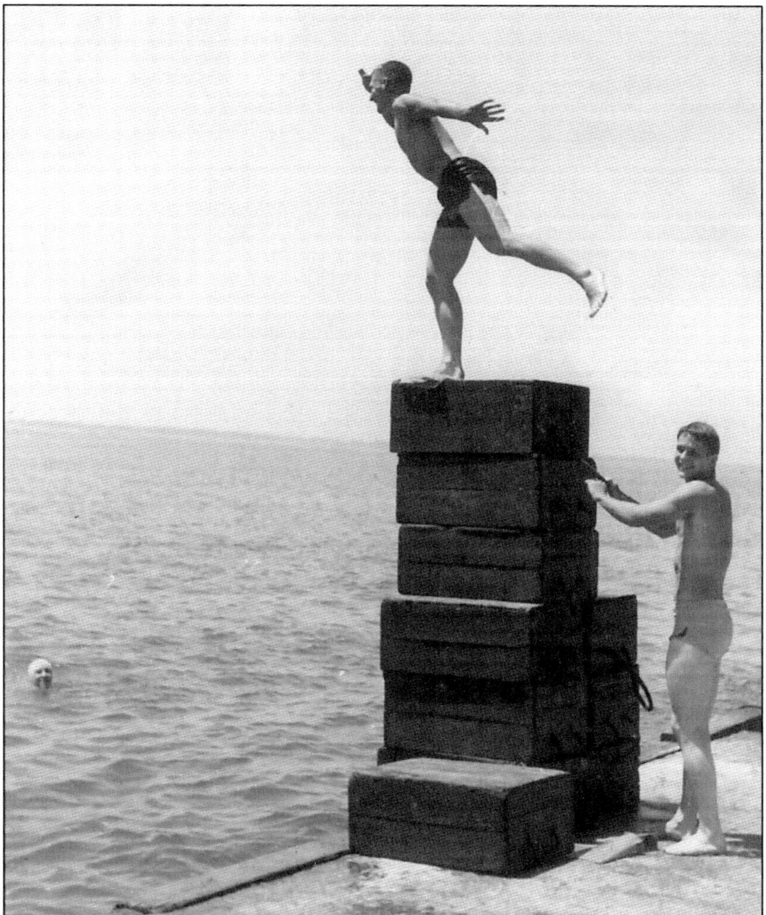

Kelleys Island's insularity often brings out the creativity in people, particularly the young—even in the mid-1950s. Here, Bill Wagner gets ready to take a dive off of a tower of fish boxes at Koster's dock (now the Unique Marker Yacht Club) as Don Millward steadies the makeshift diving platform. Already in the water is Rosemary Funk. Don't try this at home. (Courtesy of Ed and Carol Frindt.)

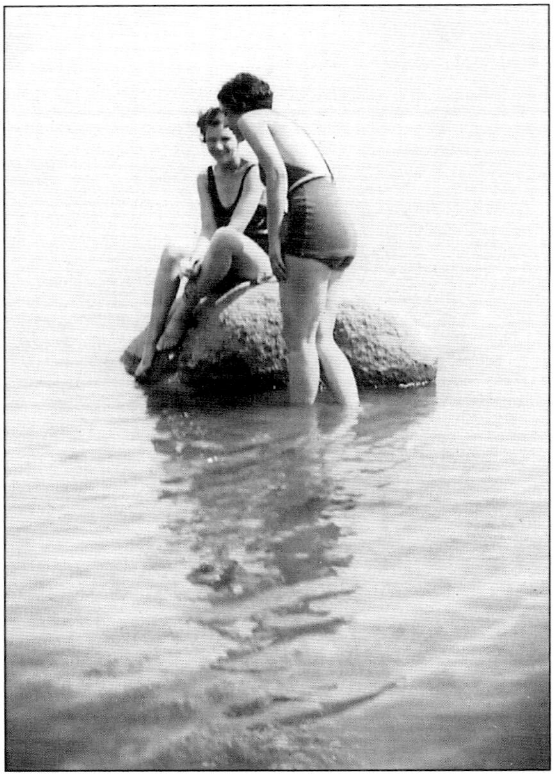

The Kelleys Island shoreline varies widely over its 18 miles, with stone and flat-rock beaches on the southeast side and a sand beach in the North Bay. The Bauman family, which settled along the southeast shore, had the advantage of a welcoming lake. Here, Esther Bauman Smith (left) and Mary Ellen Bauman Wilke take advantage of their family's beach in the 1930s. (Courtesy of Judy Du Shane.)

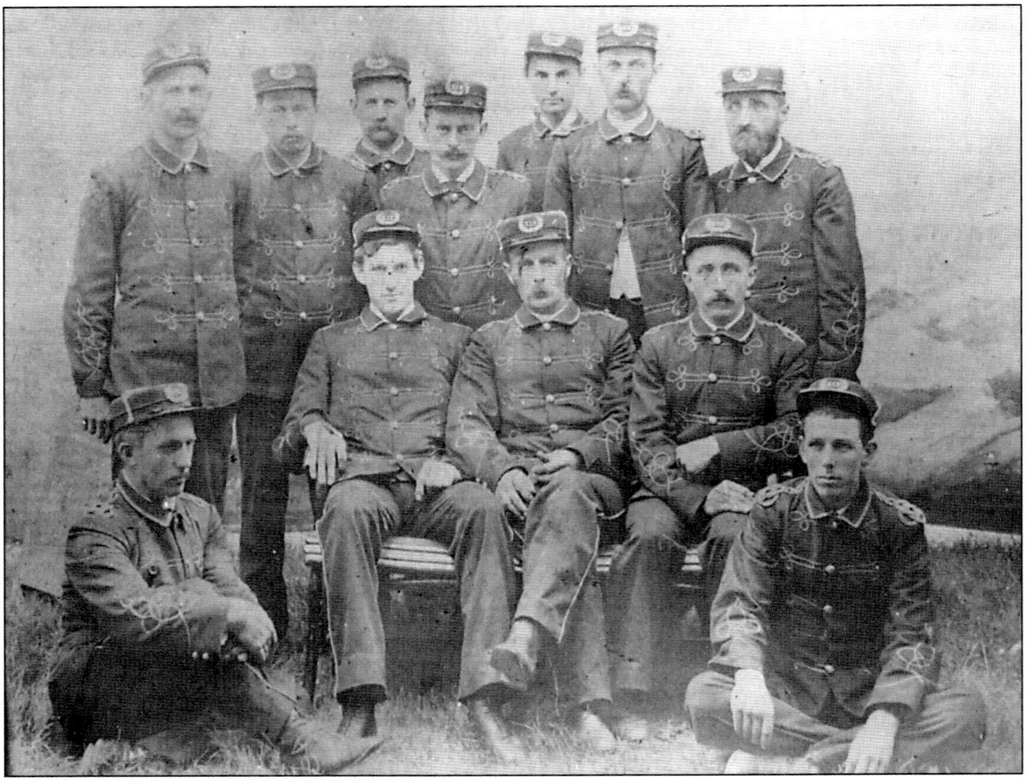

The Kelleys Island Band is decked out in full-dress uniforms, possibly in the years before World War I. Admittedly, it is a small band—but it is a small island. From left to right, these talented musicians are (on ground) unidentified and Ralph Dwelle; (second row) Gus Elfers, Charles Quinn, and Philip Roswurm; (third row) unidentified, unidentified, John Coutcher, Henry Riedy, Charles Yeager, John Moysey, and Charles Seeholzer. (Courtesy of Carol Perruchon.)

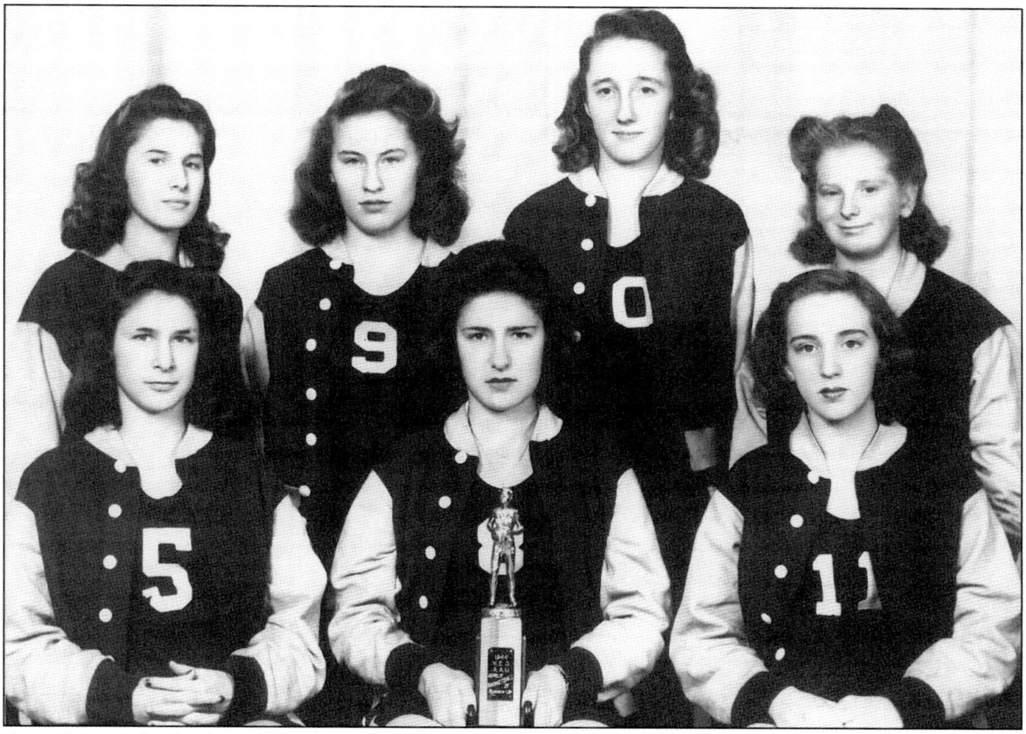

Estes School also had a girls' basketball team in the mid-1940s. The team includes, from left to right, (first row) Geraldine Beatty, Ila Beatty, and Bonnie Bickley; (second row) Laura Jean Seeholzer, Rosemary Elfers, Nancy Ward, and Elaine Martin. (Courtesy of Frank and Laura Jean Pohorence.)

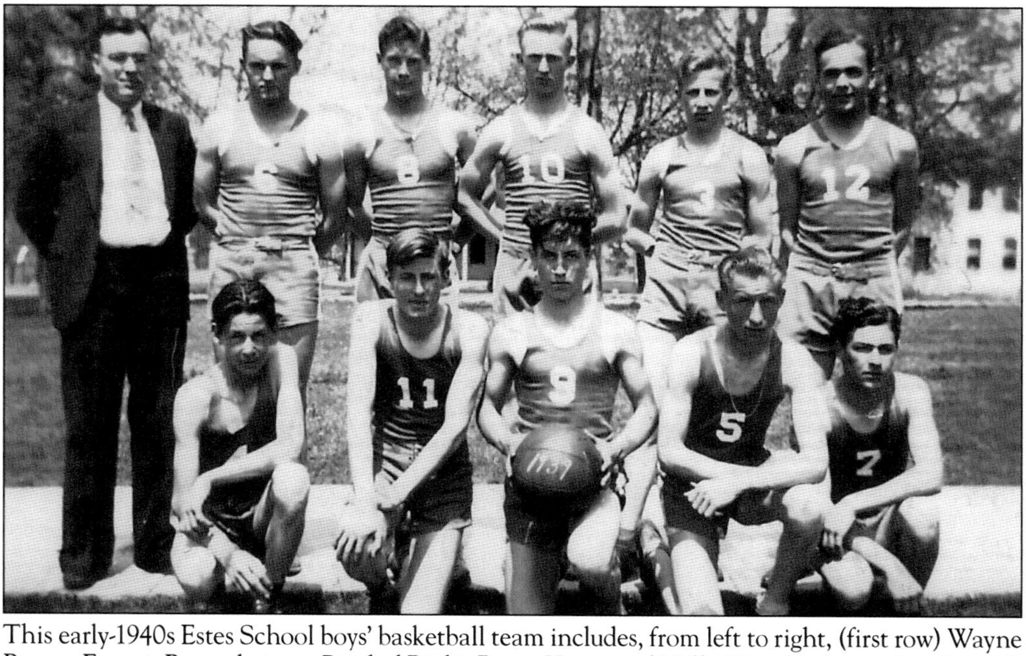

This early-1940s Estes School boys' basketball team includes, from left to right, (first row) Wayne Beatty, Francis Betzenheimer, Paschal Righi, Roger Kurtz, and Nello Bianchi; (second row) coach and school superintendent Burdette Corthell, Mike Mervo, Lawrence Walland, Billy Brown, Jimmy Brown, and Lawrence Feyedelem. (Courtesy of Bob and Carol Schnittker.)

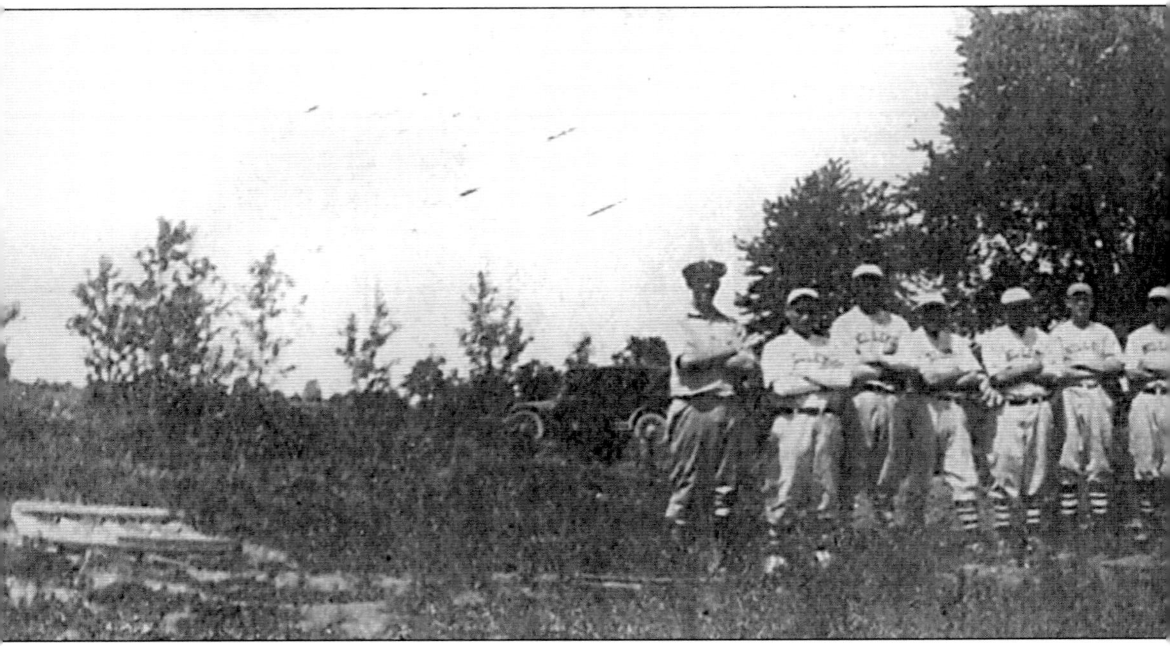

Baseball is a long-standing tradition on Kelleys Island. The exact year this team took the field is not known, but it is in the same place it is today, at the corner of Addison Road and Chappel

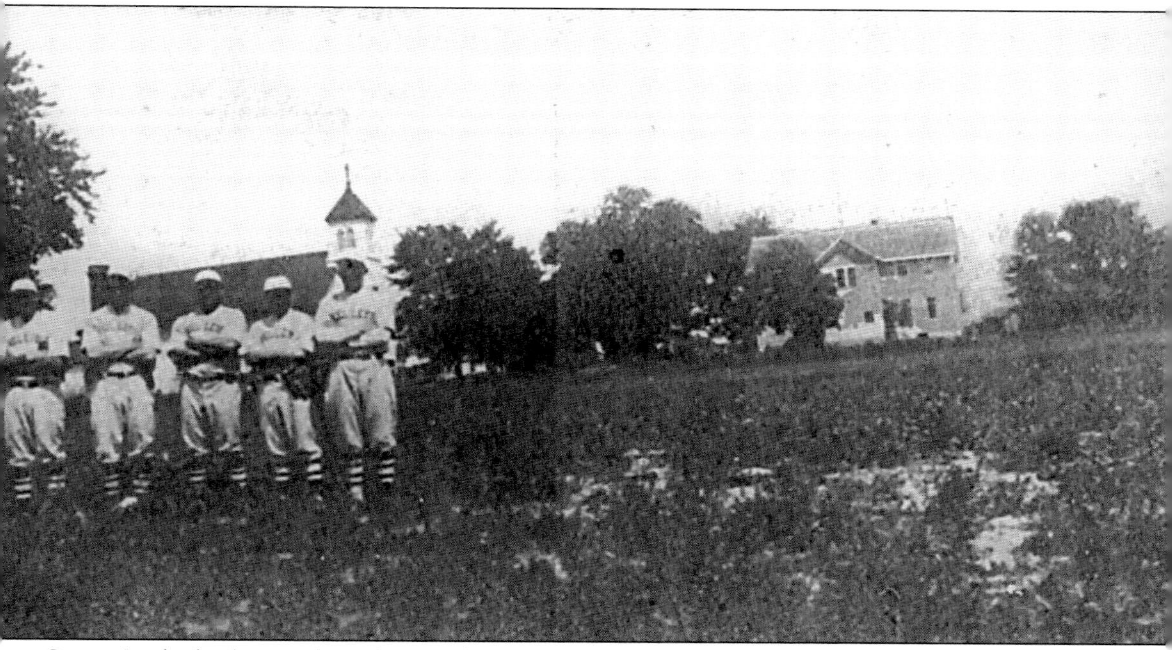

Street. In the background are the steeple of St. Michael Church and Marquette Hall, which was built in 1905 and housed the St. Michael Parish School. (Courtesy of Gary and Jackie Finger.)

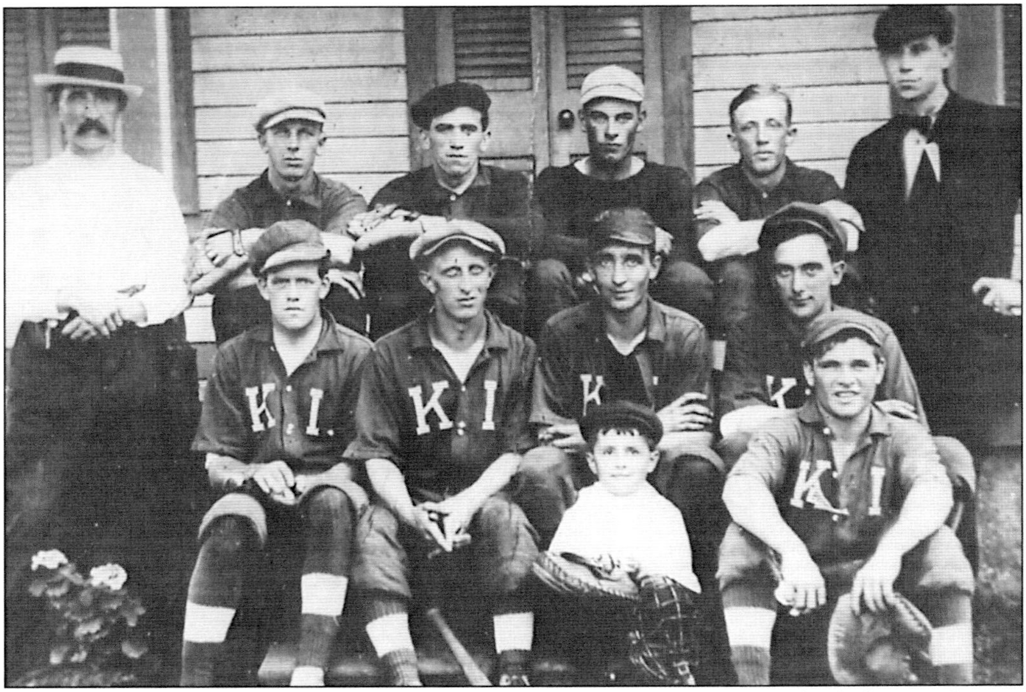

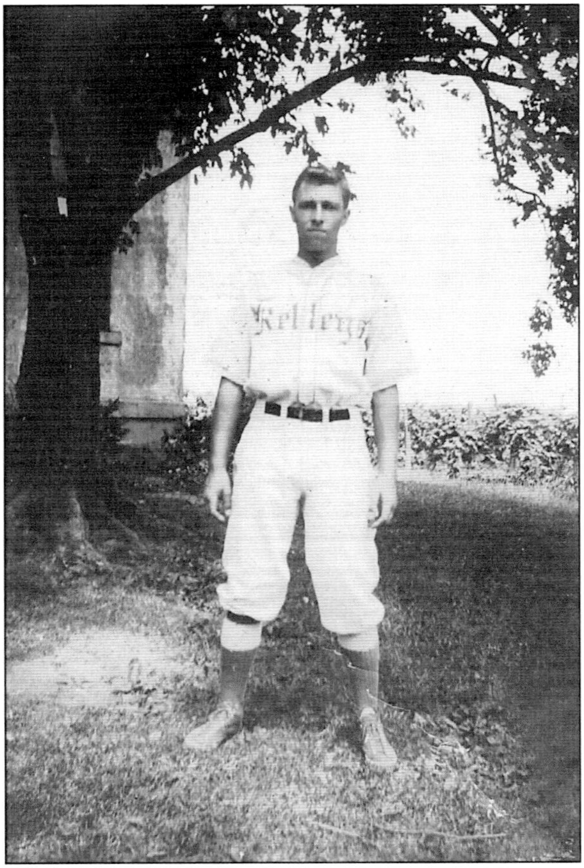

A July 1912 *Cleveland Plain Dealer* article reports that, after defeating all their opponents, the Kelleys Island Liners "declared a willingness to meet the best men that Put-In-Bay, Middle and North Bass and the Sister Islands can produce." Seen here from left to right are (first row) possibly Eldon Roswurm and unidentified; (second row) Irving Moross, Lee Brown, Leonard Roswurm, and unidentified; (third row) Philip Roswurm, Elko Sennish, Pat Murphy, Alfred Moysey, Roland Brown, and Elmer Maag. (Courtesy of Carol Perruchon.)

Samuel B. Bauman is suited up and ready for baseball in the 1930s. According to Leslie Korenko's book *Kelleys Island 1866–1871: The Lodge, Suffrage & Baseball*, the game was first played on the island in 1870. By 1905, the island team, known as the Liners, was getting notoriety in the sports pages of the *Cleveland Plain Dealer*. (Courtesy of Judy Du Shane.)

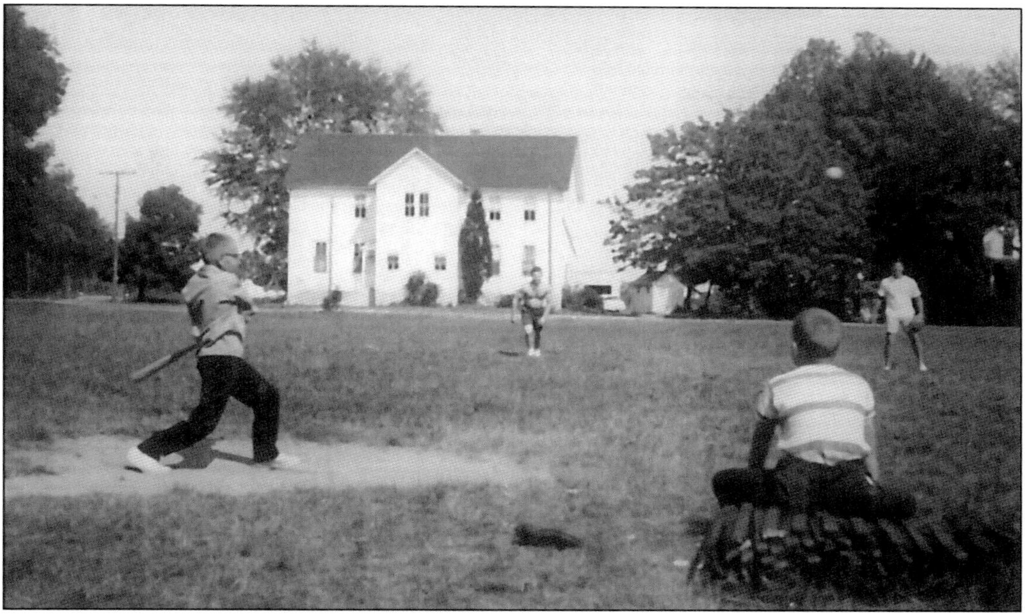

In modern times, these Kelleys Island boys play on the same field—at Addison Road and Chappel Street—that island teams have always played, with Marquette Hall still in the background. The hall, which formerly housed the island's Catholic school, was torn down in 1968. (Courtesy of Gary and Jackie Finger.)

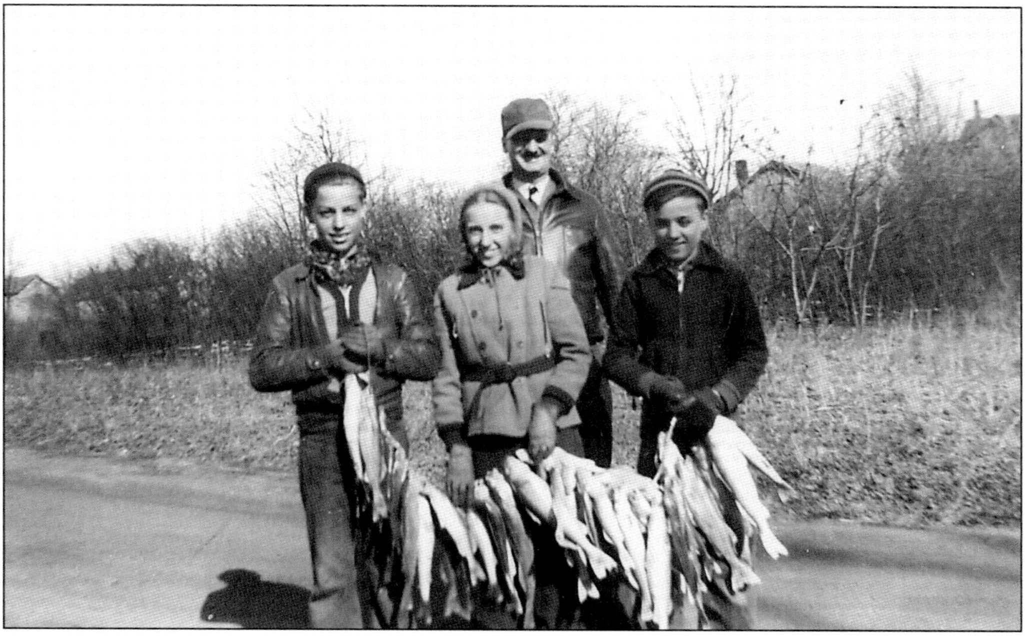

Seen here with their day's catch after fishing on Kelleys Island's south shore are, from left to right, Logan Bickley Jr., Barbara Bickley, Ed Sennish, and Lyle Bickley. Children growing up on Kelleys Island quickly learn how to catch the big ones. (Courtesy of Ted Blatt.)

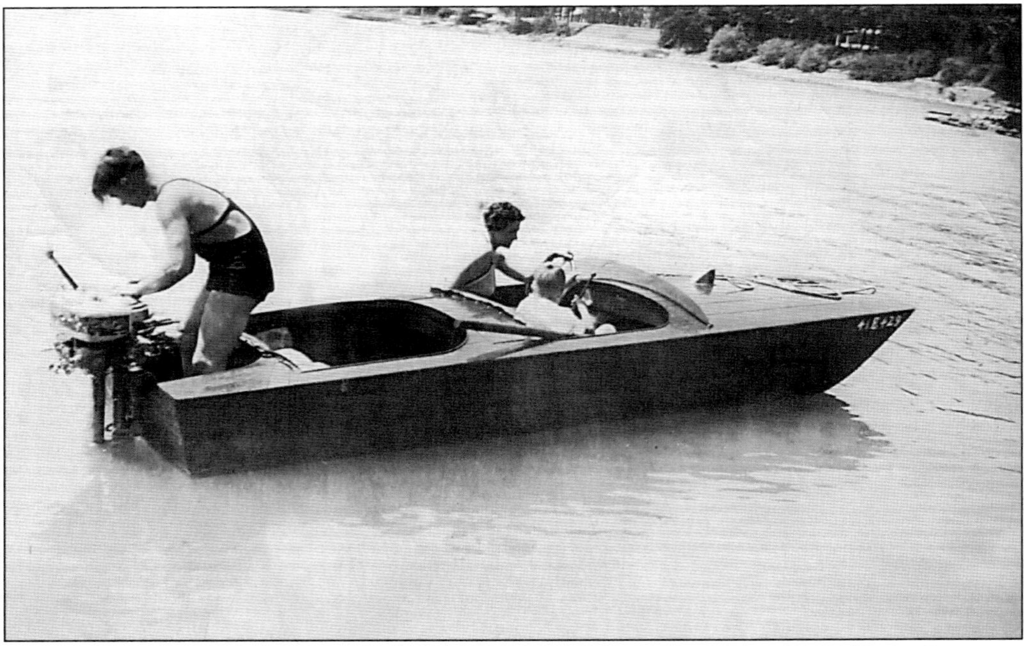

A warm summer day is a perfect day for a boat ride on Lake Erie in the 1930s and now. Sitting in the front seat of *The Stooge* are Esther Bauman Smith (left) and an unidentified boy. Tinkering with the engine is Claude O. Smith, who had a distributorship for the boat, which is made of mahogany. (Courtesy of Judy Du Shane.)

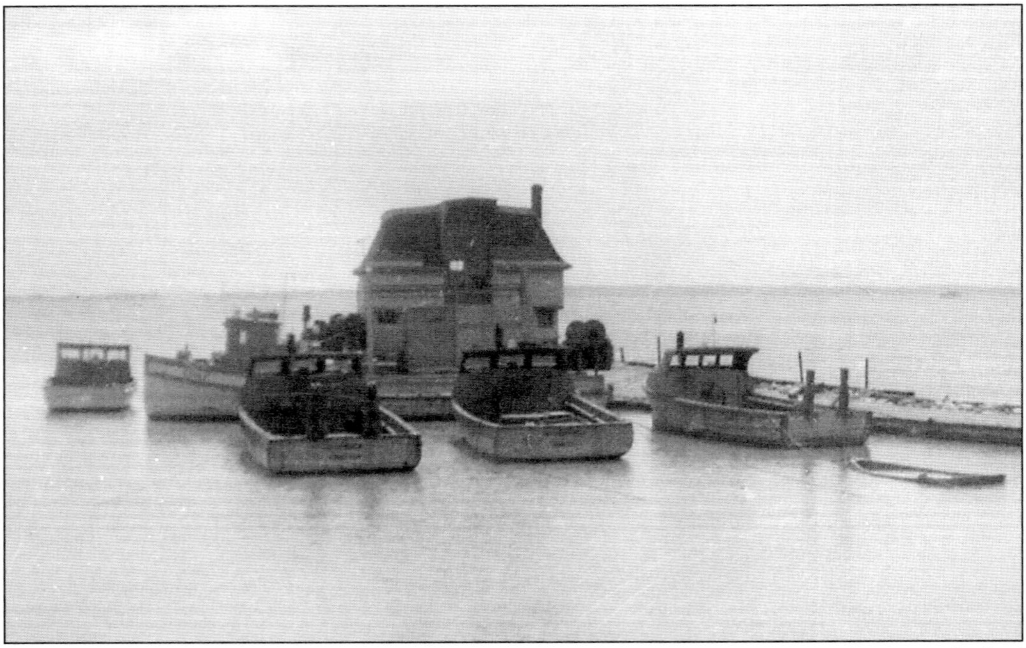

Koster's dock (now the Unique Marker Yacht Club) on East Lakeshore Drive has served all of Kelleys Island's major industries. Built in 1889, it was used by Koster's Winery and two other wine companies. The Kelley Island Lime & Transport Co. then bought the dock and eventually leased it to Lay Bros. Fish Co., which bought it in 1945. It is the last remaining wine dock on the island. (Courtesy of Barbara Schock.)

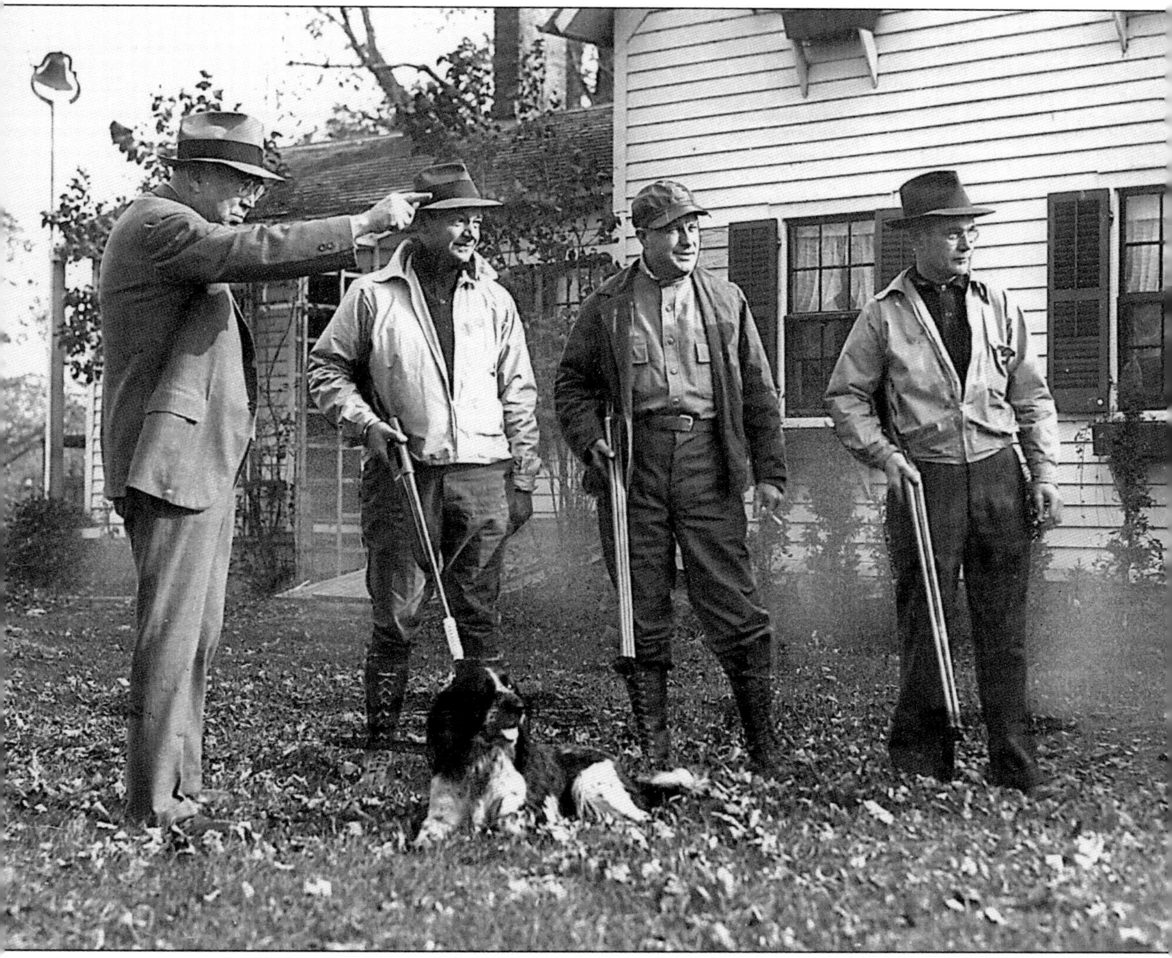

For many years, Kelleys Island's pheasant population was a big draw for hunters in November. According to the *Cleveland Press*, in 1941, some hunters could bag their legal limit of two pheasants and leave the island three hours after arriving. William Minshall (left), who was active in Cleveland and national politics, gives pheasant-hunting guidance to (from left to right) Henry Du Lawrence Jr., Ed Keal, and Henry Canning of Cleveland. Although the Kelleys Island Sportsmen's Club stocked the island with pheasants, the birds thrived, feeding off the grains raised on island farms. The pheasant population was so large that they had to be chased off the airport runway so planes could land. A bird census conducted in 2012 showed no ring-necked pheasants on the island. (Courtesy of the Cleveland Press Archives, Cleveland State University Library Special Collections.)

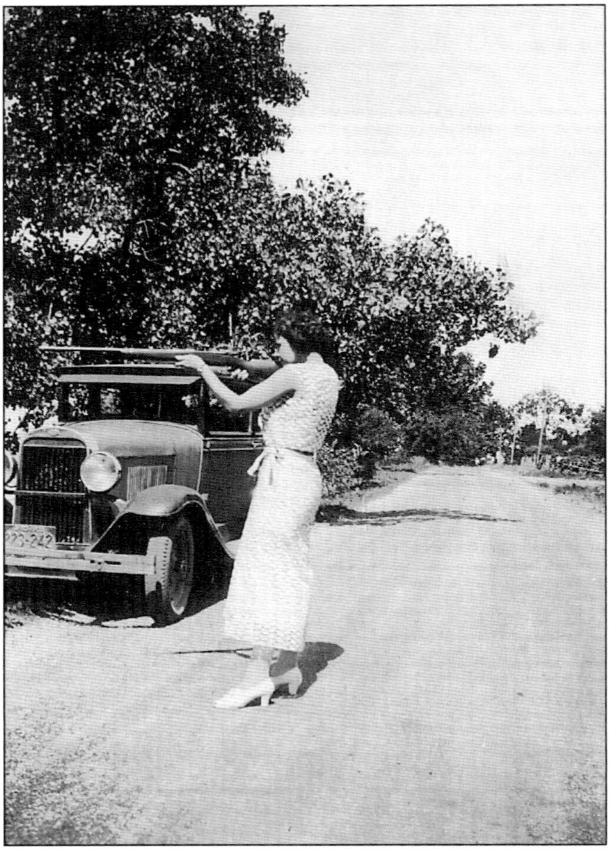

All Detsy Erne needed to know was how many guests to expect for dinner, and, armed with a rifle or shotgun, she would provide the main course. Detsy, the daughter of Samuel Bauman, was married to Andrew Erne. (Courtesy of Judy Du Shane.)

Don Schneider and Marie Ehrbar are seen below at the Ehrbar house on Addison Road, probably during hunting season. With the prospect of plentiful game, hunting has always been a popular off-season island attraction. A 1953 report indicates that 113 hunters bagged 117 pheasants and 92 rabbits. (Courtesy of Jack and Linda Hostal.)

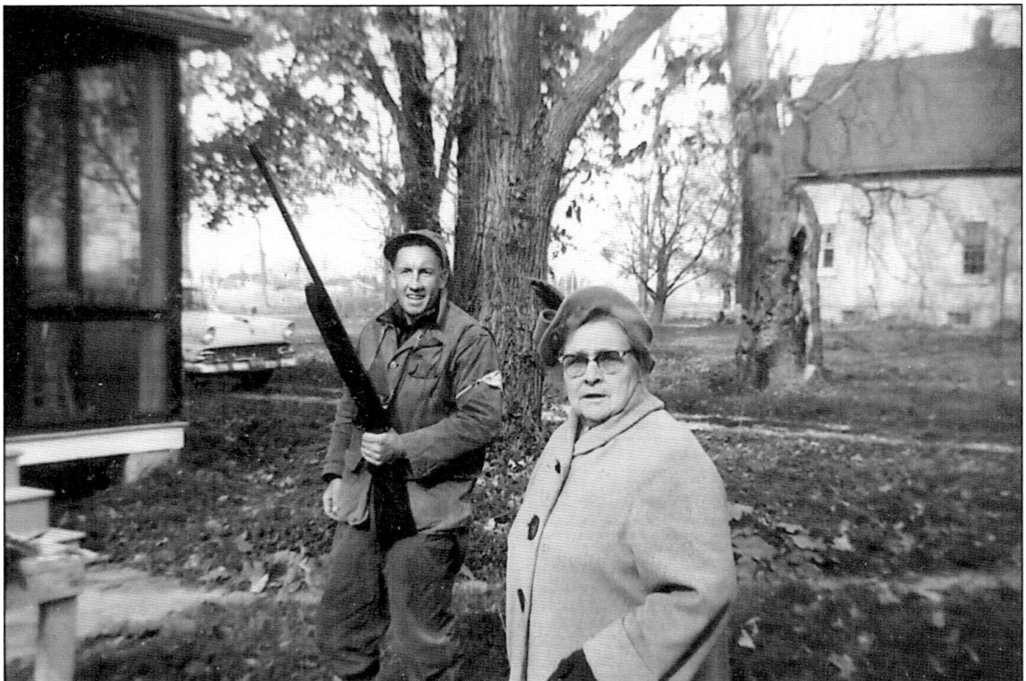

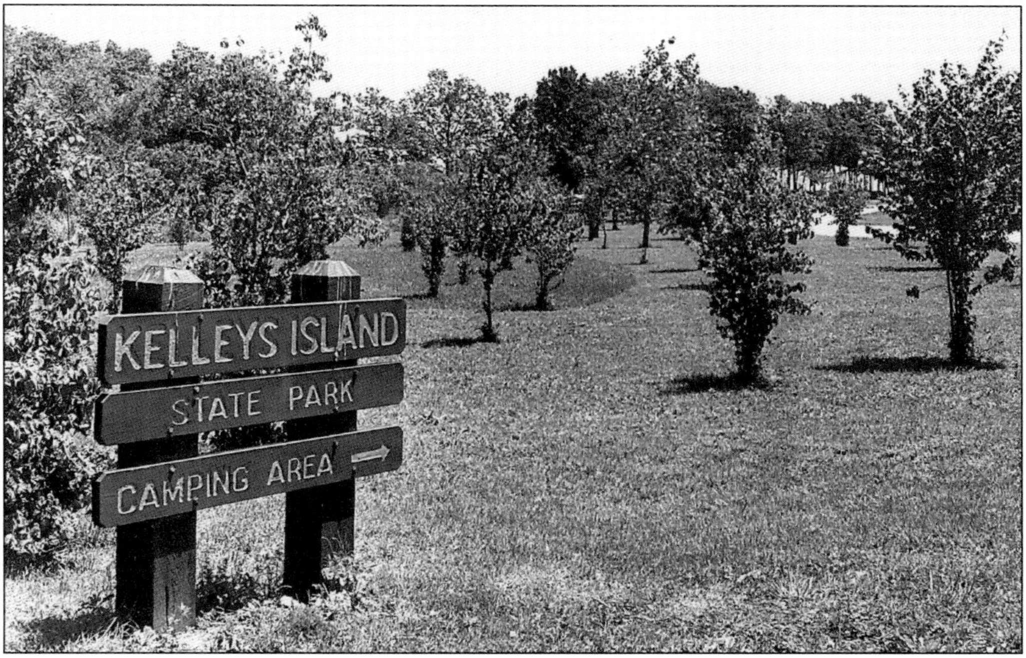

The Kelleys Island State Park campground, off of Division Street and overlooking Sandy Beach, was only three years old when this photograph was taken in 1966. The area is a linchpin in the island's parks complex, close to hiking trails, Sandy Beach, fishing, and a public boat launch. (Courtesy of the Cleveland Press Archives, Cleveland State University Library Special Collections.)

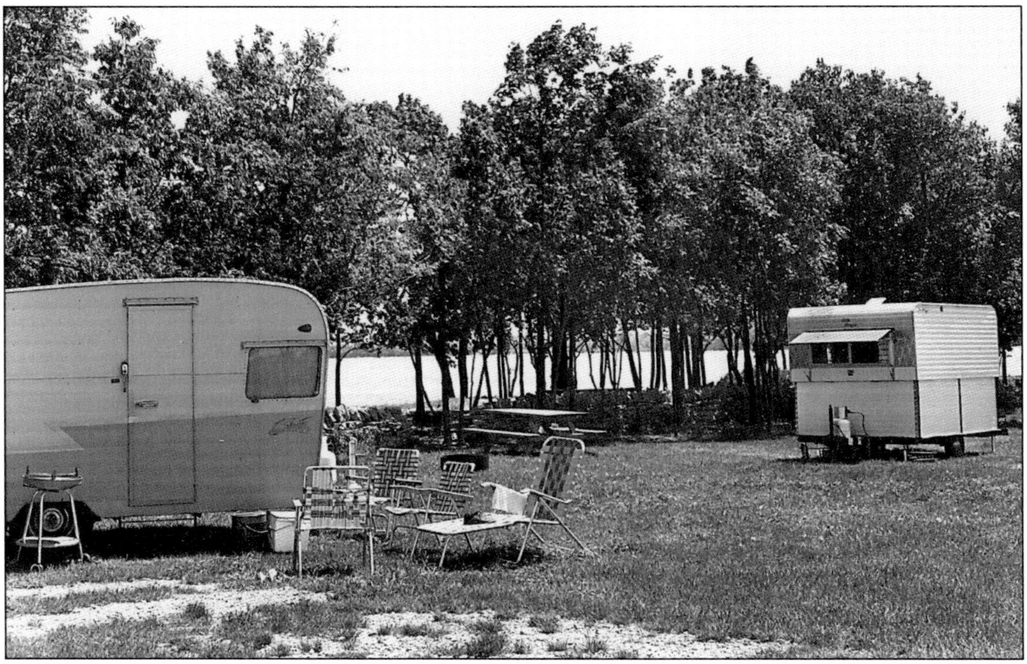

In 1965, the campgrounds had about 30 campsites on its 450 acres. At that time, the State of Ohio was planning to spend $100,000 on improvements. The campground has since grown to 129 sites and is filled on most summer weekends. (Courtesy of the Cleveland Press Archives, Cleveland State University Library Special Collections.)

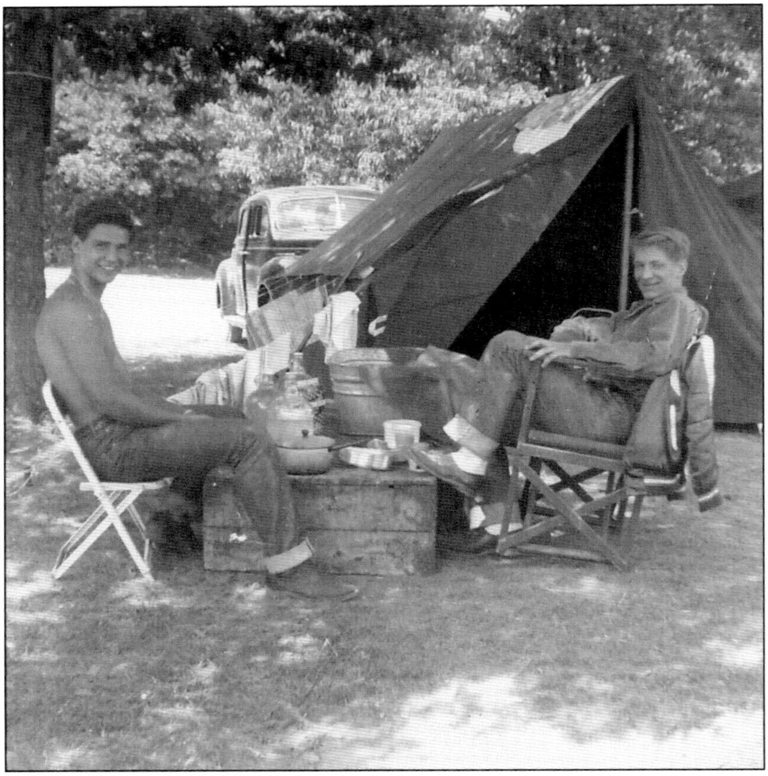

In the years before the state campground was mapped out above Sandy Beach, there were designated spots for camping, including this one just north of the current campground on Division Street. Dave Zachar (left) and Bill Wagner are seen here in the mid-1950s. (Courtesy of Ed and Carol Frindt.)

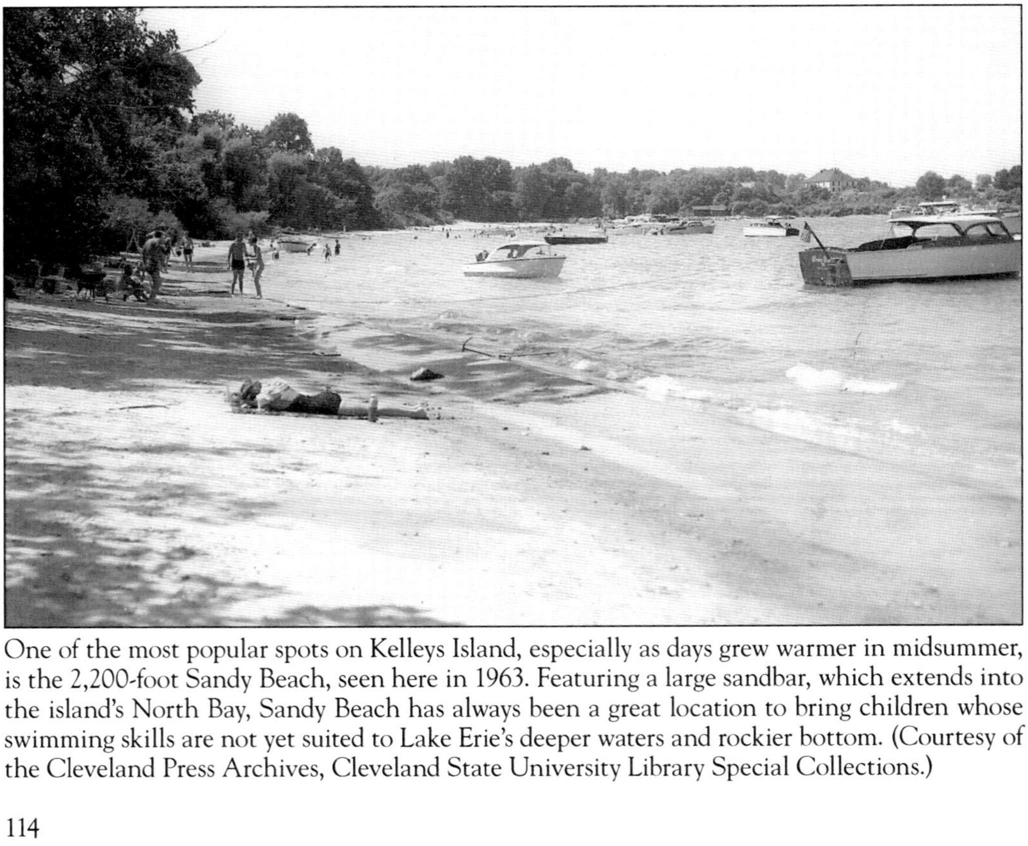

One of the most popular spots on Kelleys Island, especially as days grew warmer in midsummer, is the 2,200-foot Sandy Beach, seen here in 1963. Featuring a large sandbar, which extends into the island's North Bay, Sandy Beach has always been a great location to bring children whose swimming skills are not yet suited to Lake Erie's deeper waters and rockier bottom. (Courtesy of the Cleveland Press Archives, Cleveland State University Library Special Collections.)

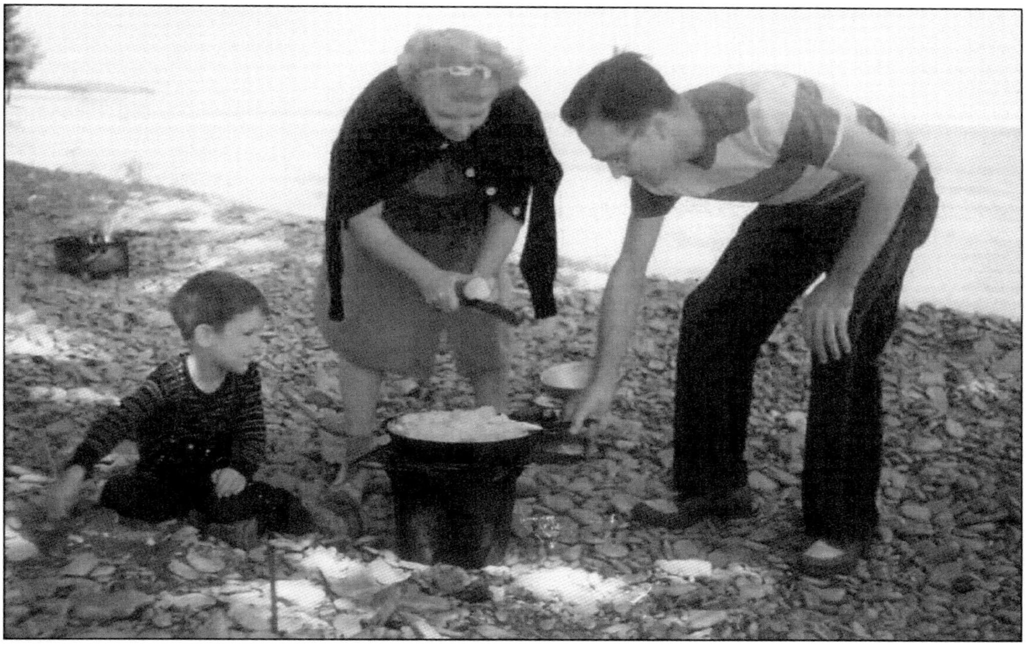

Nothing beats a meal cooked at the beach, and this trio in the 1950s shows how it is done. Chuck Herndon looks on as Jeanette and George Cleary cook some fish. Sandy Beach is currently rated as one of the cleanest beaches in Ohio. (Courtesy of the Kelleys Island Historical Association.)

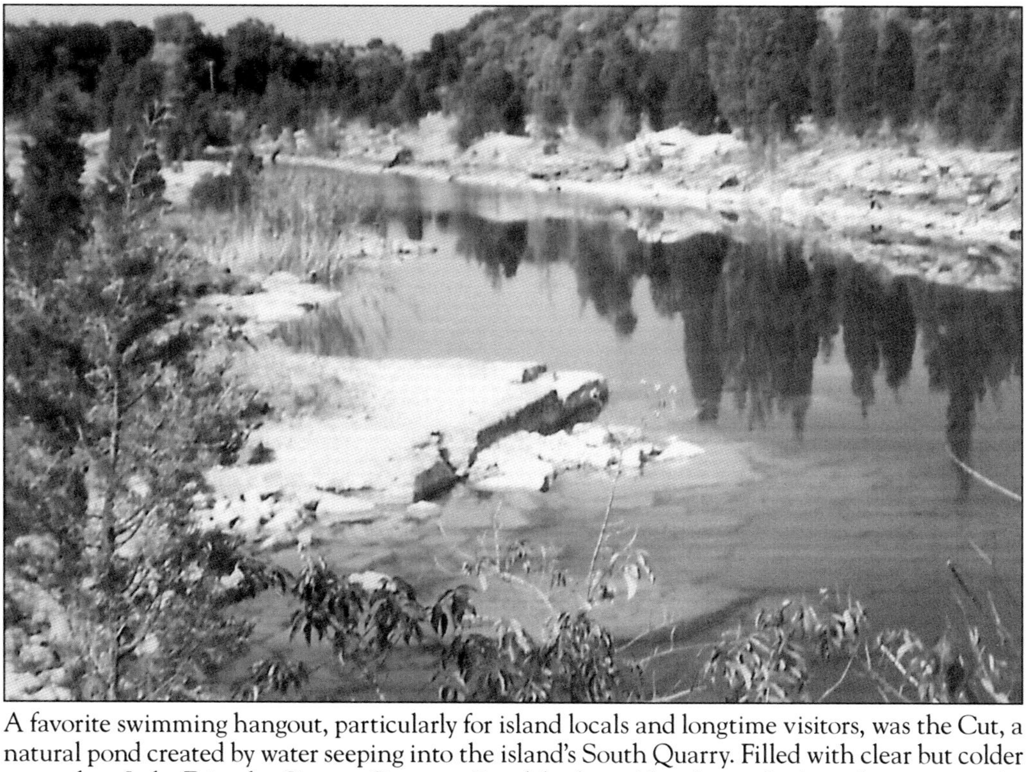

A favorite swimming hangout, particularly for island locals and longtime visitors, was the Cut, a natural pond created by water seeping into the island's South Quarry. Filled with clear but colder water than Lake Erie, the Cut, on Cameron Road, had a sudden drop, which made it a venue for experienced swimmers. (Courtesy of Ted Blatt.)

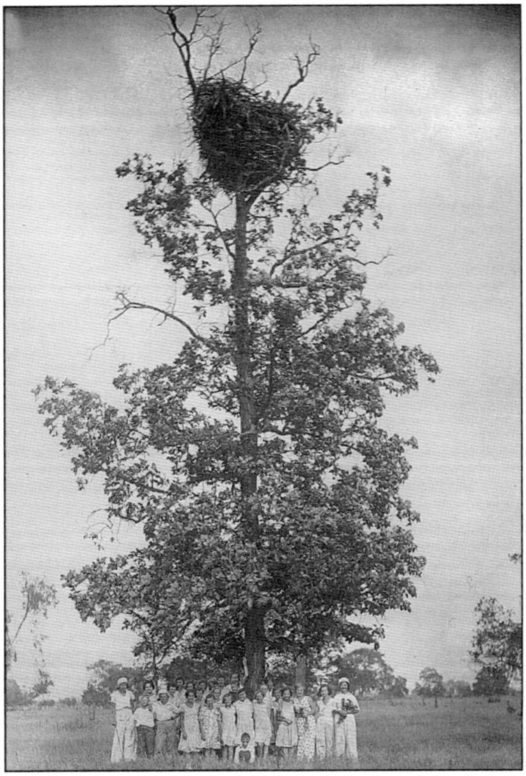

Kelleys Island has been home to several bald eagle families, including the one in this nest, which stood for many years near Monagan Road between Woodford and Ward Roads. It was regarded as an island attraction and was marked on most tourist maps. Girls in this group camping at the Villa (now Camp Patmos) in the 1930s probably thought it was well worth the visit. (Courtesy of John T. Sabol.)

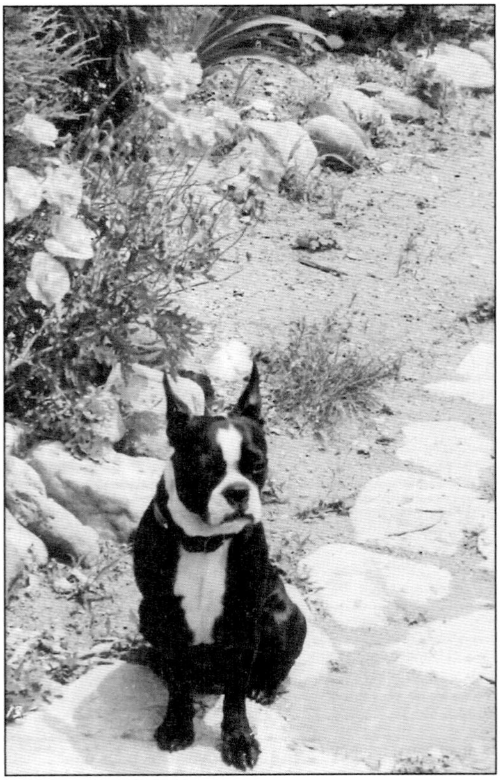

One of the most famous celebrities to live on Kelleys Island was Tarzan, a Boston Terrier who could "talk." With a 38-word vocabulary, including hamburger, liver, and onions, Tarzan held forth at the Casino on Kelleys from 1947 until he was killed by a motorist in 1958. Tarzan's owners, Ray and Ann Tacke, owned the Casino from 1945 until the 1960s. Tarzan's talent won his owners $2,000 on a national television program. (Courtesy of John T. Sabol.)

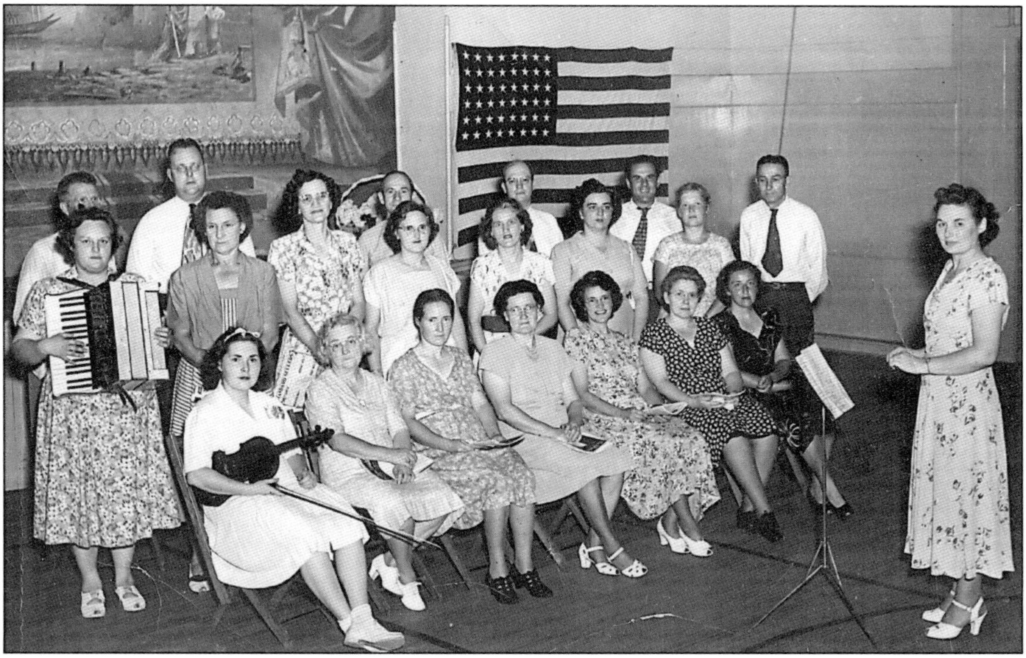

The Kelleys Island Choral Group directed by Lillian Brown (right) in the 1940s includes, from left to right, (first row) Roberta Hummell, Ella Hummell, Mary Hummell, Ruth Schnittker, Ellies Hughes, Effie Moorehead and Mary Betzenheimer; (second row) Jane Schlesselman, Rosella Beatty, Mary Augusta McKillips, Rita Betzenheimer, Dorothy Jean Schlesselman, Nadine Brown, Hazel Heischman, and Bob Moysey; (third row) Charlie Schnittker, Lynn Brown, Roy Fenwick, Rev. Calvin Moorehead, and Russ Heischman. (Courtesy of the Kelleys Island Historical Association.)

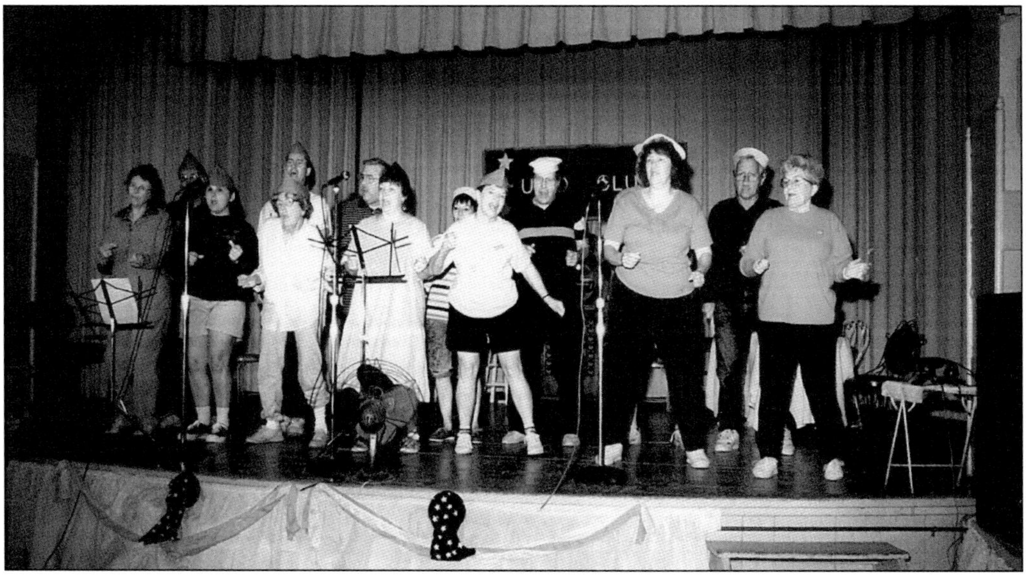

Today, the Island Singers have become a Kelleys Island institution and perform at many major events. Currently directed by Jennifer Koba, the group seen here in 1997 includes, from left to right, (first row) Lois Giles, Connie Morsher, Gye Landis, Annalee, Shirley Crabill, Carol Frindt, and Betty Jones; (second row) Byron Crabill, Tim Ullrich, Tim Koba, Judy Lahrs, Bill Crotzer, Bob Behlen (barely visible), and Knute Lahrs. (Courtesy of the Kelleys Island Historical Association.)

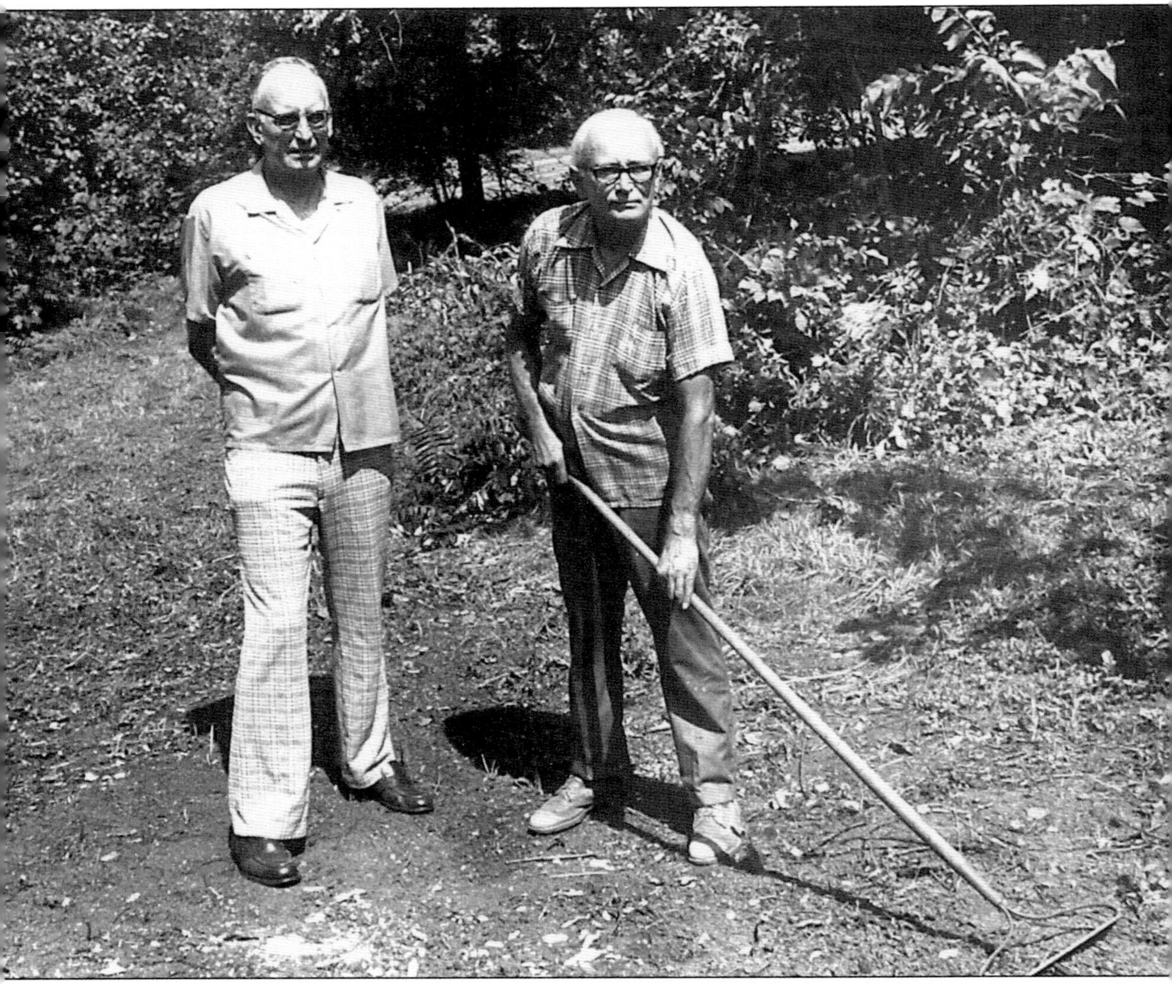

The glue that has bound the Kelleys Island community together through the years has included Dr. Heinz Boker (left) and Kurt Boker. These brothers, serving as the island physician and the schoolteacher/superintendent, respectively, excelled at what they did and were respected by islanders. Heinz was noted for the attention he paid to patients and the care he took in treating them. Kurt, according to the Kelleys Island Historical Association newsletter, lived, studied, and collected Kelleys Island. Seen here in 1977, they were both born in Germany. Heinz died in 2003, and Kurt died in 2006. Much of the Kelleys Island–related material collected by Kurt Boker is held at the Sandusky Public Library. In it are documents related to snakes and snake stories of Kelleys Island and the surrounding areas. (Courtesy of the Cleveland Press Archives, Cleveland State University Library Special Collections.)

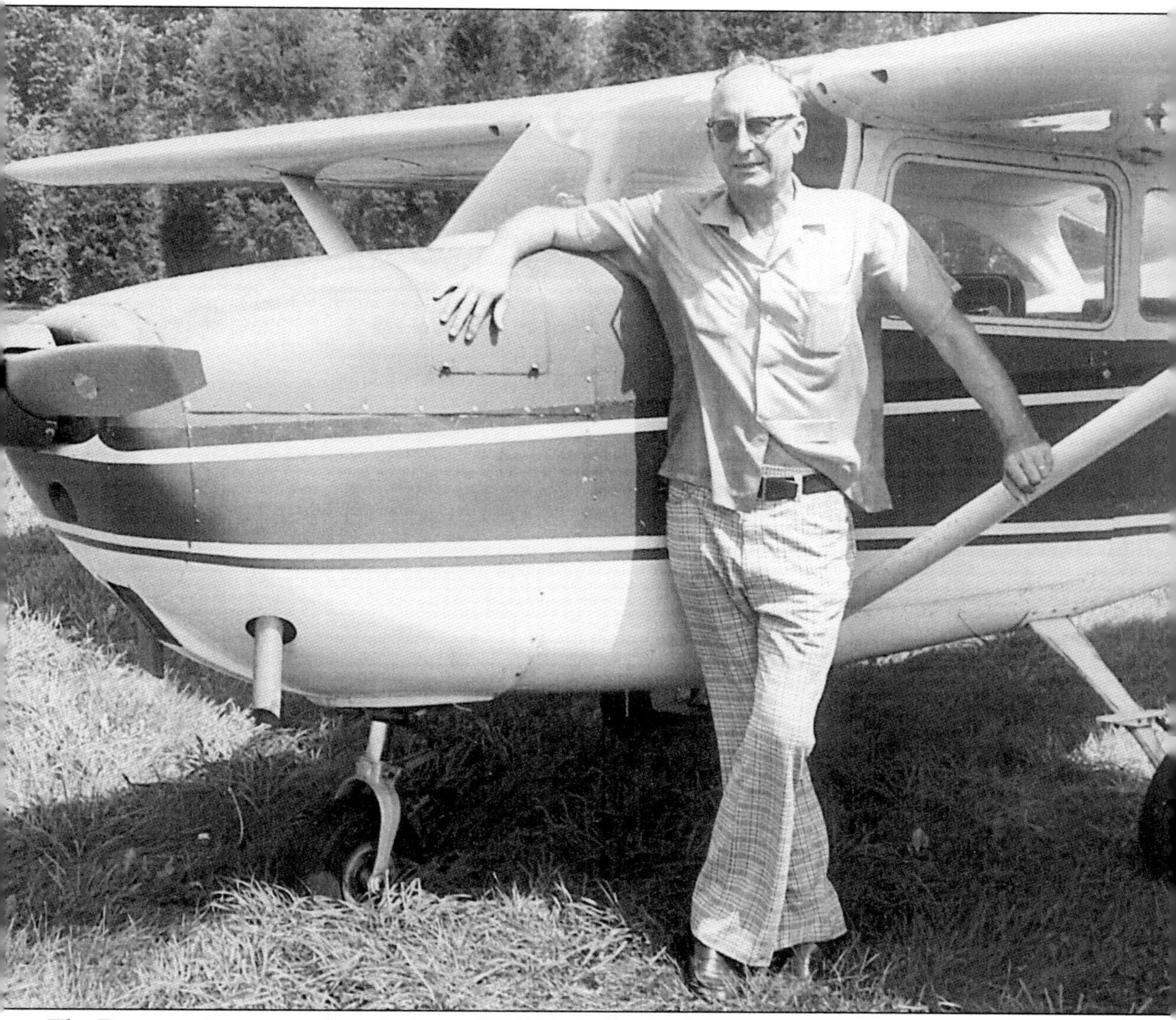

The Doctor is In sign on the side door of Kelley's Hall was always a comforting sign to islanders, as it meant that Dr. Heinz Boker, the island physician, was available. Beginning his practice in 1955, Dr. Boker served mainly on Kelleys, on nearby islands, and on the mainland, and sometimes even provided care for free. By 1968, he had obtained a pilot's license and was hopscotching to see patients by airplane. At one point, he gave up his Kelleys Island life to serve the natives on a small atoll in Micronesia. (Courtesy of the Cleveland Press Archives, Cleveland State University Library Special Collections.)

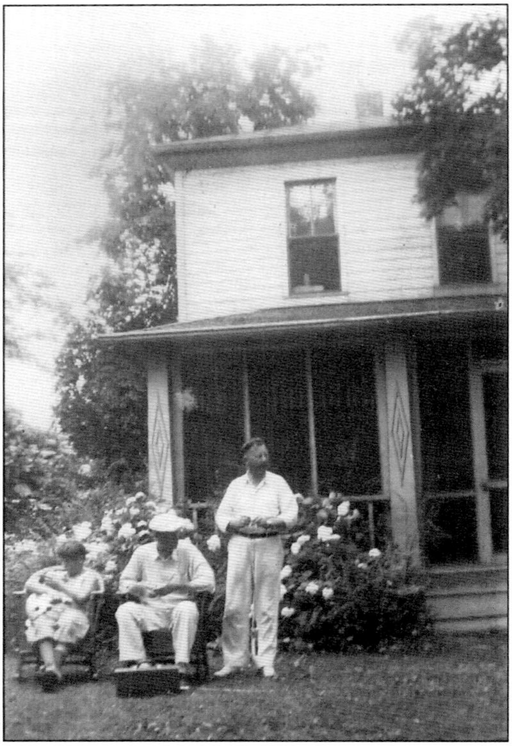

The Ehrbar house, on Addison Road, was built by the Kelley family. Oral tradition says that the house was built by Addison Kelley around 1880 for employees of the Kelley Mansion. The Ehrbar family purchased it in 1927. Seen here in the front yard in the 1930s are, from left to right, Del Ehrbar (holding his dog Pepper), a Mr. Hurley, and Lawrence Ehrbar. (Courtesy of Jack and Linda Hostal.)

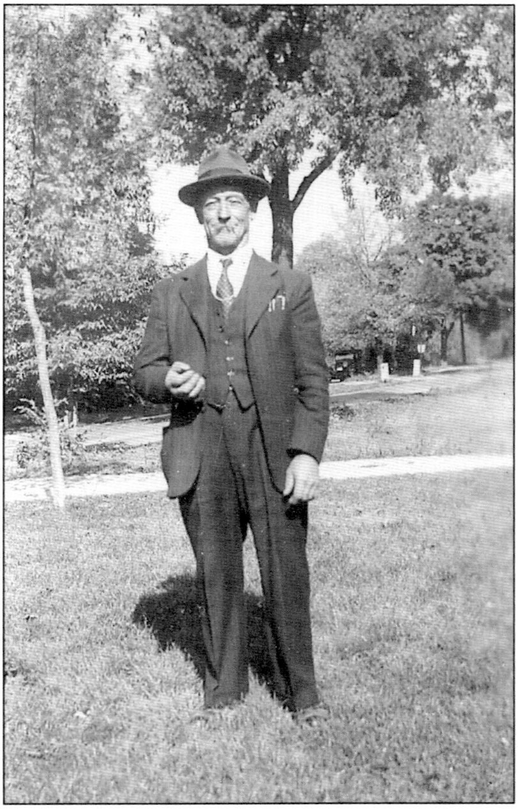

Born in Italy, Max Perruchon came to the United States with his wife, Elizabeth, and his children Ann and Paul in 1912, eventually moving to Kelleys Island, where he worked in the quarries. The Perruchons had 11 children and lived on Ward Road. A very athletic man, it is said that he could shinny up a flagpole upside down. (Courtesy of Barbara Schock.)

Godfried Schock, a fisherman for Lay Bros., put aside that livelihood to work with another Kelleys Island product—stone. As a stonemason on the island, Godfried built many island fireplaces and chimneys as well as two houses. But he still had time to build a house for himself (background). Schock, who died in 1989, is seen here with his wife, Mary, and his son Jack. (Courtesy of Barbara Schock.)

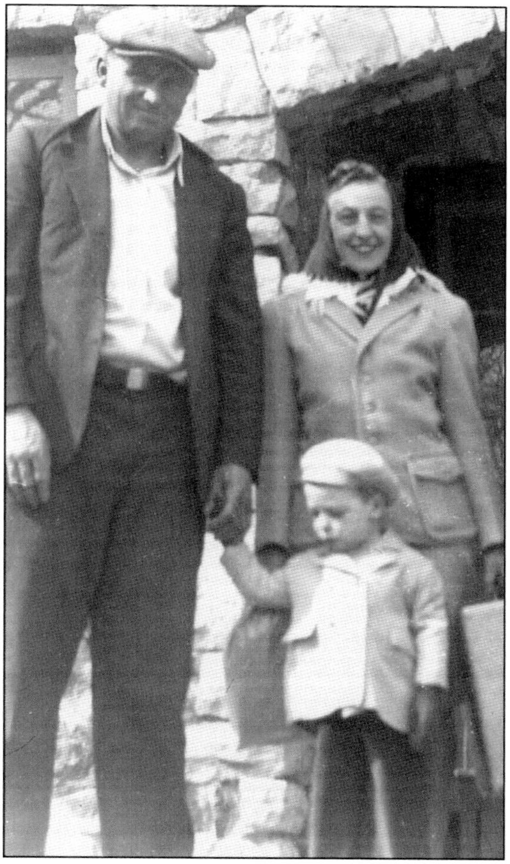

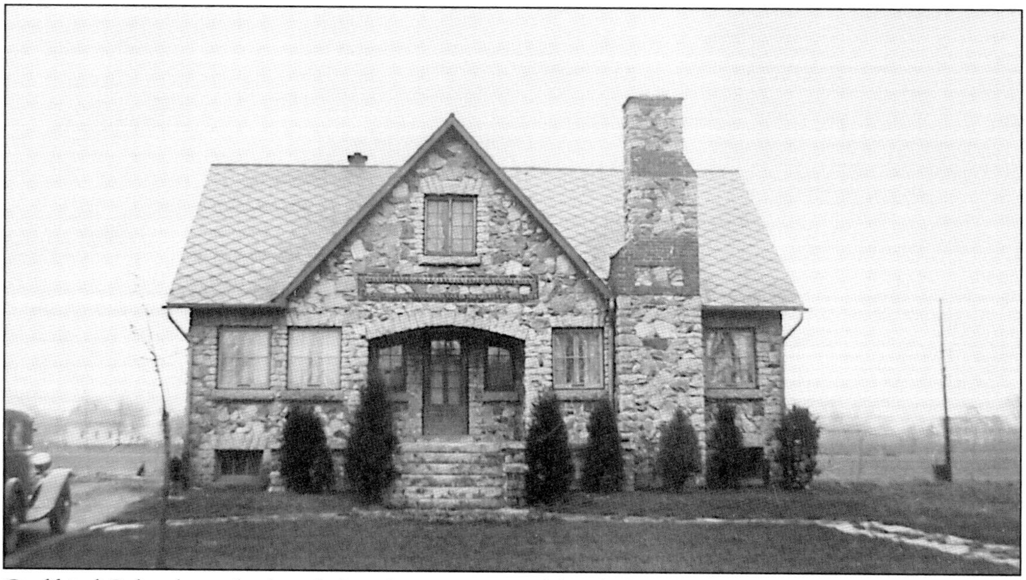

Godfried Schock worked with hand-cut stone and brick, building this home for his family on Division Street south of Chappel Street. This residence and the one just south of it, which he also built, are the only two Tudor-style houses on the island. The open front porch seen here was later enclosed. (Courtesy of Barbara Schock.)

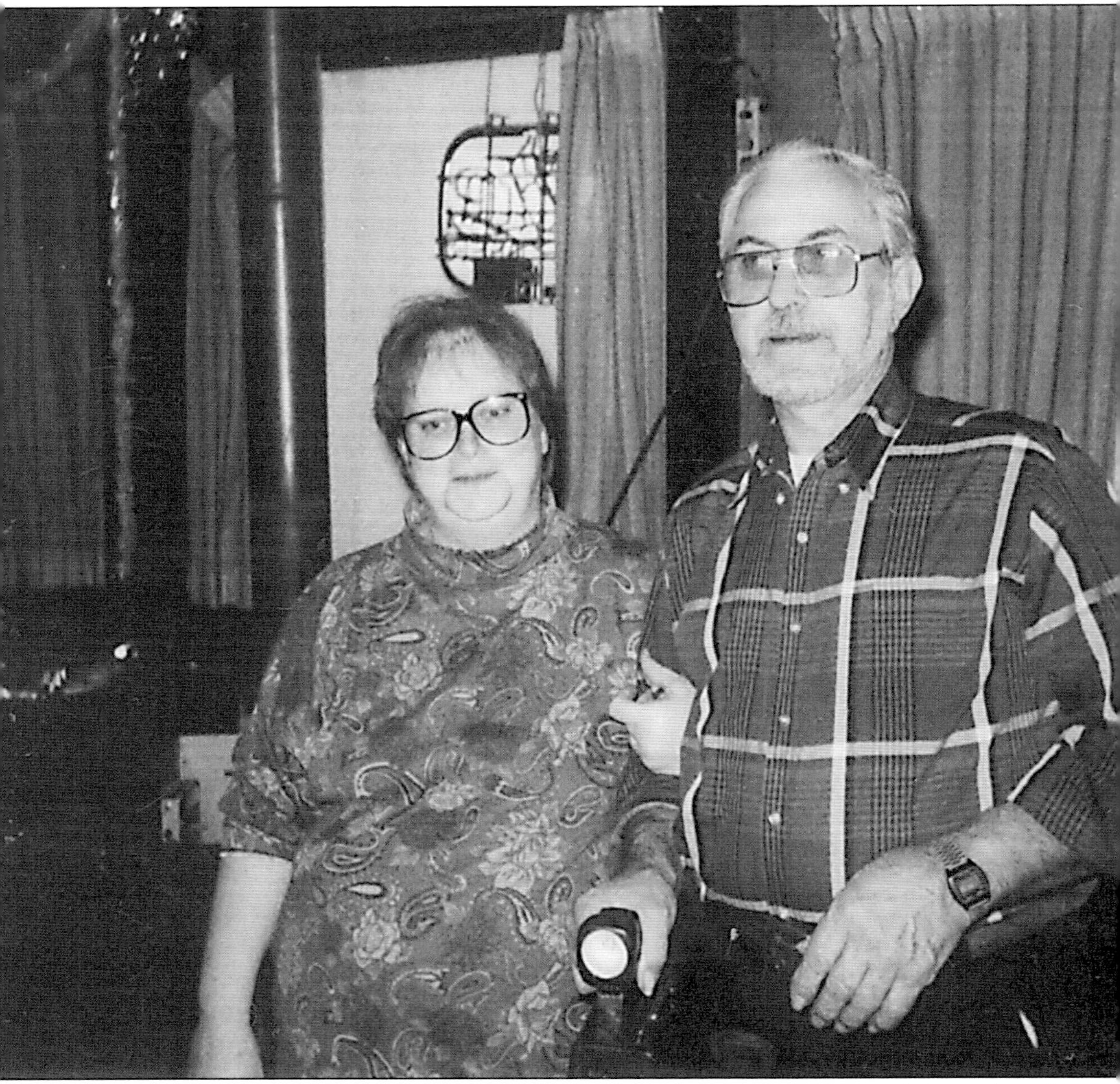

Russ and Bea Matso held forth as proprietors of Matso's Place (now the Captain's Corner), in the center of Kelleys Island's business district, for many years. Russ was the second generation to own the bar, succeeding his father, Joe Matso. Besides running a business, Russ was also the island's jack-of-all-trades, doing repairs and remodeling for island homeowners as well as opening and closing houses for summer residents. He pursued island history with the same energy, collecting photographs and postcards and recounting stories and facts about his lifelong home. He was well aware that his business occupied the same space as the Store on the Corner, known as the Lodge, where early island news was disseminated and discussed. A big part of the island was lost when Russ died in September 2006. (Courtesy of Barbara Schock.)

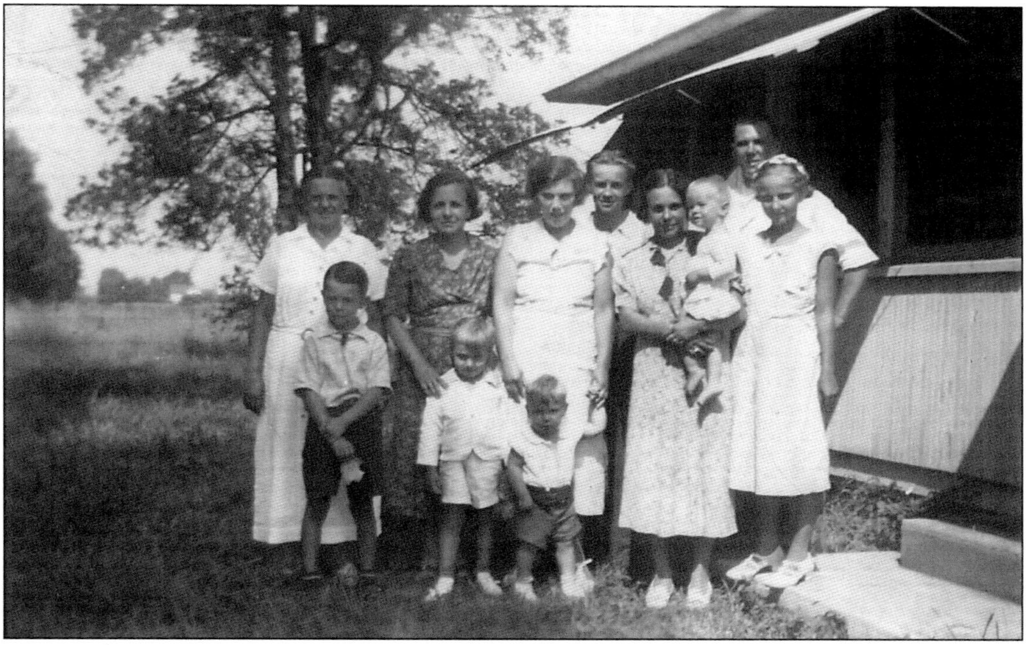

In 1939, these visitors vacationed at the Wigwam, owned by Fr. Vaclav Chaloupka of Cleveland and located at the time on Woodford Road. The group includes, from left to right, (first row) Robert Sabol, Donald Kuchar, and Edward Kuchar; (second row) Anna Ausperk, Gertrude Slivka, Jeanette Kuchar, Florence Sabol, Daniel Sabol, and Lillian Sabol; (third row) Gilbert Ausperk and Frank Slivka. The Wigwam, now located on Harbor Lane, was rented for $25 per week. (Courtesy of John T. Sabol.)

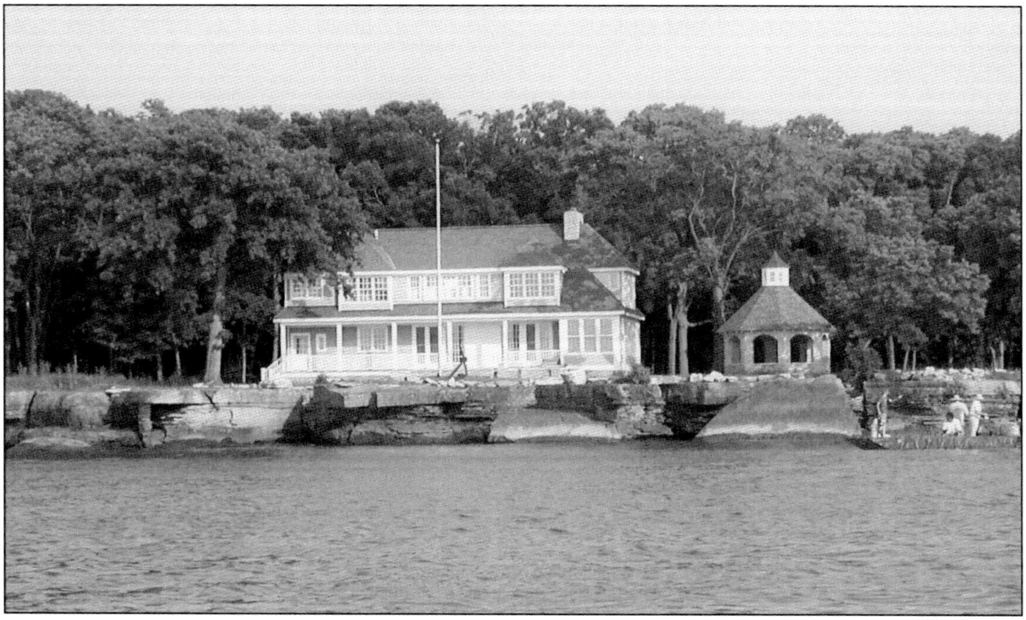

Long Point, at the northeast corner of Kelleys Island, has changed radically through the years. Table Rock has since crumbled into Lake Erie, and the area has been developed with luxury homes such as this one. The area itself is generally not accessible, except by a private road. (Courtesy of John T. Sabol.)

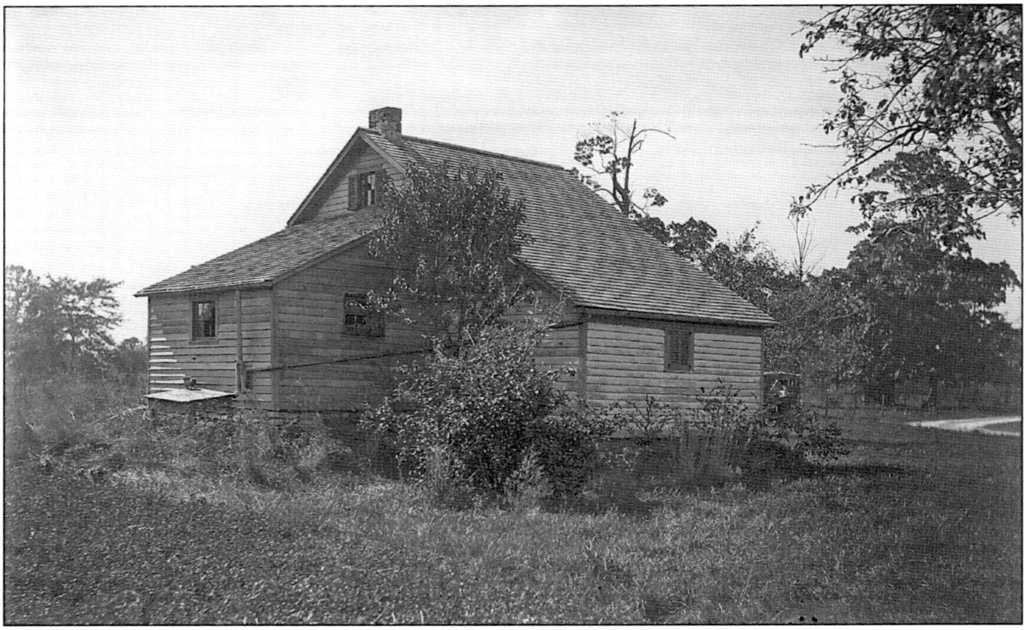

Fr. Vaclav Chaloupka of Nativity of the Blessed Virgin Mary Parish in Cleveland, the owner of the Villa (later Camp Patmos), also owned rental cottages on Kelleys Island. Seen here is Cozy Corner, at the corner of Ward and Hamilton Roads, at the time he purchased it, in the early 1920s. (Courtesy of John T. Sabol.)

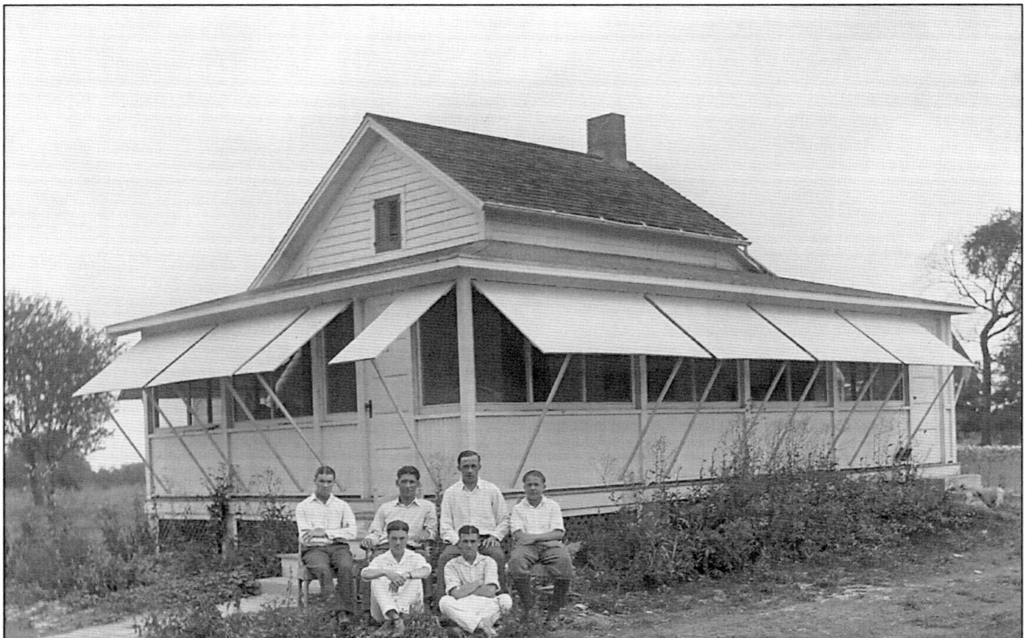

Cozy Corner is seen here after it was renovated by Father Chaloupka. The renovation included the addition of a wraparound sleeping porch. The furnished, three-bedroom cottage slept eight and rented for $20 a week. It was advertised as "the ideal place for a really restful vacation." (Courtesy of John T. Sabol.)

Burt Miller, seen here in 1932, owned a garage in Lorain, Ohio. After several fishing and hunting trips to Kelleys, he fell in love with the island and moved there in 1952. Besides establishing two businesses, he cleared land, hauled stone, and mowed grass. In the 1960s, Miller and four partners purchased a grape vineyard on the southeast corner of the island and established the Sweet Briar Allotment. (Courtesy of Jim Miller.)

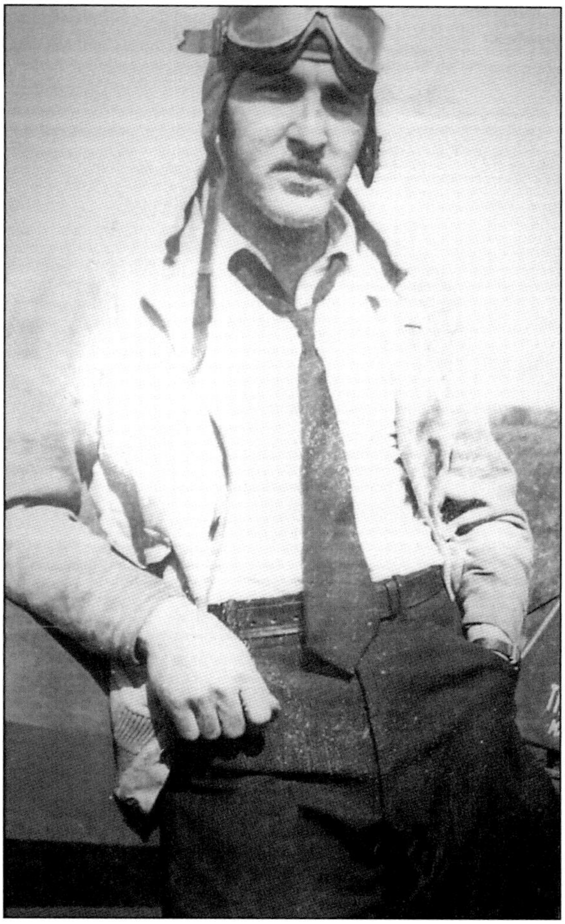

Jake Martin (below) and the Martin family have been known to generations of island residents and visitors. The family owned Martin's Ice Cream Parlor, which became Martin's Bar and is now the Village Pump, on West Lakeshore Drive. Jake was a builder of many homes, a land developer, and a council member. His wife, Jessie, taught at Estes School and wrote two books of island history. Here, Jake loads a biplane at the island airport. (Courtesy of Carol Perruchon.)

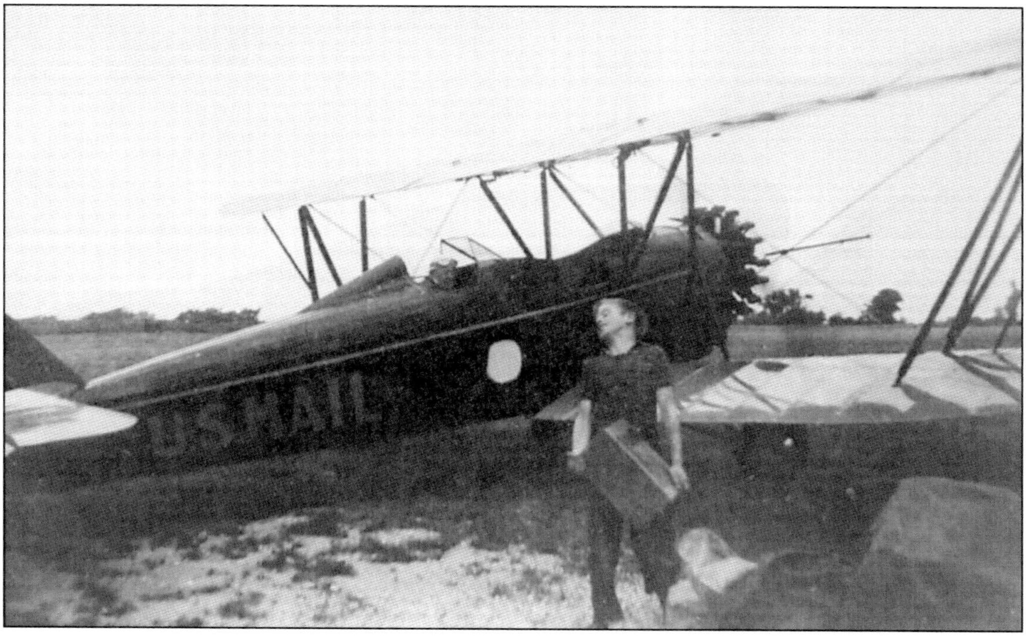

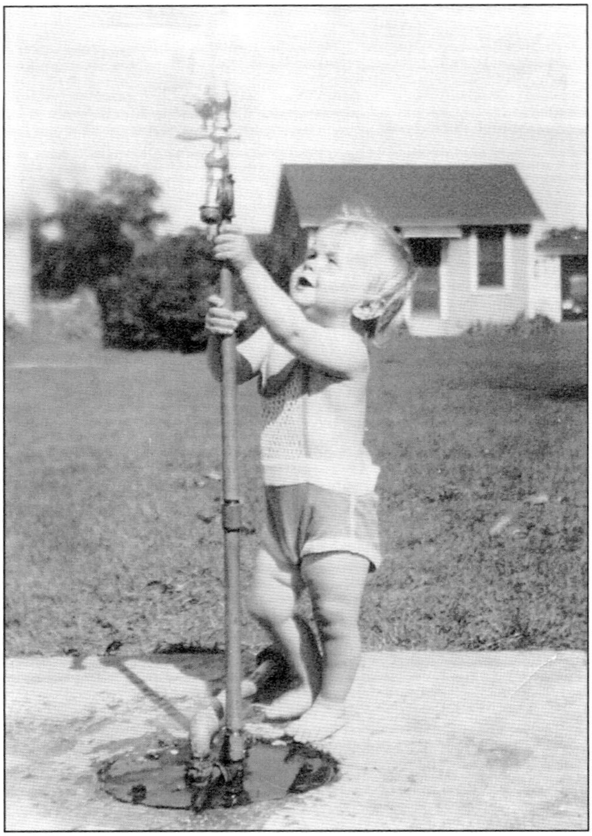

Even though he was too young to fully enjoy the Villa on Kelleys Island in 1938, Dan Sabol explored the whole place. He would have been with his mother, Florence, who was cooking at the camp run by Fr. Vaclav Chaloupka of Nativity Parish in Cleveland. It was the start of his lifelong love of Kelleys Island. (Courtesy of John T. Sabol.)

Homecoming is a major late-summer event on Kelleys Island sponsored by the Kelleys Island Landowners Association. This one-day event provides an opportunity for current and former residents and vacationers to reconnect with the island and the great memories it brings back. In this scene from a recent homecoming, bagpipers brought to the island by KILA member John Carrig parade toward the center of town. (Courtesy of Jack and Linda Hostal.)

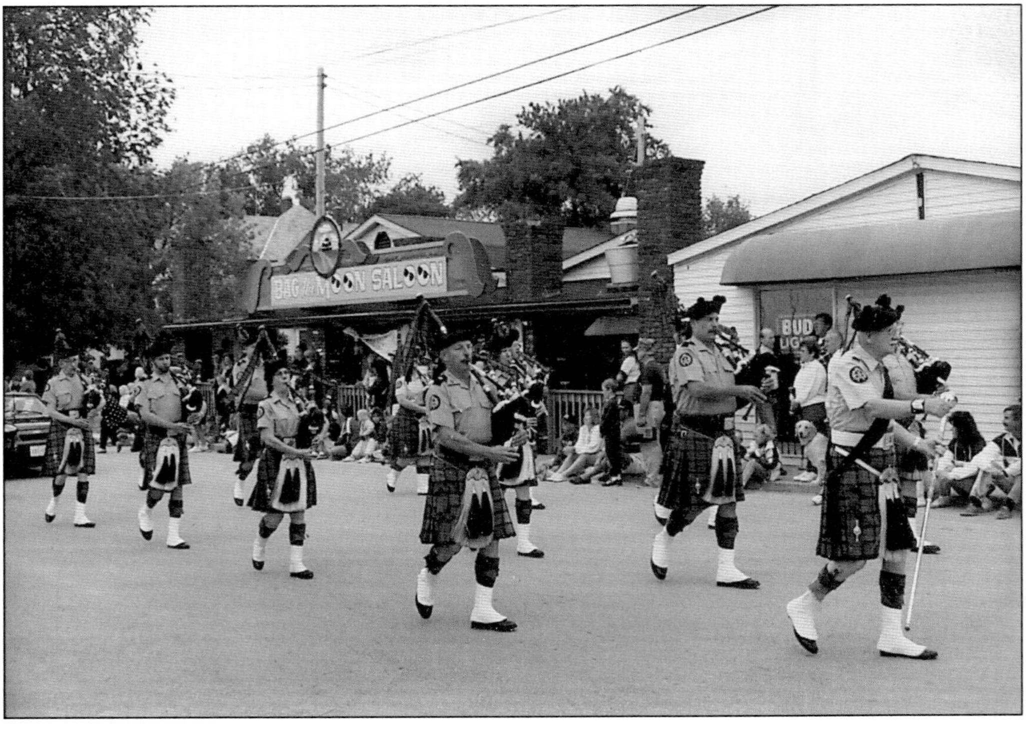

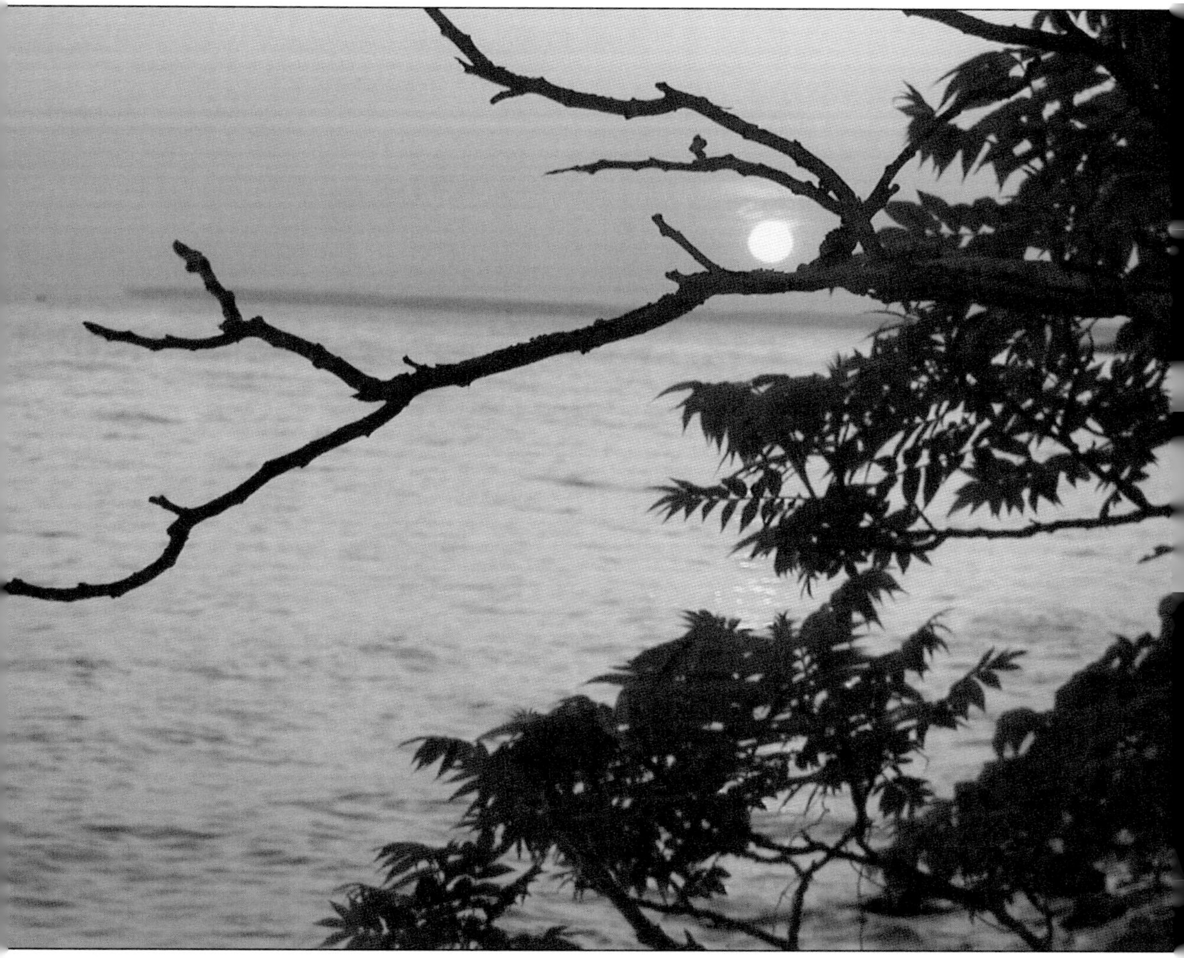

As dusk approaches in the summer on Kelleys Island, foot, car, and bike traffic builds up along the island's south shore as people gather to watch the sun go down, look back on the day they have had, and look forward to more of the same. After all, on Kelleys Island, it is all about the sunset. (Courtesy of John T. Sabol.)

Consistent with our mission to preserve history on a local level, this book was printed in South Carolina on American-made paper and manufactured entirely in the United States. Products carrying the accredited Forest Stewardship Council (FSC) label are printed on 100 percent FSC-certified paper.

MADE IN THE USA